Complete Guide to Provincial and National Park Campgrounds

Sixth Edition

CAMPING
British Columbia

JAYNE SEAGRAVE

Victoria • Vancouver • Calgary

Heritage House Publishing Company Ltd.
#108 – 17665 66A Avenue
Surrey, BC V3S 2A7
www.heritagehouse.ca

Heritage House Publishing Company Ltd.
PO Box 468
Custer, WA
98240-0468

Library and Archives Canada Cataloguing in Publication

Seagrave, Jayne, 1961–
    Camping British Columbia: a complete guide to provincial and national park campgrounds / Jayne Seagrave. — 6th ed.

ISBN 978-1-894974-60-8 (pbk.)

    1. Camp sites, facilities, etc.—British Columbia—Guidebooks. 2. Outdoor recreation—British Columbia—Guidebooks. 3. British Columbia—Guidebooks. I. Title.

FC3813.S42 2009   796.5409711   C2008-907208-1

Library of Congress Control Number: 2009920211

First edition 1997, second edition 1998, third edition 2001, fourth edition 2004, fifth edition 2005

Edited by Holland Gidney
Book design by Darlene Nickull
Proofread by Meaghan Craven
Cover design by Frances Hunter
Front-cover photo of Ruckle Provincial Park by Sean Wood/iStockphoto
Except where captions indicate otherwise, all photographs provided by the author. Uncredited photographs appearing on pages 53, 91, 93 and 184 were provided by BC Parks. All photographs used are reproduced with permission, and copyright for these images remains with the respective photographers and organizations.

Printed in Canada

Heritage House acknowledges the financial support for its publishing program from the Government of Canada through the Book Publishing Industry Development Program (BPIDP), Canada Council for the Arts, and the province of British Columbia through the British Columbia Arts Council and the Book Publishing Tax Credit.

The Canada Council | Le Conseil des Arts
for the Arts | du Canada

BRITISH COLUMBIA
ARTS COUNCIL
Supported by the Province of British Columbia

ACKNOWLEDGEMENTS

In 1996, I met nervously with Rodger Touchie, the relatively new owner and publisher of Heritage House Publishing, and suggested a book on camping in British Columbia's provincial parks to him. I had moved to BC five years earlier and since that time had been in constant awe of their magnitude, diversity and beauty, and I was amazed that no one had written a guidebook about them. At this time neither Rodger nor I could have envisioned the book would be so well received and become so popular. Each edition of the text is an improvement on the last, and for that I am indebted to Rodger and his colleagues at Heritage House for their knowledge, expertise and guidance. They have all been, and continue to be, a delight to work with.

Information contained in this sixth edition has been gained from personally visiting and camping in almost every BC provincial and national park campground. It also comes from the numerous conversations I have had over almost 20 years with the staff who work in these huge "open-air hotels" and who have, without exception, been willing and enthusiastic to share their vast knowledge with me.

Finally, I have to thank my husband, Andrew Dewberry, who continues to actively encourage me to camp and who has been instrumental in taking many of the photographs for this book, and my children, Jack and Sam, for their sincere *joie de vivre* and obvious *joie de camping*.

CONTENTS

BRITISH COLUMBIA PARKS WITH VEHICLE-ACCESSIBLE CAMPGROUNDS

Facilities vary between parks. Some provide playgrounds, solar showers and amphitheatres.

INTRODUCTION

Camping British Columbia was written out of a love of camping and a deep respect for British Columbia. As Canada's third largest province, BC covers 950,000 square kilometres, including 18,000 square kilometres of inland water. BC has more land designated to provincial parks than does any state in the U.S. except for Alaska and Hawaii, and it boasts over 400 different locations for day use and camping. In addition, six national parks are found in the province, four of these with developed camping facilities, plus the Gulf Islands National Park Reserve. With all this space for exploration and over 12,000 camping spots, it is little wonder that the "camping experience" has become an integral part of recreational life for BC residents and visitors alike.

Written both for those who camp in tents and those who use recreational vehicles (RVs), this book describes the location, facilities offered and recreational activities available for all BC provincial and national parks with campsites that are accessible by vehicle (with the exception of Sidney Spit and Newcastle Island) and which provide at least the basic amenities of drinking water, picnic tables, fire pits and pit toilets. No privately owned campgrounds are included, although many of the ones in BC offer wonderful camping facilities.

For convenience, these campgrounds are grouped into six regional chapters (The Islands, Vancouver Coast and Mountains, Thompson Okanagan, BC Rockies, Cariboo Chilcotin Coast, and Northern British Columbia) while the introductory chapter of this guide details important background information on camping in British Columbia. To offer guidance to the novice and provide reminders to the seasoned camper, I describe selecting a camping spot, packing for a camping trip, the reservation process, potential hazards and camping with kids. For those wanting to visit multiple campgrounds, I have suggested 7-, 14- and 21-day camping itineraries, which are found in the "Multi-day Camping Tours" chapter. The selections are based on my personal experiences and amenity evaluations and cover reasonable daily travel distances.

This sixth edition of *Camping British Columbia* builds upon and updates the information contained in my previous books. Additionally, for various reasons, six campgrounds are no longer included but five new ones have been added (Babine River Corridor, Beaver Creek, Cedar Point, Kin Beach and Kitty Coleman). Four of these additions are designated "Category C" campgrounds, meaning they are jointly administered by BC Parks and a local community group. A few other provincial parks included in this book have also become Category C. The facilities offered in these parks may be significantly different to those that are solely under the auspices of BC Parks, for example they may not recycle and the vegetation may be overgrown, but some offer recreational opportunities not available in the more tradional parks, such as tennis courts. Since these Category C parks are listed on the BC Parks website and do provide vehicle camping, drinking water, picnic tables, fire pits and toilets, they have been included.

Camping is a personal experience; what appeals to one person may not appeal to another. However, British Columbia is blessed with some of the most breathtaking scenery in the world. Many of the provincial and national parks are nestled in the heart of this beauty and are yours to experience at relatively little cost. Over the last 18 years I have travelled and camped in every region of BC and have been amazed at the stunning beauty the province offers. It still surprises me that many residents of BC are not campers. I hope this book encourages more individuals to take the plunge and use the excellent facilities provided in their province's parks. A wealth of adventures and experiences can be enjoyed by those of every age. So, what are you waiting for?

Camping is a popular and enjoyable activity for families.

THE CAMPING EXPERIENCE

The aim of this chapter is to provide some of the basic ground rules for camping in BC's national and provincial parks. While the contents of this chapter are intended primarily for the uninitiated to show them what to expect, those who camp regularly will find the information on making reservations, what to take and how to deal with bears and other hazards useful reminders. I've also added new sections on security issues, green camping and camping with kids.

Arriving at a Provincial or National Park Campground

All national and provincial park campgrounds are well signposted from major highways. A sign (blue for provincial parks, brown for national parks) 2 kilometres before the campground turnoff is the first warning you will receive, followed by another one 400 metres from the campground, which will direct you to the access road. The park operator will post notices on these roadside signs to state when a campground is full or closed. You will come to appreciate what a real advantage this is if the campground is located 60 kilometres from the highway on a rough gravel road.

Selecting your Spot and Setting up Camp

Presuming you do not have a reservation (see "Reservations"), excitement upon arrival is selecting your spot. Depending on the season, time of day and location of the park, this decision may already be out of your hands. The park may be full or there may be only one place left. Some parks have areas specifically designated for tents, but most have spots suitable for both RVs and tents. A number of parks offer "double spots," ideal for two families camping together, and pull-through spots for larger RVs. A map of the campground at the park entrance shows where these spots are found. If the park offers a reservation service, the reserved sites will be listed at the park's entrance. Once you have established which campsites are available, you should "cruise" the campground to select your spot. Campsites by any beach, lake, river or creek are the most desirable locations, so head for them first, making a mental note of where the water tap is located. Try to avoid areas of stagnant water (mosquito breeding grounds) or spots close to the "thunderboxes" (pit toilets), which, during the park's warm summer months, may exude unpleasant odours, attract flies and whose banging doors can cause a disturbance. At first glance, spots near the flush toilets and showers may seem convenient, but remember that between 5:00 p.m. and 11:00 p.m., and between 7:00 a.m. and 11:00 a.m., most people at the campground will be visiting these facilities at least twice and walking past your site in order to do so. On the other hand, if you have children in your party or want to meet people, you may deem these spots ideal.

Once you have driven around and made a mental note of your preferences, return to and claim your first choice. Should you not want to pitch camp immediately, leave a plastic tablecloth or water jug on the picnic table to state to the world that this is your spot then head back to the gatehouse to register and pay the associated fee. If there's a staffed gatehouse or welcome centre at the campground, that's generally where you'll register and pay for your campsite (unless you have a reservation). You will be asked to provide your name, the number of people in your party, vehicle license-plate number and where you are from. You can request a particular spot to camp if you've picked one out, or you'll be given a choice of available sites. You can pay for as many nights as you want, up to a maximum of 14 nights in both provincial and national parks (some parks, such as Haynes Point and Pacific Rim, may limit your stay to 7 nights). A receipt displaying the date on which you intend to leave will be posted on your spot.

In most parks, if you don't register and pay upon arrival, you can drive around and select your own spot and an attendant will come and collect payment (cash only) during the early-evening hours. (Park attendants are good sources of information on weather conditions, local activities, the best fishing locations and so on.) Some parks operate an honour self-registration system whereby you deposit the campground fee in an envelope, place it in a box at the entrance to the park and secure a receipt. For such instances, it is good to ensure that you have small bills and change, although fellow campers are usually willing to help you out. Instructions on self-registering will be printed on a sign at the park's entrance and on the deposit envelope. Once you've completed the self-registration form, you post the receipt at your spot.

If you delay pitching your tent or going to collect water, just don't forget what time it gets dark. This is particularly relevant if you are camping in the shoulder seasons of early spring and late summer, when darkness falls as early as 7:00 p.m. Arriving at a campground late, pitching your tent in the dark and cooking dinner by flashlight is challenging to say the least. In contrast, relaxing by the fire while the sun goes down and the stars come out is a highly pleasurable experience when you know your bed is made, dinner is over and the dishes done. Once established in your new home, you are ready to explore the campground. The first port of call should be a return visit to the information board at the park's entrance, where you will find a map of the campground and details about any hazards in the area.

Fees

During the early-evening hours in most parks, an attendant will come and collect payment (cash only). Camping fees vary depending on the facilities provided; campgrounds with showers tend to be the most expensive, whereas less developed campgrounds cost less. Fees include GST and in 2008 ranged from $10.00 to $24.00 for provincial parks and up to $38.80 for national parks. A daily entrance fee is charged by national parks even if you are staying overnight ($7.80/adult, $3.90/child, $19.60/family; or you can purchase an annual pass good for all national parks). Before June 15 and after Labour Day, residents of BC who are 65 or older may camp for half price in provincial parks (and at Prior Centennial and McDonald parks); from June 15 to Labour Day, full rates apply. With the correct documentation, Persons with Disabilities who are residents of BC may be exempt from campsite fees. For the most up-to-date fees for particular provincial parks, visit the BC Parks website at www.bcparks.ca; and for national parks, www.pc.gc.ca.

If camping in the same park, you generally do not have to pay the vehicle fee for parking in day-use areas as long as you display your camping receipt in your vehicle but some of the more popular provincial parks have started charging ($3.00–$5.00 per day, or you can purchase an annual pass for $25.00). If you intend to fish in national parks, you will have to purchase a permit ($9.80/day, $34.30/year) and any angler over the age of 16 needs a Freshwater Fishing Licence to fish in provincial parks ($10.00/day, $36.00/year for BC residents; $20.00/day, $55.00/year for non-residents—see www.fishing.gov.bc.ca). Parks also may also request payment for firewood ($5.00 to $10.00 per bundle—and the bundles do vary considerably in size), or for the privilege of having a campfire ($8.80 in national parks, which includes firewood). If a sani-station is provided, there is usually a fee to use it ($2.00 in provincial parks, $8.00 in national parks).

Notice boards near park entrances provide useful information for campers.

Facilities

All campgrounds included in this book provide at least the basic amenities of drinking water, wood for sale, picnic tables, fire pits and pit toilets; some larger campgrounds may also have sani-stations, flush toilets, showers, wheelchair access, interpretive programs, visitor centres and/or group camping. Washroom facilities are generally well maintained, clean and, unlike many campgrounds I have stayed in abroad, they never run out of toilet paper. (I was preconditioned in Europe, so it took me years to stop carrying a spare roll with me.) Gravel camping spots are tidied and raked after each visitor departs, garbage is regularly collected and recycling is encouraged. Overall, the facilities provided in BC's national and provincial parks are excellent.

Reservations

In 1996, BC Parks created a new service that enabled advance reservations to be made in 42 of the more popular provincial parks. Today, reservations can be made at 66 provincial parks in BC (plus two national-park campgrounds) through the Discover Camping Campground Reservation Service and 68,000 people made a reservation through this service in 2006.

For those who have found a full house at a popular campground on the times they have tried to visit, making a reservation in advance provides a way to avoid uncertainty. While reservations offer the advantage of assuring accommodation for the night, unless you have the option of choosing your spot, you may end up next to a particularly well-used thunderbox (pit toilet) or at the busy entrance to the campground.

To make a reservation in a provincial park (or at Prior Centennial or McDonald, which are part of the Gulf Islands National Park Reserve), phone

Campgrounds Included in this Book that Accept Reservations

Alice Lake
Bamberton
Bear Creek
Beatton
Beaumont
Birkenhead Lake
Blanket Creek
Champion Lakes
Charlie Lake
Cowichan River
Crooked River
Cultus Lake
Elk Falls
Ellison
Englishman River Falls
Fillongley
Fintry
French Beach
Gladstone (Texas Creek)
Golden Ears
Goldstream
Gordon Bay
Green Lake
Haynes Point
Herald
Juan de Fuca
Kekuli Bay
Kettle River Recreation Area
Kikomun Creek
Kin Beach
Kiskatinaw
Kokanee Creek
Kootenay (National)
Lac la Hache
Lac Le Jeune
Lakelse Lake

Liard River Hot Springs
Little Qualicum Falls
Loveland Bay
Manning
McDonald (National)
McDonald Creek
Miracle Beach
Moberly Lake
Monck
Montague Harbour Marine
Morton Lake
Mount Fernie
Mount Robson
Moyie Lake
Nairn Falls
Okanagan Lake
Otter Lake
Paarens Beach
Pacific Rim (National)
Porpoise Bay
Porteau Cove
Premier Lake
Prior Centennial (National)
Rathtrevor Beach
Rolley Lake
Saltery Bay
Sasquatch
Shuswap Lake
Smelt Bay
Sproat Lake
Stamp River
Strathcona
Syringa
Ten Mile Lake
Tyhee Lake
Wasa Lake

Discover Camping at 1-800-689-9025 (if calling from outside the Lower Mainland) or 604-689-9025 (from Vancouver and surrounding area) or visit www.discovercamping.ca to book online. In 2008, the fee to reserve was $6.30 per night to a maximum of $18.90 for 3 to 14 nights. Campers pay the reservation and campsite fees when making their reservation. Payment is taken by MasterCard or VISA and includes GST. Reservations are taken seven days a week from March 1 to September 15, and sites can be reserved up to three months in advance and as late as two days prior to arrival. Reservations for the holiday weekends of Victoria Day, BC Day or Labour Day must be for a minimum of three nights.

In addition, reservations are now accepted for certain campgrounds in Kootenay and Pacific Rim national parks through the Parks Canada Campground Reservation Service. To make a reservation using this service, go to www.pccamping.ca or call 1-877-737-3783 (from within Canada) or 1-514-335-4813 (from outside Canada). While dates vary from year to year, Pacific Rim generally begins accepting reservations on March 1 while Kootenay campsites can be reserved beginning in April. You can reserve a campsite up to midnight on the day prior to your arrival. In 2008, the cost to make a reservation was $10.80 per stay, and you pay the campsite fee for the number of nights included in your stay at the same time. (However, you will still be required to pay the park's daily-entry fee upon arrival at the park.) You will also be charged to change or cancel a previously confirmed reservation. You can pay by VISA, MasterCard or American Express, and by certified cheque or international money order if using the phone system.

Campfires

For many people, myself included, building and enjoying a campfire is an essential part of camping. In 2004, BC Parks started to charge for bundled firewood and national parks now require that you purchase a campfire permit for each fire. A few campgrounds (e.g. Porpoise Bay and Stawamus Chief) have even gone so far as to ban individual campfires at all times while others, such as Juan de Fuca, actively discourage fires for environmental reasons. When conditions are excessively hot and dry, as they were in the summer of 2003, campgrounds in arid areas ban fires altogether. If you need a campfire to make your camping experience complete, contact the campground you want to stay in to determine if fires are allowed, or check the campground notice board when you arrive.

Security Issues

Over the last 10 years, and since the publication of the first edition of *Camping British Columbia*, I have taken part in a number of radio phone-in interviews and given advice and guidance on a number of camping issues. A sad development in these yearly events is the increase in the number of people calling the radio station to relay stories of being victims of crime at a campground, usually the theft of unsecured possessions. I still maintain that camping is very safe, but it cannot be denied that crimes do take place. Generally, they tend to occur in the larger campgrounds nearer to centres of population (e.g. Golden Ears, Cultus Lake, Chilliwack Lake). Many of these parks now have security patrols to deter theft and to ensure their campgrounds remain peaceful and secure for everyone. Crime can occur anywhere and it is the responsibility of the camper to minimize the opportunity for it to take place, especially in parks that have been targets for deviants in the past. BC Parks frequently displays signs informing campers that the campground has been a target for crime in the past and suggesting extra vigilance.

Potential Hazards

Any hazards to be found in a particular park are posted at the campground entrance, but here are the more common problems and how to avoid them.

- **Swimmer's Itch**
  Parasites living in freshwater snails and waterfowl can cause swimmer's itch (a.k.a. cercarial dermatitis), a temporary skin irritation caused by the parasites' larvae entering the skin. The larvae thrive close to the shore in the warm waters of lakes and ponds where Canada geese and other waterfowl are found. Because children go in and out of the water frequently and have tender skin, they are particularly vulnerable. Swimmer's itch can be avoided by applying an oil to the skin such as baby oil before swimming, towelling off briskly and showering after swimming. The presence of swimmer's itch is indicated by small red spots that can develop into small blisters. Although unpleasant, the condition can be treated with calamine lotion and the condition usually clears up by itself within a week. The information board at the campground entrance will indicate whether swimmer's itch is a problem at the lake you plan to visit.

- **Poison Ivy**
  This low, glossy plant with three green leaves and white berries can produce severe skin rashes. It is prevalent in sunny areas on Vancouver Island and in the Okanagan. Calamine lotion is an effective treatment.

- **Sunburn**
  You are living largely outdoors when camping, and it is easy to forget how long you have been exposed to the sun. Always remember to apply and reapply sunscreen, wear a hat and be especially careful when you're around water or snow, which reflect the sun and can increase your chance of sunburn.

The Rules of Park Camping

Although few formal rules exist, there is a definite camping etiquette that should be observed for the benefit of all. Most of the items in the following list are common sense and serve only as a gentle reminder.

1. A camping party is regarded as a family from the same address, or if not a family, a maximum of eight people, up to four of whom may be 16 years or older.

2. Usually only one vehicle and trailer is allowed per site. Either one (but not both) may be an RV. A second vehicle (not an RV) may be allowed on the site for an additional nightly charge.

3. Keep pets on a leash in campgrounds and all other restricted areas.

4. Quiet time starts at 11:00 p.m. when the park gates are closed. Campsite visitor restrictions apply, and park gates are generally closed between 11:00 p.m. and 7:00 a.m.

5. In season, the threat of forest fires is immense, so extreme caution should be taken. At all times, light fires only in metal fire pits or designated campfire areas. Observe campfire restrictions and burn only as much wood as you need—help preserve the environment. Do not use your fire pit for garbage disposal. Partly burnt food tempts wildlife, and blackened beer cans are an annoyance.

6. Store food in your vehicle in airtight containers. If you do not have a vehicle and are in an area frequented by bears, and no food storage facility is provided, hang food in bags suspended on a tree branch, at least four metres above the ground. (With 100,000 black bears in BC, this is not a rule to ignore.)

7. To protect the vegetation, camp only in the designated areas and use tent pads when provided.

8. Dispose of garbage properly and recycle as much as possible.

9. Cutting trees and branches, and picking flowers, berries or mushrooms, is prohibited in all parks. Enjoy the flora and fauna by looking, smelling and photographing, but leave it undisturbed so that others may have the same pleasure.

10. Respect boating restrictions and do not take powerboats near swimmers; try not to disturb the tranquility of those enjoying the beach.

11. Observe fishing restrictions, trail closures and any other rules specific to the park or campground.

12. Alcohol is allowed at your campsite. I camped for years before I learned it was okay to consume a glass of wine with dinner. I guiltily hid my drink from the park attendant I thought would expel me for my transgression. On one occasion, discovered and expecting to meet the full wrath of the BC Parks employee, I cowered and apologized. All he said was, "You can drink here. This is your home away from home. It is only in the public sections of the park that alcohol is prohibited." From that point on, I've always thought of the spot where I'm camping as my "home away from home."

13. Checkout time is usually 11:00 a.m., and the maximum length of stay is 14 days per year in any one park (though a few parks restrict your stay to 7 nights).

14. Clean your campsite on departure. Remove all garbage.

- **Water**

  Lifeguards are not employed in BC parks, so a watchful eye must be kept on those who cannot swim. Some parks have designated swimming areas; others do not. Weather conditions may change rapidly in some locations, with winds suddenly developing and causing a hazard for boating enthusiasts. Again, information on the park's notice board will state whether this is a problem.

- **Bears**

  BC is home to almost one-quarter of all the black bears in Canada and about half of all grizzlies. Although encounters between people and bears are rare, campers should remember they are always in bear country in BC. Respect bears as strong, fast, wild animals, and act responsibly at all times.

  Generally, bears go out of their way to avoid people, but all bears are dangerous. They can rip apart tents and vehicles in their search for food, run as fast as a racehorse and they have excellent sight, hearing and sense of smell. They are strong swimmers, and black bears and young grizzlies are agile tree-climbers. Upon leaving the city, you are in bear country and should use caution.

  Anyone planning to camp or spend time in the outdoors should learn how to recognize a black or grizzly bear and how to respond accordingly. Black bears can be black, brown, cinnamon or blond with a straight-face profile, short curved claws and a small shoulder hump. Grizzly bears can also be black, brown or blond, but they are bigger than black bears and have long curved claws and a prominent shoulder hump. When walking in bear country, watch for warning signs, such as tracks, overturned rocks, clawed trees, chewed roots and droppings. Talk loudly, wear bear bells or sing to make your presence known. If you see a bear in the distance, leave the area immediately. If you encounter one at close range, avoid eye contact, move away slowly and stay calm. If the bear stands up as it approaches you, it is trying to identify what you are. Talk quietly so it knows you are human. If it is lowering its head, flattening its ears, snapping its jaws and snorting, the bear is displaying aggression. This is serious. Do not run, but continue to back away. If a grizzly shows aggression, consider climbing a tree. Generally, the key is to do nothing to threaten or arouse the animal. If a grizzly attacks, play dead and adopt a tight, curled-up position with your head on your knees and your hands behind your neck. Do not move until the bear leaves the area. If a black bear attacks, try to retreat to a safe place and use weapons, such as rocks and branches, to deter the animal.

  Never approach or feed bears. Food-conditioned bears—those that scavenge food from garbage cans and picnic tables—begin to associate food with people, lose their natural fear of humans and become a threat to campers and to themselves. With caution and sensible behaviour, you can safely camp in and enjoy bear country.

BE BEAR AWARE

- Avoid cooking fish, as the smell strongly attracts bears.

- Cook and eat away from your tent.

- Clean up immediately and do not leave cooking utensils, coolers or dishwater around.

- Never bury garbage. Bears normally dig for food, and they may remember the location as a food source, thus endangering those visitors that follow.

- Avoid getting scents or food smells on clothing or sleeping bags.

- Women should consider using tampons if menstruating.

- Always use a flashlight if walking at night.

What to Take Camping

To the uninitiated, it would appear that some people take everything camping. On one occasion, I camped next to a couple who had a large RV with two mountain bikes tied to the front, a boat on the roof and a small four-wheel-drive vehicle towed behind. Their picnic table displayed several coolers of assorted sizes, wine glasses, a breadbasket and a red-checked tablecloth; overhead was an ornate striped awning. Artificial grass, potted plants, lanterns and numerous plastic lounge chairs with cushions were strategically positioned around a huge barbecue. This campsite had more accoutrements than my home (and was certainly worth more). It is impossible to provide the definitive list of necessities, but there are a number of items that will make your camping experience more enjoyable, whether you are a tenter or an RVer.

I started my BC camping career in 1992 with a two-person tent (designed for two very small people) and toured the province in a 1974 Ford Pinto. On this first excursion I was totally unprepared. My partner and I had no axe, so to make a fire we had to arrive at a campground early enough to collect the unused wood that had been cut by our predecessors. On one occasion this option was not available, so we approached a neighbouring site and asked a camper if we could borrow his axe. He came over from his well-equipped RV to supply the tool and chat. After surveying our meagre tent and picnic table (displaying two plastic plates, two plastic mugs, and one plastic grocery bag of food), he started to explain how he started as we were doing, with barely the basics, but assured us that as each year progressed our commitment to camping would grow and more "comforts" would be acquired. He was right. We now arrive at our campsite in a 2007 seven-seater van, sleep on self-inflating thermarests in a six-person tent we can stand up in, have tarps, a red-checked tablecloth, clotheslines, coolers, a hibachi and, yes, even an axe. On three separate occasions we have been lucky enough to camp in a 28-foot recreational vehicle—real luxury. On occasion we see novice campers starting out as we and many others have done, and we look knowingly at each other, content in the thought that it will not be long before they, too, start to collect the camping necessities. One of the tremendous joys of camping is learning how to do it. That said, there are a few "essentials" you'll want to pack right from the beginning. See the sidebar on the opposite page.

Green Camping

Some would argue that true tent camping is, by its very nature, green, but like the rest of our society this has changed over the last 50 years with the introduction of recreational vehicles. In some campgrounds, tents are the exception rather than the rule. But while huge RVs with their own generators and heavy gas consumption remain a regular sight in many BC parks, there are ways that camping is reverting back to its more traditional roots as our concern for preserving the environment increases. Some evidence of this shift includes:

- **Recycling:** Most parks have recycling facilities. When camping as a family we now take along a separate bag for collecting bottles and cans, so even if the campground does not recycle we can.

- **Fires:** Ten years ago, firewood was provided free of charge and fires burned all day. With the concern for air quality and the environment, provincial parks now charge for wood, and national parks now require you to pay for campfires. Some campgrounds also prohibit individual fires.

- **Boating:** An increasing number of lakes are being closed to powerboats, water skiers and those dreaded Jet Skis. Other parks have instituted restrictions on the types of motors allowed.

- **Fuel costs:** The cost of fuel in BC rose by 40 percent in 2008. That summer it cost over $300.00 to fill the tank of a 24-foot RV so there may be a return to car-camping using tents. With transportation costs for all vehicles being prohibitive to long road trips, we may also witness a change in campground attendance in certain areas. Campgrounds near population centres may become more crowded and those in the remoter areas of the province, and on islands only accessible by increasingly expensive ferry rides, may suffer a decline in attendance.

Camping Essentials

- aluminum foil
- axe
- barbecue, hibachi or camping stove (plus briquettes or fuel)
- biodegradable dish soap and scrubbing pads
- bungee cords
- digital camera, or camera and film
- candles or camping lantern
- first-aid kit, including calamine lotion
- flashlight
- food
- garbage bags
- insect repellent
- matches and newspaper if you intend to have a campfire
- paper towels
- pocket knife
- pots, dishes and cutlery
- rainy-day activities (books, portable radio, travel games)
- rope
- sleeping bag, pillow and camping mattress
- sunglasses, hat and sunscreen
- tarp
- tent and fly, tent trailer, camper or RV
- toilet paper
- towels
- water container and funnel

Camping with Kids

Ten years ago, I did not have children and camping was a wonderful, tranquil experience. Now my two boys are 8 and 10 years old and camping is anything but a "wonderful tranquil experience." As a family we camp every summer and as the boys have grown older so their love of camping has increased. In 2007, I asked my oldest son what his best summertime experience had been. I expected him to say the three-week trip we'd had to visit relatives in England, but instead it was the four-day trip we'd taken to Alice Lake Provincial Park. Often when you reflect on your childhood it is the outdoor summer activities that are the most memorable. Camping and all it entails is a wonderful thing to do with kids, who are totally oblivious to the weather and seem to be able to play in a lake whatever the water's temperature.

While camping is a popular affordable family vacation, what you can and cannot do when camping with kids depends on the age of your offspring, as each age brings unique experiences, joys and challenges.

- **Camping with Babies or Toddlers**

  If your baby is not yet a crawler, camping is easy. Okay, you do have to take more stuff, but you can leave the baby happily goo-gooing in the car seat on the picnic table while you erect the tent. Playpens are great and can be used for a baby to sleep in as a crib, and a mosquito net can be easily laid over the top, should bugs be a problem.

  Camping with toddlers, however, is another matter. This age can be the most challenging because of all the equipment they require, their need for diapers and their propensity to put everything in their mouths. The great outdoors, replete with animals, rocks, stones, water, dirt, vegetation and insects, can't be childproofed as easily as can your home. I believe the secret to camping with toddlers is being relaxed about it. So they don't have a wash before going to bed, or they sleep in the clothes they've been in all day, or they delight in treading on the ants and poking the banana slugs with pinecones; let them do it. The biggest

problem I found while tent camping with toddlers was in their early-morning waking. The dawn arrives and their excitement over seeing you sleeping next to them stimulates their delight and curiosity; so you get up at 5:30 a.m. and experience the campground at a time few others will. Afternoon naps may also be a challenge if you try to get them to sleep in the unfamiliar tent. A better option is a gentle push in the stroller around the campground's roads, especially if these are gravel—an almost surefire way to send them to sleep.

Most of the difficulties of this tent-based experience are, of course, avoided by camping in a recreational vehicle, camper, tent trailer or towing trailer. If there is ever a time when you get rid of the tent and choose an RV, it is at this age. On the plus side, kids of this age are still quite portable, so you can hike with them in a backpack—something that is not an option with the preschooler.

- **Camping with Preschoolers**

While you can't send these young ones off to explore the campground on their own, children at this age are a real delight to take camping. The under-fives can actively get involved with camping and what it means to set up home outdoors away from the urban centre. They can help select flat ground to put up the tent, get sticks for toasting marshmallows, explore adjacent undergrowth without eating it, take a ride on the tricycle and run around and make noise. Expect them to stay up late, get dirty, make friends with the kids from the next campsite, play the best imaginary games and have a ball.

Camping with this age group also means you can vacation in May, June or September and avoid the crowds and the added expense. Make the most of it and remember to teach them your campsite number upon arrival, as well as basic safety information. Also remember to pack fishing nets, water shoes, sidewalk chalk and toys.

- **Camping with Schoolchildren**

By setting boundaries and following a few simple rules, children this age will learn to love the camping experience. Provincial and national parks provide wonderful safe environments for children to explore by themselves. Parents do not have to worry about unsafe roads and fast drivers, video arcades or TV. Children can gain some independence by exploring safely on their own. Parks are fantastic for cycling, rollerblading, swimming and exploring with newfound friends or with friends brought from home. Remember their board games, art supplies, sidewalk chalk, balls, bikes, rollerblades and books and they will be sure to entertain themselves. The big disadvantage with this age group is the restriction of having to camp during school holidays and weekends when parks are most crowded. A little planning ahead helps a lot, though; these are the times when you really appreciate the reservation system (see "Reservations").

British Columbia Regions

1. The Islands
2. Vancouver Coast and Mountains
3. Thompson Okanagan
4. BC Rockies
5. Cariboo Chilcotin Coast
6. Northern BC

THE REGIONS AND THEIR PARKS

This section is divided into six chapters that reflect the main geographical regions of the province: The Islands; Vancouver Coast and Mountains; Thompson Okanagan; BC Rockies; Cariboo Chilcotin Coast; and Northern British Columbia.

Maps at the beginning of each chapter show the location of each campground and the main highways and centres of population. However, these maps should serve only as a guide: more accurate information should be obtained by referencing a good map of the province, such as the *British Columbia Road & Recreational Atlas* or *British Columbia Road Map and Parks Guide*. Additional information on parks in the various regions can be found on the Internet; a list of useful websites is included at the back of this book.

Blanket Creek Provincial Park is located in the BC Rockies. Camping is an excellent way to explore the different regions of the province. (BC Parks photo)

To reach campgrounds on Vancouver Island or the Gulf Islands, you will have to take one of the BC Ferries vessels, such as these seen at Pender Island.

Ferry Schedules

Current BC Ferries schedules are always available at Tourism BC centres, in some newspapers and on the BC Ferries website at www.bcferries.com, or by calling 1-888-223-3779 from anywhere in North America.

THE ISLANDS

This chapter includes campgrounds located on Vancouver Island and the Gulf Islands. Vancouver Island is the largest North American island in the Pacific and stretches 450 kilometres. Named after Captain Vancouver, one of the first European visitors in 1778, this varied region includes mountains, farmlands, miles of breathtaking coastline (lots of it inaccessible by road), and unique wildlife. The Gulf Islands are situated between Vancouver Island and the Mainland and for many residents offer a serene and alternative lifestyle away from the populations of the Lower Mainland and southern Vancouver Island. Tourists, too, find the islands a delight. Despite the number of campgrounds available, the popularity of the region and the convenience of its location close to large centres of population mean that many idyllic spots are busy, especially during July and August.

Bamberton Provincial Park borders on Saanich Inlet and has a great beach that is connected to the camping area by several trails. (BC Parks photo)

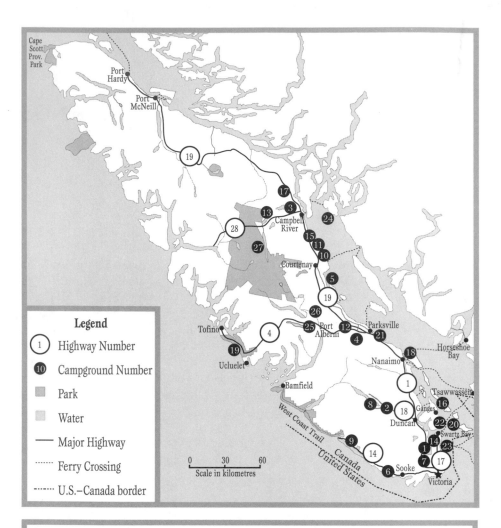

The Islands

BAMBERTON

Location

A true family-friendly campground and a really picturesque location, Bamberton looks onto Finlayson Arm of the Saanich Inlet, across the Gulf Islands to Mount Baker and beyond. Bamberton is situated about half an hour's drive from Victoria, 1 kilometre east of Highway 1 at Malahat Drive. Services are available on the highway, in Victoria to the south and in Duncan to the north.

Facilities

Nestled in a lightly forested area, which includes arbutus trees unique to the West Coast, are 53 well-appointed, private camping spots. There are flush and pit toilets but no sani-station or showers. The park is wheelchair-accessible and reservations are accepted. This is one of the few campgrounds open year-round.

Recreational activities

This is a popular family recreational area, as the warm waters of the Saanich Inlet together with over 225 metres of beach make it a pleasant place for families to congregate, play and rest. Creeks that run through the park have little fishing potential, but it is possible to catch salmon in the inlet. Small trails lead from the campground to the beach area, and intrepretive programs are offered in the summer months. As this provincial park is so close to Victoria, 30 minutes to the south, and Duncan, 20 minutes north, there are many additional things to see and do outside the immediate area. For example, Duncan has a forest museum displaying logging artifacts and giving the history of an industry that is very much a part of Vancouver Island's heritage.

Additional information

Bamberton was given to the people of BC by the British Columbia Cement Company, and the name was chosen to commemorate H.K. Bamber, a former managing director of the company. Its proximity to Victoria and the population of southern Vancouver Island means Bamberton is a popular place for locals to spend weekends and therefore can become very busy. It is far more desirable than a nearby competitor, McDonald.

COWICHAN RIVER

Location

This is one of BC Parks' newer provincial parks; Cowichan River was designated a Provincial Heritage River recently because it is internationally renowned for its wild salmon and steelhead. Although less than 10 years old, this park has become very popular, especially amongst the angling community. Located between Cowichan Lake and Duncan, the 1,414-hectare park can be reached from Highway 18 on a good gravel road or from Highway 1 south of Duncan by a 17-kilometre paved and gravel road. Services are available in both Cowichan Lake and Duncan.

Facilities

There are two campgrounds in this park. Forty-three vehicle and four walk-in camping spots are located at Skutz Falls (*skutz* means "waterfall" and comes from the Cowichan word *skewts*). Most of these campsites are open and quite close together, offering little privacy. An additional 29 are located at Stolz Pool on the Cowichan River. Water, pit toilets, picnic tables and fire pits are all provided. Reservations are available at the Stolz Pool campground.

Recreational activities

The Cowichan River is one of Vancouver Island's most popular fishing environments. It flows 47 kilometres from its headwaters at Cowichan Lake to the sea and is known as an angler's paradise with rainbow and steelhead trout and excellent salmon runs. A section of the Cowichan River Footpath, a 20-kilometre trail leading to some of the best fishing holes, is within the park boundaries. As well as the excellent fishing potential, the park has swimming, canoeing, kayaking, hiking and tubing possibilities and is therefore attractive to all ages. A section of the Trans-Canada Trail runs through the park (see www.trails.bc.ca).

Additional information

In addition to being the delight of many fishers, this location is ideal for exploring the communities of Cowichan Lake and Duncan. Duncan calls itself the "city of totems" and is home to over 80 totem poles, which have been erected primarily in the downtown area. Some employ traditional design while others are less traditional. Duncan also houses the Quw'utsun' First Nations cultural centre, a fascinating place found on the banks of the Cowichan River that has a longhouse, theatre and arts and craft centre. When we stayed at Stolz Pool there seemed to be hundreds of teenagers sunbathing on the large slab rocks, with huge tubes lying by their sides. Every vehicle in the parking lot had an inner tube tied to it. In this respect, at the height of summer it is a place that attracts a younger crowd. However, these youths were not loud and seemed aware of the "rules of camping." I imagine that during the shoulder season this campground is a wonderful (and quieter) place for people of every age to visit.

Elk Falls

Location
This is a beautiful 1,087-hectare provincial park that features a cascading 25-metre waterfall created by the Campbell River falling into a walled canyon. In spring, the waters tumble (or, in late summer, trickle) over a deep gorge and provide a beautiful vista. Elk Falls is located on Highway 28 just 2 kilometres north of Campbell River, where all services are available.

Facilities
Elk Falls boasts 122 large, private camping spots surrounded by trees. Approximately 25 of the more desirable spots are situated along the banks of the Quinsam River; the rest are among an area of second-growth forest. There are a couple of flush toilets and a sani-station, however, only some park areas are wheelchair-accessible. Reservations are accepted. The day-use area is separate from the campground, making for quite a peaceful provincial park.

Recreational activities
The primary attraction of the area is fishing, which is excellent in both Campbell River and Quinsam River. Depending on the time of year, steelhead, rainbow and cutthroat trout and Dolly Varden can be caught. Another feature of this provincial park is the extensive 12-kilometre trail system. The Quinsam River Trail leads to the Quinsam Salmon Hatchery, and the Canyon View Trail takes explorers to the John Hart power-generating facility and an impressive bridge over the river. Other trails lead through woodland to wonderful waterfalls and wildlife-viewing opportunities. For children there is an adventure playground and sports field, and swimming and paddling are possible in the river at the day-use area. The nearby community of Campbell River is a pleasant town to explore and provides a number of attractions, including a pier where you can rent fishing rods and buy ice cream. Keep an eye out for the logger up the pole by the shopping centre, and watch for seals in the Strait of Georgia.

Additional information
In 1997, a magazine produced by BC Parks stated: "The undisputedly cheapest overnight rate in the salmon capital of the world is located in Elk Falls Provincial Park. Just $9.50/night buys a quiet river setting, a campsite, a convenient location and a fishing extravaganza. " In 2008, the price had increased slightly, but it is still a real bargain for those who love fishing and those who just want an idyllic place to camp.

ENGLISHMAN RIVER FALLS

Location

Established in 1940, this 97-hectare provincial park is a delight to visit at any time of the year. Englishman River Falls is found 13 kilometres southwest of Parksville off Highway 4 on a paved road. Qualicum, Parksville and Nanaimo are nearby.

Facilities

The campground has 105 spacious campsites set in a forest of Douglas fir interspersed with Rocky Mountain maple trees and ferns. There are no showers, flush toilets or sani-station, and only the basic camping facilities exist (pit toilets, drinking water, picnic tables, fire pits). This park is not wheelchair-accessible. Reservations are accepted.

Recreational activities

In this park you can walk to the beautiful waterfalls amidst a mixed forest of cedar, Douglas fir and hemlock. Three kilometres of trails offer views of the river, and you can swim in the swimming holes at the base of the lower falls. A deep pool at the bottom of the canyon is a good place to seasonally view spawning salmon, steelhead and trout (fishing in this park is prohibited). The park's proximity to Nanaimo (48 kilometres away), Port Alberni (50 kilometres) and Courtenay (88 kilometres) means the activities and facilities of these communities are easily accessible, as is the beach at Parksville (14 kilometres), where at low tide the sea recedes nearly 100 metres and leaves a vast expanse of sand and pools to explore and beachcomb.

Additional information

Once named *Rio De Grullas*—"River of Cranes"—by the Spanish explorers of the 18th century, this river was renamed a century later in memory of an English immigrant who died here. The campground is frequently used when the one at Rathtrevor Beach is full. It is well worth visiting in the fall when the trees are turning beautiful shades of golden and red, or in the spring when the wildflowers are at their best.

FILLONGLEY

Location

There is something for everyone in this 23-hectare provincial park that includes a beach, a marshy estuary, a forest rich in old-growth firs and the remnants of what was once a large estate. Found on Denman Island and featuring views of Lambert Channel, Fillongley is reached by taking a ferry from Buckley Bay, south of Courtenay, to Denman and then driving the 4-kilometre paved road to the east side of the island where the campground is situated. Denman Island has food, gas and basic supplies.

Facilities

The biggest drawback of Denman Island's only provincial park is that there are only 10 camping spots available here, and they are lined up side by side at the parking area. For more privacy, it is possible to pitch tents under nearby trees. All the basic amenities are provided (drinking water, pit toilets, picnic tables, fire pits). The park is wheelchair-accessible. Since 2000, reservations have been accepted.

Recreational activities

The campground is situated near a lovely rocky beach from which it is possible to swim, kayak, beachcomb and look for oysters and clams. Hiking trails through old-growth forest have also been developed and offer an alternative to the shoreline recreational pursuits. The island is ideal for cycling enthusiasts as there is little traffic (except near the ferry terminals) and it is relatively flat. Denman Island is a delightful place to explore, for it has a beautifully relaxed atmosphere and many arts and crafts shops. In addition, nearby Hornby Island, which is also easy to reach, has hiking trails and lovely beaches.

Additional information

The park was created from a bequest by George Beadnell, one of the first pioneers to settle in the area. He named his estate Fillongley after his home in England and built a tennis court, bowling green, clubhouse and greenhouse, as well as a large impressive home. Following Beadnell's death in 1958, these facilities fell into disrepair and were eventually destroyed. Beadnell is buried in the park. This is a fantastic, tranquil camping spot with a rocky beach and shallow waters. I spent a wonderful night here watching the sun set after having dinner on the beach. It's one of the best-kept secrets of BC Parks but is often full, so be sure to make a reservation.

FRENCH BEACH

Location

French Beach Provincial Park, which boasts 1,600 metres of beach and exceptional views across the Strait of Juan de Fuca toward the Olympic Mountains in Washington State, is a marvellous place to visit. The 59-hectare park is located just 20 kilometres west of Sooke on Highway 14 (Sooke is 38 kilometres from Victoria). Services are provided by a small store adjacent to the campground, as well as stores in Sooke and Jordan River (11 kilometres away).

Facilities

Set in a forest of Douglas fir, Sitka spruce, western hemlock and western redcedar are 69 shaded camping spots. There is a sani-station, but the campground has only pit toilets. The park is wheelchair-accessible and reservations are accepted. The campground is open year-round.

Recreational activities

One of the biggest attractions here is whale watching. Magnificent grey whales migrate to their feeding grounds in the spring and return in the fall. If you're lucky, you can view them from the beach or, if you are an experienced paddler, at closer range in a kayak. Roaming pods of killer whales are also sometimes observed. Looking offshore, it is not unusual to see river otters, seals and sea lions playing, while ospreys and bald eagles frequent the skies overhead. The extensive sand-and-gravel beach, rimmed by the forest, is a beautiful place to swim from—although it is considerably wilder than the beaches on the other side of the island. Small nature trails wind through the second-growth forest, and there is a playground for children. Once you have had enough of the natural beauty, go and explore Victoria's many attractions.

Additional information

A friend of mine tried to persuade me not to include French Beach in this book; she wanted to keep it all to herself and hated the thought of it becoming too well known. The biggest draw for her and for me to this provincial park is the huge beach—a beautiful place to sit and watch the sun go down or to stargaze. This is a rugged beach that is great to explore at any time of the year.

GOLDSTREAM

Location

The BC Parks webpage for Goldstream reads: "Massive trees, majestic waterfalls, a meandering river that meets the sea, flowers, birds and fascinating fish are but a few attractions that draw people to Goldstream Provincial Park." This description, coupled with the fact that the park is only 16 kilometres northwest of Victoria off Highway 1, makes it a very popular location for both locals and tourists. A small store and pub are located at the park entrance.

Facilities

This 477-hectare park has 173 well-appointed camping spots available for every type of recreational vehicle. There are showers, a sani-station, flush and pit toilets and wheelchair accessibility. Reservations are accepted and strongly advised. The campground is open year-round but certain services (water, firewood, sani-station) are only available between March and October.

Recreational activities

Goldstream is blessed with a number of hiking and walking routes, some accessible to mountain bikers. Trails take hikers through Goldstream's two distinctive vegetation zones to views of 600-year-old Douglas fir trees and many other deciduous and evergreen trees and plants. The Gold Mine and Lower Falls trails lead to Niagara Falls, which is higher than its namesake (and fortunately much less commercialized—no honeymoon suites here). Swimming and fishing are possible within the park, and in the summer months, naturalists conduct interpretive programs in the outdoor theatre. An excellent visitor centre is also located here, which has exhibits, snacks and offers programs throughout the year.

Additional information

Goldstream River was first named Gold Creek in 1858 by Lieutenant Peter Leech, an engineer with the Vancouver Island Exploration Committee, who discovered gold in the waters. Subsequent exploration revealed only small deposits, but there is nothing stopping the fortune seeker from further exploration. The Goldstream River is now the site of chum salmon spawning, and from mid-October to November it draws many thousands of visitors and millions of salmon. BC Parks produces a leaflet detailing the salmon spawning process. Long ago, this area, like many others on Vancouver Island, was used as a fishing ground by the Coast Salish people. Whether you are a fortune seeker, an angler or just a holidaymaker, Goldstream is a lovely place to visit.

GORDON BAY

Location

Be sure you have the sunscreen if you plan to holiday at Gordon Bay Provincial Park, which is one of Canada's hottest spots. This 51-hectare park is found at the southern end of Lake Cowichan, 35 kilometres northwest of Duncan and accessed by taking Highway 18 just north of Duncan. The nearby community of Lake Cowichan has most services, and there is a small store at Honeymoon Bay, 2 kilometres from the campground.

Facilities

Positioned in an area of second-growth Douglas fir, this campground has 126 large, well-structured camping spots (those numbered 1 to 14 are closest to the bay). There are flush and pit toilets, a sani-station, showers and full access for wheelchairs. Reservations are accepted and highly recommended, as this is one of the Island's most popular locations. The campground is open year-round.

Recreational activities

Gordon Bay is located in one of the warmest valleys on Vancouver Island. The mountains pressing close to Cowichan Lake produce a heat trap that ensures the highest average daily temperature in Canada. The waters of Lake Cowichan supply relief from this heat (as do the shady camping spots). For the angler, the lake has reserves of Dolly Varden, rainbow and cutthroat trout, chum, coho and spring salmon. There is a boat launch in the park and water skiing is permitted. An adventure playground has been constructed for children within the camping area. Two of the biggest attractions are the excellent pebble beach—fantastic for children of every age—and the clear weed-free waters. Trails lead from the park over a forest floor covered with thimbleberry, salal and salmonberry plants, and, in the spring, wonderful wildflowers. (Remember, picking the vegetation in BC parks is prohibited.) Interpretive programs are available in the summer.

Additional information

In addition to the beauty of the park itself, the immediate surrounding area provides many alternative activities. A small museum at Saywell Park offers local interest, and you can tour the Lake Cowichan Earth Satellite station. Lake Cowichan is also the hometown of Dawn Coe-Jones, a repeat winner on the LPGA tour, who learned to golf at March Meadows, the attractive nine-hole public golf course in Honeymoon Bay. Because Gordon Bay is a delightful family-oriented camping location equipped with all amenities, it's not surprising that it's one of the most popular campgrounds on southern Vancouver Island—and frequently full.

JUAN DE FUCA

Location

This is one of the province's newest campgrounds. Its quick addition to the list of reservable sites illustrates BC Parks' recognition that it would be immediately popular. Juan de Fuca Provincial Park consists of three main areas. In addition to the campground and day-use area (known as China Beach) there is the Juan de Fuca Marine Trail, a 47-kilometre stretch of wilderness that was used at the turn of the century as a life-saving trail. It is adjacent to the shoreline, known as the "graveyard of the Pacific" because a number of boats ran aground here. The third area of the park is Botanical Beach, a unique shoreline and one of the richest tidal areas on the west coast. The campground is situated on the west coast of southern Vancouver Island, 35 kilometres west of Sooke and 36 kilometres east of Port Renfrew.

Facilities

China Beach features 75 vehicle-accessible campsites in a lightly forested area. Although fire pits are available, the parks administration stresses the use of stoves to conserve the environment. There are only picnic tables, pit toilets and drinking water. Some campground facilities are wheelchair-accessible. Reservations are accepted.

Recreational activities

The main feature of this park is the Juan de Fuca Marine Trail, which was developed as an alternative to the increasingly popular West Coast Trail. Although 47 kilometres may be pretty tough going for some, it is easy to select a small section of beach to wander along. From the day-use area there is a one-kilometre trail through the forest to the beach, while Second Beach is a two-kilometre return trip from China Beach. Nearer to Port Renfrew is Botanical Beach, where a wonderful array of shoreline and marine life is revealed at low tide. Red, purple and orange starfish can be seen, as well as sea anemones and blue mussels. Sea fishing is possible, as is canoeing, kayaking and windsurfing if the seas are not too rough. Personally, I think it is just wonderful to sit and watch the ever-changing sea.

Additional information

The Juan de Fuca Marine Trail was the result of the Commonwealth Nature Legacy—a reminder of the 1994 Commonwealth Games that were held in Victoria—but the area was recognized as biologically significant as early as 1901, when the University of Minnesota established a marine research station here. This is a stunning park, but take caution when enjoying it: the shoreline is prone to "rogue" waves, which hit the beach occasionally and can drag you into the sea.

KIN BEACH

Location

Kin Beach is a new addition to *Camping British Columbia* and is a Category C park, which means it's co-administered by a local community board and its facilities and services vary slightly from those solely under the auspices of BC Parks. This newly created park is located on central Vancouver Island in the Comox Valley, overlooking the Strait of Georgia and very close to the Comox–Powell River ferry terminal. Access is from Ryan Road in Comox: turn left on Little River Road then right on Kilmorley Road. Services are available in Comox or Courtenay. A small store selling some items is positioned in the park's day-use area.

Facilities

The 9-hectare park has 18 vehicle-accessible camping spots. Firewood is available for purchase, tap water is provided, and there are flush and pit toilets. Reservations are recommended during the summer and can be made by calling the park directly at (250) 339-6365.

Recreational activities

The nearest boat launch is at Kitty Coleman Provincial Park down the road, but it is possible to canoe and kayak from this park. The beach is somewhat rocky, which makes for good rock-pool analysis (remember the bucket and tell the kids to put everything back after they've finished prodding and poking). Fishing for salmon, rockfish and shellfish takes place here. There is a large day-use area with a grassy area, picnic tables, a woodstove and even a tennis court (a recreational facility rarely found in provincial parks; in fact, I think this could be the only one!). There is also a kids' playground.

Additional information

I have not as yet visited this park but it is on my "to do" list and is a welcome addition to an area of the province that frequently finds its provincial parks operating at capacity. We often camp or picnic at Miracle Beach, just down the road, so will be checking out Kin Beach and its neighbour Kitty Coleman in the near future.

KITTY COLEMAN

Location
Like Kin Beach, just a stone's throw away, Kitty Coleman has been designated a Category C provincial park and is managed by a local community board, which means it provides a different camping experience than other provincial parks. The 10-hectare park is found on the southern side of Georgia Strait, 6 kilometres north of Courtenay, off Highway 19A. Take Coleman Road off Highway 19, turn on Left Road then right on Whittaker Road. All services are available in Courtenay or Comox.

Facilities
The campground here has 65 sites, some of which overlook the park's 900 metres of shoreline. There are flush and pit toilets but no showers and only pump water. Firewood is available for purchase from the park administrator.

Recreational activities
The park is characterized by a mature forest of western hemlock, western redcedar and the estuary of Kitty Coleman Creek. A series of trails meanders through the park, and canoeing, kayaking and swimming are popular pastimes. There are two pay-to-use boat launches, and you can fish for salmon or harvest shellfish, which at times are abundant in the area. The park is also good for spotting a variety of wildlife, including seals, sea lions, porpoises and bald eagles.

Additional information
BC Parks says there is a single majestic old-growth Douglas fir in the park and wild onions growing in the area. I am a little nervous about including Category C parks where I haven't camped, as the facilities and upkeep is very much dependent on the local community boards charged with their administration. Since Kin Beach and Kitty Coleman are both are close to each other, campers have the luxury of checking them both out (and, if neither is appealing, Miracle Beach is just a short drive away).

LITTLE QUALICUM FALLS

Location

Impressive waterfalls cascading into a rocky gorge characterize this 440-hectare provincial park, claimed by some people to be the most magnificent park on Vancouver Island. Little Qualicum River drops several hundred feet down the slopes of Mount Arrowsmith in a series of waterfalls. This remarkable vista is located on Highway 4, 19 kilometres west of Parksville on Little Qualicum River. Services are available at Port Alberni and Parksville.

Facilities

Ninety-five camping spots are here for the taking in the Upper and Lower campgrounds, set amongst a pleasant fir and pine forest setting. The park is accessible to wheelchairs, and there are flush and pit toilets but no showers or sani-station. The campground is quite close to the road and railway line. Reservations are accepted.

Recreational activities

Swimming in this provincial park is wonderful and can be undertaken in lovely little green pools at the Cameron Lake picnic site just a short drive away. (Be advised that at certain times of the year swimming is prohibited—check the park notice board.) There are over 6 kilometres of graded walking trails, and fishing in the river is rewarding. Just outside the park is MacMillan (Cathedral Grove) Provincial Park, where magnificent western hemlocks, Douglas firs, and western redcedars stand over 60 metres tall, like the columns of a cathedral. Some of these trees are more than 800 years old. Cathedral Grove has trails that lead into the depths of the spectacular old-growth forest.

Additional information

The area around Beaufort and Cameron lakes contains salamanders and newts, which like the cool, damp cedar and fir forest area. This provincial park is conveniently located for exploring the eastern Parksville/Qualicum area and the western town of Port Alberni. From Port Alberni, it is possible to take the famous MV *Lady Rose* (www.ladyrosemarine.com) through the fjord scenery of the Alberni Inlet to Bamfield on the west coast, an unusual and rewarding trip that starts at 8:00 a.m. and returns around 5:00 p.m. If it is not raining, you are guaranteed to see some spectacular scenery and unusual wildlife.

Loveland Bay

Location

Loveland Bay is one of BC Parks' most recent additions. I first visited in May 2002, well before the crowds arrived and when wonderful birds were singing their hearts out. It is situated 18 kilometres west of Campbell River on Lower Campbell Lake and is reached by taking the John Hart Dam gravel road from Highway 28, then Camp Road 5 (gravel). Both gravel roads are good and suitable for every type of vehicle. It is a relatively small 30-hectare site but was immediately popular once opened (likely because it is so close to some of the best fishing in the province).

Facilities

There are 31 vehicle/tent campsites. All but five have direct access to the lake via a small pebbly beach and boast fantastic views of Lower Campbell Lake. There are 10 pit toilets and pump water is provided. The park is wheelchair-accessible and, surprisingly, reservations are accepted.

Recreational activities

There are few organized activities here — indeed, this campground is not geared for children. But it is an ideal place for reading and relaxing, and there is a small wharf to sunbathe on. Recreational activities include boating, swimming, fishing and canoeing on picturesque Campbell Lake. There is a boat launch, but be careful of the many submerged stumps and also of the wind, which can be quite strong on the lake. In the town of Campbell River, only 20 kilometres away, it is possible to rent or buy all the fishing equipment you could ever require. With the recent decline of the fishing industry, Campbell River has promoted itself as a tourist destination and is now a lovely place to wander around and people-watch. The 180-metre-long, 6.6-metre-wide pier regularly draws crowds; you can watch seals swimming below while you eat ice cream sold on the pier. Other attractions outside the park include mountain-bike trails, hiking and the Snowden Demonstration Forest.

Additional information

As mentioned previously, a number of provincial park campgrounds on Vancouver Island fill up during the peak summer season. For those who cannot find accommodation at Elk Falls, Miracle Beach or Strathcona, Loveland Bay provides an ideal alternative. Only 3 percent of the population of Vancouver Island lives north of Campbell River, so for those who want to explore the less commercialized, quieter side of Vancouver Island, Loveland Bay is an ideal choice.

McDonald (National)

Location

If you have missed the last ferry to the Mainland, you will be thankful for this park at the end of the Saanich Peninsula. Part of the Gulf Islands National Park Preserve since 2003, this former provincial park has good views of the nearby islands and is geared to overnight stays. Located 2 kilometres from the Swartz Bay ferry terminal, the park primarily provides accommodation for travellers waiting to take the ferry from Swartz Bay.

Facilities

This campground has 56 functional treed drive-in camping spots. Despite being near considerable development, McDonald Park has only the basic facilities (fire pits, picnic tables, pit toilets, drinking water), but it does have wheelchair access. Reservations can be made through Discover Camping.

Recreational activities

As already mentioned, McDonald is used primarily by people waiting to catch a ferry, or by those who have just taken a ferry and are only staying one night. The park therefore offers little in the way of recreational pursuits. The town of Sidney, which has a pleasant harbour, bookstores, craft shops and cafés, is within easy access and can be explored. In the summer, a small passenger ferry can be taken to Sidney Island, a park that has delightful scenery and allows camping.

Additional information

Victoria, only a 30-minute drive from Swartz Bay, offers a host of cultural and recreational activities for those who have time to explore. Victoria is the capital of British Columbia and houses the Provincial Legislature. Along streets lined with trees and flowers, the fascinating Royal British Columbia Museum, Empress Hotel, Parliament Buildings, Inner Harbour and China-town are all within easy walking distance of one another. Shopping here is also a real treat. For those who have a choice and a vehicle, Bamberton Provincial Park is preferable to McDonald, but if you're tired after a long day of travelling and just want a place for the night, McDonald delivers the goods.

MIRACLE BEACH

Location

Blessed with a wide sand-and-pebble beach and excellent views across the Strait of Georgia to the Coast Mountains, this campground is attractive to both adults and children and is an ideal spot for a family vacation. Miracle Beach is located on the protected shores of Vancouver Island's east coast, midway between Courtenay (22 kilometres south) and Campbell  River (22 kilometres north), 1.5 kilometres from Highway 19 on a paved access road. The campground has all required services conveniently located on the highway and in nearby communities. A small store is located in the nature house.

Facilities

Miracle Beach is 137 hectares and boasts 201 large private camping spots in a second-growth forest of Douglas fir, hemlock and western redcedar. All amenities are here, including showers, flush and pit toilets, a sani-station and wheelchair accessibility. Reservations are accepted and advisable. The campground is open year-round, but full services are only provided from April to September.

Recreational activities

One of the main attractions is the lovely long sand-and-pebble beach, perfect for swimming, sunbathing and exploring tide pools when they are accessible. Miracle Beach also has one of the best visitor centres I've visited. To supplement personal investigations, the excellent visitor centre has saltwater aquariums and nature displays, and interpretive programs are offered here, including the Jerry's Rangers program for kids. Black Creek, which runs through the park, has a coho salmon run, and there are two small walking trails. For those who choose to travel farther afield, the salmon fishing in the area is good, and short boat trips can be taken to the nearby islands of Denman, Hornby, Quadra and Cortes. At night, clear skies make for excellent stargazing from the beach or your camping spot.

Additional information

Miracle Beach is said to have received its name because it was miraculously missed by two severe forest fires that devastated much of the surrounding forest area in the recent past. Whenever I stay here, children seem to outnumber adults 10 to 1. This provincial park is an extremely popular camping location, especially during the summer months. If you have young children, it is the perfect place to spend a vacation.

Montague Harbour Marine

Location

When Montague Harbour Marine Provincial Park on Galiano Island opened in 1959, it was the first provincial park to serve both visitors who arrived in their own boats and those who came by car or on foot. The park encompasses an 89-hectare area that starts 5 metres below sea level and rises to 180 metres above. Galiano Island can be reached via BC Ferries, either from Swartz Bay on Vancouver Island or Tsawwassen on the Mainland (and from some other Gulf Islands). From the ferry dock at Sturdies Bay, you drive 10 kilometres northwest to the park. Full services are at Sturdies Bay, and the nearby marina has a small store and coffee bar with basic supplies.

Facilities

There are 40 beautifully positioned camping spots in this 97-hectare park, 25 of them suitable for vehicles and set in a forested area. Many of the 15 walk-in sites overlook the harbour and therefore have better views than the drive-in spots. Facilities are restricted to the basic ones found in provincial parks (pit toilets, drinking water, picnic tables, fire pits); there is no sani-station, but some facilities are wheelchair-accessible. Reservations are accepted and strongly advised. The campground is open year-round, but full services are only offered from March to October.

Recreational activities

This gorgeous park has scenic hiking trails that lead through a forested area of arbutus, Douglas fir, hemlock and Garry oak to beautiful beaches of white sand and shell, ideal for sunbathing or swimming. The abundant salmon and shellfish in the area attract a wide array of birds, including bald eagles, which can easily be seen fishing for their dinner. Canoes and kayaks can be hired from the adjacent marina, and there is a boat launch within the park. Intrepretive programs are offered in a glass-bottomed hut, which provide an entertaining and educational introduction to the marine life of the area. Galiano Island has quite a unique feel about it. Many artists and craftspeople have chosen to live here, and the area around Sturdies Bay has a small number of restaurants, craft shops and an excellent bakery.

Additional information

On weekends in the summer months, the Hummingbird Pub offers a free hourly bus service in the evening to and from the park's gate. Galiano's only neighbourhood pub has live music and good food. The marina next to the park serves excellent cinnamon buns and coffee in the morning. The island is named after the Spanish explorer Captain Galiano, the first European to visit the Gulf Islands in 1792. Smaller and less commercialized than Salt Spring Island, but with more amenities than Pender, Galiano is a fantastic place to spend some time. It's also a wonderful place to cycle around, and bikes can be rented at Sturdies Bay. The sunsets from the Montague Harbour campground are astoundingly beautiful. It's one of my favourite camping spots.

Morton Lake

Location

A really serene camping experience can be had at this exquisite little park nestled in the Sayward Forest northwest of Campbell River on Mohun and Morton lakes. The park is reached by travelling north on Highway 19 past the pulp mill and then taking the Menzies Main logging road (gravel) for 12 kilometres and Morton Lake Road for 7 kilometres. Services are at Campbell River, 27 kilometres to the south.

Facilities

There are only 24 camping spots in this 74-hectare park, but many of them have access directly onto Morton Lake and are quite charming. Only the basic amenities are available (pit toilets, drinking water, fire pits, picnic tables). Reservations are accepted.

Recreational activities

Visitors to this area can enjoy fishing for Dolly Varden and rainbow and cutthroat trout, boating, swimming and canoeing in Mohun or Morton lakes. Mohun Lake provides access to the Sayward canoe circuit, a 47-kilometre roundtrip. Alternately, a trail leads to Andrew Lake, which provides a different venue for water-based recreational pursuits just 30 minutes away. There is a good sandy beach by the campground, and since this location is away from the nearest population centre, sunbathing and swimming can be a tranquil experience—you may even consider skinny-dipping.

Additional information

The forest around the lake was destroyed in the Great Campbell River Fire of 1938 and has subsequently been replanted with Douglas fir and pine; cedar and hemlock have all grown back naturally. The scars of the fire are still clearly evident in the area. Morton Lake is the northernmost provincial park on Vancouver Island with basic camping amenities. Marble River and Schoen Lake provincial parks do not have potable water, and when I tried to stay at Schoen Lake in September 1995, the park was closed. In contrast to the roads south of Campbell River, Highway 19 north is a very quiet and beautiful drive; it is a great pity that there are not provincial parks located along this stretch of highway. In all my years of camping, it is only in the northern part of Vancouver Island that I have out of necessity stayed in a private campground. Although BC may have a large number of provincial parks in comparison to other provinces, states and countries, there is still a need for more campgrounds, especially on northern Vancouver Island.

Newcastle Island Marine

Location

A small island barely a kilometre from Nanaimo, with spectacular views across to the mountains on the Mainland, Newcastle can only be reached by water. Newcastle Island Marine Provincial Park is a popular cruising destination for recreational boaters. From Nanaimo, a charming little paddlewheeler operates from Maffeo Sutton Park, behind the civic arena, to ferry foot passengers to the island (in 2008, return fares were $8.00 for adults and $4.00 for children under 11). Services are available in Nanaimo, although food can be purchased in the tearooms located in the pavilion on the island.

Facilities

The 336-hectare park has only 18 designated camping spots, beautifully positioned at the edge of the forest, but a vast grassland meadow accommodates all additional campers. Many prefer this open space, as it is closer to the water. There are flush and pit toilets, two coin-operated showers and the park is wheelchair-accessible. The pavilion offers food from 10:00 a.m. to 7:00 p.m. during the peak summer season. The campground is open year-round, but full services are only offered between April and October.

Recreational activities

The island is rich in history; the Coast Salish people inhabited the area for centuries prior to the Spanish exploration in 1791. With the help of the indigenous people, the Hudson's Bay Company opened a coalmine on the island and named it Newcastle after the famous British mining town. Coal was extracted until 1887. From 1869 until 1955, a sandstone quarry was in operation. Evidence of the past can be seen when you take the 22 kilometres of hiking trails that zigzag their way around and across the park. Bikes are permitted on two of these trails. There are a number of beaches, caves and bays to explore and a calm sea to swim in. Canoeing along the shoreline is a favourite pastime, and there is a children's play area. Deer can be seen grazing in the early evening, and the area is also noted for its shoreline bird life.

Additional information

In July 1995, 1996 and 1997 the CAMPA big band played the Newcastle Island Pavilion. On each of these occasions we left Vancouver with rucksacks on our backs, caught two buses to the ferry at Horseshoe Bay, took the ferry from Horseshoe Bay to Nanaimo and walked the 30-minute route from the ferry terminal to the paddlewheeler to go and camp on the island, hike the trails during the day, eat on the verandas of the licensed tearooms during the evening and then dance the night away to the sound of brilliant jazz music. On these occasions I think we were the only couple wearing shorts, but we had great fun, and for under $20.00 each. This campground is not accessible by car and really should not be included in this book . . . but it's one of my favourites and I believe everyone should know about it! The park's website is www.newcastleisland.ca.

PACIFIC RIM (NATIONAL)

Location

Pacific Rim National Park Reserve is located on the west coast of Vancouver Island on Highway 4. Three distinctly different locations make up this 51,300-hectare (including 22,300 hectares of ocean) national park, and in order to see all aspects of it you need at least two weeks. The park's features include the famous West Coast Trail, a 77-kilometre rugged excursion into west coast rainforest scenery (reservations are required if you intend to take this hike); the Broken Group Islands, a group of over one hundred islands in Barkley Sound; and Long Beach with its fantastic sands. Services are available at Ucluelet and Tofino, as well as along Highway 4, which runs between these two centres.

Facilities

Developed vehicle-accessible camping facilities are only available in the Long Beach area of the park (backcountry camping is possible in other areas). Located between Ucluelet and Tofino, the Green Point campground has 94 blissful spots located high above the beach where campers are lulled to sleep by the sound of the ocean. There are also 18 non-reservable walk-in forest sites available. Facilities include a sani-station, flush and pit toilets, a visitor centre and wheelchair accessibility (in addition, the park has two wheelchair-accessible trails and the Wickaninnish Centre has an all-terrain wheelchair for visitor use). During the summer months this campground is almost always full, so reservations are essential. Book through www.pccamping.ca or call 1-877-737-3783. The maximum stay here is 7 nights and 2008 fees ranged from $17.60 to $23.50.

Long Beach.

Recreational activities

Long Beach boasts 22 kilometres of pristine beach, providing a superb expanse of shoreline for surfers, windsurfers, swimmers and kayakers to demonstrate their skills. The ocean temperature varies from 6 to 12°C. As the wild waves of the Pacific Ocean pound along the sands, beachcombing and hiking are invigorating activities here in any season—as long as you have the correct attire. There are nine short (1- to 2-kilometre) walking trails covering 12 kilometres in total, which can be used to explore the rainforest or coastal flora and fauna (bald eagles frequent the area). Hikers should be very cautious on rocky points and headlands as three people were swept to their deaths in 1997 by large waves. Remember, the next wave can be higher than the one before! There are nightly indoor interpretive programs offered from late June to early September. The Wickaninnish Intrepretive Centre is currently undergoing a $1.7-million facelift, which should be complete in September 2009. The community of Tofino is rapidly developing into a tourism hub and offers many commercial services, including guided excursions in the area.

Additional information

National parks charge a daily entrance fee, even if you are staying overnight (in 2008, the fees were $7.80/adult, $3.90/child, $19.60/family; or you can purchase an annual pass good for all national parks). Parks Canada has produced a number of leaflets about Pacific Rim, including one listing all the hiking trails, which can be obtained from the visitor centre. Long Beach is extremely popular in the peak summer months but offers just as many delights for those who choose to avoid the crowds and visit during cooler wetter times of year. The region receives 300 centimetres of rain a year, so if you are visiting out of season, dress accordingly. If you do manage to camp in the campground, you may well wake to find the previous evening's ocean view obscured by a heavy morning mist. During the course of the day the mist usually disappears, allowing you to again enjoy the sight, as well as the sound, of the ocean. Pacific Rim has its own website: www.pc.gc.ca/pacificrim.

Contemplating the surf.

Prior Centennial (National)

Location

For a get-away-from-it-all camping experience, you cannot go far wrong in selecting North Pender Island's Prior Centennial, a former provincial park that has been part of the Gulf Islands National Park Reserve since 2003. Ferries to the island can be taken from Tsawwassen on the Mainland or from Swartz Bay on Vancouver Island, and from some of the other Gulf Islands. The campground is located 6 kilometres from the ferry terminal on Canal Road. There are stores in Port Washington, Hope Bay and Port Browning.

Facilities

This is a relatively small 16-hectare park nestled in a pleasant forested area. Seventeen well-spaced vehicle/tent sites are available; unfortunately, they are close to the road. All basic services can be found here (drinking water, fire pits, pit toilets, picnic tables). Reservations are accepted through Discover Camping.

Recreational activities

The campground's location a few hundred metres from Medicine Beach on Bedwell Harbour makes it ideal for beachcombing and shoreline explorations. Hiking trails exist, and Pender Island is great to explore by bike. Watch for the historical markers that give details of the island's past. The small settlement of Hope Bay is a pleasant place to relax and watch the world go by.

Additional information

This park was donated to BC Parks in 1958 by Mr. and Mrs. F.L. Prior, hence its name. Pender Island is only a short ferry ride from Galiano Island and Salt Spring Island, which both have provincial parks. Many tourists vacation in the Gulf Islands by "island hopping," while residents of the Lower Mainland and Vancouver Island visit to enjoy the altogether different ambience created by the island lifestyle. Access to South Pender Island is via a wooden bridge a kilometre from the campground, and while there is more to explore on North Pender Island, it is also interesting to travel south, as the feel of the island changes.

Rathtrevor Beach

Location

Cool ocean water lapping a long white beach is just one of the many attractions of Rathtrevor Beach Provincial Park. Situated on Highway 19A, just 3 kilometres south of Parksville, with views over the Strait of Georgia to the Coast Mountains beyond, Rathtrevor Beach is the most popular park on Vancouver Island for camping. Services are available in Parksville, while a small concession selling pop, coffee, candy and other sundries recently opened in the park's visitor centre.

Facilities

The 165 camping spots are located in the Douglas fir-forested area of the 347-hectare park and accommodate every type of recreational vehicle. This year-round campground is fully equipped with a sani-station, three shower buildings and flush and pit toilets. It is wheelchair-accessible. Reservations are accepted, and you won't get a space without one in June, July or August (in fact, they are required between the last week of June and Labour Day).

Recreational activities

Famed for its beautiful sandy shingle on 2,000 metres of beach leading to warm clear waters, Rathtrevor Beach is described by BC Parks as "unbeatable for swimming." Windsurfing and canoeing are possible (though there is no boat launch), and there are a number of walks and self-guided nature trails. Birdwatching is reputed to be good in the springtime and during the annual herring spawn. There are two children's play areas, and in the summer months the amphitheatre is used to deliver visitors' programs. The old farmhouse is now the park visitor centre where you can rent bikes.

Additional information

Rathtrevor takes its name from pioneer William Rath, who established a farm here in 1886. After he died in 1903, his wife was left with five children but kept the farm running and eventually developed the land into a campground, adding the suffix "trevor" for effect. BC Parks acquired Rathtrevor Campground in 1967. Today this campground is extremely popular, but visitors who arrive to find it full only have to travel 13 kilometres to find alternative camping at Englishman River Falls Provincial Park. I last camped at Rathtrevor in 2008 and it was the perfect place for children: huge sites, daily interpretive programs, safe cycling, great beaches and only a 30-minute drive from the ferry. Bliss!

RUCKLE

Location

In 1974, when the Ruckle family sold a 486-hectare parcel of land to the provincial government for a nominal fee, they gave British Columbians and visitors to the province a superb camping location. The largest provincial park in the Gulf Islands, Ruckle is situated 10 kilometres from Fulford Harbour on Beaver Point Road, at the southeastern corner of Salt Spring Island. The nearest services can be found at Fulford Harbour.

Facilities

This superb park contains 78 walk-in camping spots in a grassy area beside Swanson Channel, as well as eight drive-in spaces. There is parking for RVs, but no campsites are immediately adjacent. The walk from the parking area to the campground is flat, and in less than five minutes you can pitch your tent on a site directly overlooking the ocean. All the basic amenities are found here (pit toilets, drinking water stations, picnic tables, fire pits). There is no sani-station or access for the disabled.

Recreational activities

Campers can observe otters, harbour seals, porpoises, sea lions and—if they're very fortunate—killer whales as they swim in the adjacent waters. Ruckle Park has more than 7 kilometres of shoreline, characterized by pocket beaches, rocky coves and headlands waiting to be explored. There are over 15 kilometres of walking trails, leading around the headlands and through the forested areas. While there is no designated swimming area, beachcombing, fishing, windsurfing, ocean kayaking and scuba diving are all possible here, while a maze of paved roads makes cycling a delight.

Additional information

The park area was originally settled in 1872 by the Ruckle family, which still resides and works in the area. The continuous use of the land for farming purposes from the late 1800s until today makes it one of BC's oldest family farms. The Ruckle family retains its right to life tenancy within the park. Visitors can tour the historical farm buildings and learn about farming practices of a bygone age. Descriptive markers and photographs attached to the well-maintained historical buildings give details of a past life.

SIDNEY SPIT MARINE (NATIONAL)

Location

Although it is effectively a marine park, Sidney Spit Marine Park on Sidney Island is a lovely camping facility that deserves a mention. There is no vehicle access; it is reached by taking a foot-passenger ferry that departs from Government Wharf at the end of Beacon Avenue in Sidney, a short drive from the Swartz Bay ferry terminal on Vancouver Island. Services are found in Sidney and Victoria. The former provincial park is now part of the Gulf Islands National Park Reserve.

Facilities

Once you take the 25-minute ferry ride from Sidney (2008 fares: $14.00/adult; $12.00/child, return), you'll find the park has 20 formal walk-in camping spots in addition to group-camping facilities and plenty of space for spillover camping. All the basic amenities are provided (pit toilets, drinking water, picnic tables, fire pits), as well as wheelbarrows for hauling gear, as the walk from the wharf to the campground is somewhat hilly and takes about 20 minutes.

Recreational activities

Sidney Spit has been described as "one of the most beautiful marine parks in the Pacific Northwest" as it features thousands of metres of white sandy beach backed by towering bluffs. Beyond these, the uplands contain a second-growth forest of fir, maple, western redcedar and arbutus. One of its main features is a lagoon affording one of the best opportunities to explore intertidal life. These salt marshes and tidal flats attract both human and animal forms: ornithologists, naturalists, seals, orcas and dolphins are all occasionally seen. Trails lead around the park, and the stunning beach provides opportunities to swim, sunbathe and fish.

Additional information

Some of the bricks used to build the famous Empress Hotel in Victoria and the Hotel Vancouver in Vancouver were produced by a brick factory that operated at the turn of the century near the southern wharf of Sidney Island. At its peak, this factory employed 70 workers. In 1924, the Todd family began purchasing land on Sidney Island and by 1968 owned all but the one tenth the provincial government had acquired in 1924. These 400 hectares form the marine park that's now part of the Gulf Islands National Park Reserve. The community of Sidney is an enjoyable place to take an afternoon stroll; in addition to shops that sell books, crafts and antiques, there are inviting delis and cafés that offer an assortment of refreshments to revitalize a tired camper.

SMELT BAY

Location

Located on the southern peninsula of Cortes Island, with stunning views to the south and west across a long pebble beach, 16-hectare Smelt Bay is the only provincial park on the island that permits camping. Cortes Island is not easy to reach but is well worth the effort. You must take two ferries, the first from Campbell River to Quadra Island (15 minutes), and the second from Quadra to Cortes (45 minutes). A well-signed 15-kilometre paved road leads from the ferry terminal to the campground. Services are available on the island at Whitecove, Manson's Landing and Squirrel Cove.

Facilities

Twenty-three camping spots are available in the woods, set back from the beach. Most are double sites. As one would expect, only the basic facilities are supplied (pit toilets, drinking water, picnic tables, fire pits). Reservations are accepted and advisable.

Recreational activities

Leisure pursuits in the area include beachcombing, swimming, fishing and general relaxing. At low tide the pebble beach that leads to Sutil Point reveals a fascinating array of rock pools waiting to be explored. (Sutil Point is named after the Spanish ship *Sutil* that Captain Galiano used to explore these waters in 1792.) The immediate area of the park is rich in history. For example, the mounds behind the gravel beach were built centuries ago by the Salish people to defend themselves against the Yacultas. Cycling around the island is a pleasant easy activity as the traffic is minimal and the roads are paved. Two other day-use parks—Manson's Landing and Hague Lake—are located nearby. Cortes is a quiet remote island with a unique charm that is very different from nearby Quadra Island. The island has few settlements, with most of the development concentrated at the south end.

Additional information

Smelt Bay was created in 1973 to offer camping facilities and to protect an indigenous cultural site. In the early fall, tens of thousands of smelt spawn in this vicinity, hence the park's name. In turn, these small fish attract an array of other sea life to the area, including salmon, otters, seals, herons and sea lions. A lovely quiet getaway spot, Cortes Island is one of the more scenic islands and has an intricate coastline ideal for canoeing and kayaking.

Sproat Lake

Location

Situated on the northern shore of Sproat Lake, just 13 kilometres west of Port Alberni off Highway 4, this is a popular family campground, but there is something for everyone here.

Facilities

Excellent camping can be had at Sproat Lake, which has two connected campgrounds situated in a forested area straddling the highway. The more desirable are the "lower" 15 sites nearer the lake, but all 59 spots have access to showers, flush and pit toilets and a sani-station. The park is wheelchair-accessible and reservations are accepted for both the upper and lower campgrounds.

Recreational activities

Sproat Lake is noted for its warm water, which is fantastic for swimming. There is a large boat launch and good fishing, plus there are opportunities to waterski and wind surf. Trails lead through the forested area of second-growth Douglas fir, and the ground is littered with an attractive assortment of wildflowers at certain times of the year. The prehistoric pictographs found along trails at the southern end of the park are testimony to human presence in the area over the centuries and are considered some of the finest in BC. In addition, the town of Port Alberni is a pleasant community to explore and just 15 minutes away.

Additional information

During the summer, visitors can see huge Martin Mars bombing planes take off from their lakeside base to extinguish fires. The world's largest water bombers, these planes are operated by a collective of five BC forest companies. Each plane can load 32 tonnes of water within 22 seconds by skimming across the lake at a speed of more than 110 kilometres per hour. The economy of Vancouver Island is dependent on the logging and tourism industries, and the threat of fires in this area and in the rest of BC peaks during the summer camping season. It is therefore imperative that all campfires be extinguished properly before a campsite is vacated. If the threat of fire becomes too great, fires are forbidden in provincial parks, and, as was the case in 2003, parks can be closed to campers altogether.

STAMP RIVER

Location

Formerly known as Stamp Falls, this park was renamed Stamp River when it was amalgamated with Money's Pool Provincial Park, increasing its area by 100 hectares. An angler's delight, this park is extremely popular with fishers, who visit the area for the excellent steelhead, coho and cutthroat trout that can be caught in certain designated areas. Located 14 kilometres north of Port Alberni off Highway 4, on a paved road, Stamp River has a lovely rural setting and yet is close to all of Port Alberni's amenities. It is also one of the closest provincial parks to Pacific Rim National Park, approximately 100 kilometres to the west.

Facilities

There are 23 camping spots available here, some pleasantly located in a forested area near the river. Only the basic facilities exist (drinking water, pit toilets, picnic tables, fire pits). Reservations are accepted.

Recreational activities

If you enjoy fishing, you'll love Stamp River, as the main attraction here is the fish. The campground is often used as a base camp for anglers who wish to explore the lakes and rivers in the vicinity. The park's unique feature is the fascinating display of salmon ascending the fish ladders in the summer and early fall. In July and August, some 30,000 sockeye salmon use this route; smaller numbers of chinook and coho follow in September and October (and sometimes into December). Trails lead visitors from the campground to the fish ladders and to the views of the waterfalls on Stamp River.

Additional information

This 327-hectare park was created in 1940 and is named after an early pioneer who built Port Alberni's first sawmill. It's a pleasant and interesting picnic spot for travellers heading along Highway 4. The highway between Port Alberni and Tofino is quite beautiful and follows the clear tumbling waters of the Kennedy River for half of its route. Upon reaching Pacific Rim National Park near Tofino, the traveller is rewarded with dramatic views of the Pacific.

STRATHCONA

Location

Established in 1911, Strathcona is BC's oldest provincial park. Located in a majestic wilderness of old-growth forest, mountain peaks, clear rivers, waterfalls and lakes, it encompasses more than 245,000 hectares. The main route to the park is from Campbell River on Highway 28, which runs through the park and connects to Gold River on the west side of the Island. All services are available in Campbell River, and there is a private lodge in the park that offers food, accommodation and canoe/kayak rentals. Fuel is not available in the park.

Facilities

In addition to wilderness camping, you can camp at two locations on Buttle Lake: Buttle Lake campground, which has 85 spots (and the better beach), and Ralph River, 35 kilometres away, which also has 85. Facilities at both locations include wheelchair-accessible pit toilets, wood for sale, drinking water, fire pits and picnic tables. There is no sani-station (the nearest one is at Elk Falls). Reservations are accepted.

Recreational activities

As would be expected, there is a great deal to see and do in Strathcona Park, and it is easy to spend a week here. From Buttle Lake there are 12 hiking and walking trails that take explorers on a variety of hikes, and there are shorter nature walks too. There are climbing routes at Crest Creek Crags, and other areas of the park have developed trail systems. Swimming in Buttle Lake is good from both of the campgrounds, and there are two boat launches. Waterskiing is permitted on the lake, and the nearby lodge rents canoes and kayaks. A wealth of streams, rivers and lakes provides angling opportunities, and there are excellent wildlife-viewing opportunities, as well. The southern section of the park contains Della Falls, one of Canada's highest waterfalls at 440 metres, and the 10th highest in the world. With the spring runoff in May and June, the falls are particularly spectacular. Westmin Mines is located in the park, and guided tours of the operation are offered on weekdays during the summer. Details of these activities and the park's many other recreational options are listed in a leaflet produced by BC Parks.

Additional information

Strathcona is named after Donald Alexander Smith, Lord Strathcona, who was a Canadian pioneer and one of the principals involved with the construction of the Canadian Pacific Railway. Strathcona is an excellent location for those who enjoy hiking and the outdoor life and is definitely worth more than a one-night stay. It is not particularly kid-friendly, especially if you have young children. Interestingly, the wildlife in the park differs from that on the Mainland: chipmunks, rabbits, coyotes, foxes, grizzly bears, skunks and moose are not found here. The road from Campbell River to Gold River traverses much of the park and is a pleasant quiet drive.

VANCOUVER COAST AND MOUNTAINS

With the highest population density in the province, southwestern BC is undoubtedly the most popular region for provincial-park camping. Twenty provincial parks, all within a four-hour drive of downtown Vancouver, meet the demand for weekend getaways, and the spectacular scenery en route makes the commute enjoyable. Whether you head north on the meandering Sea to Sky Highway, east on Highway 7 to follow the mighty Fraser River, or to the Sunshine Coast via BC Ferries, your journey will include breathtaking views of mountains, clear rivers and streams, forests and fields, as well as the comforting knowledge that services are never far away.

Birkenhead Lake is surrounded by breathtaking snow-capped mountains.

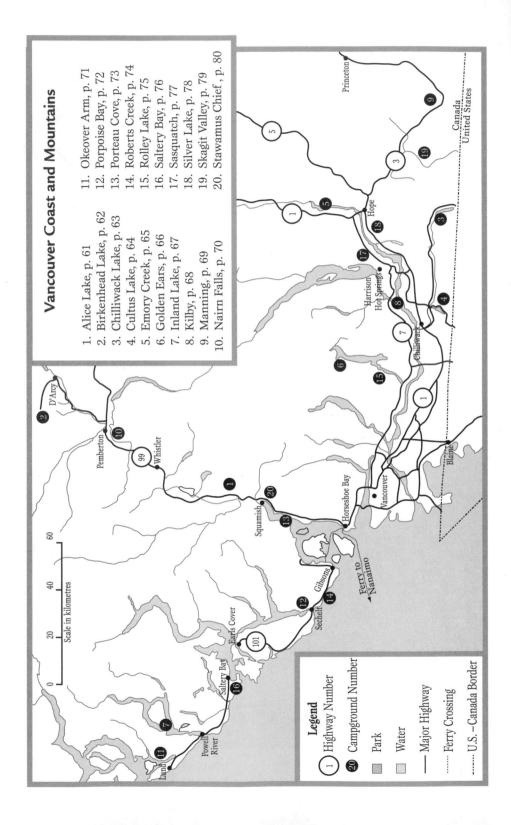

Vancouver Coast and Mountains

1. Alice Lake, p. 61
2. Birkenhead Lake, p. 62
3. Chilliwack Lake, p. 63
4. Cultus Lake, p. 64
5. Emory Creek, p. 65
6. Golden Ears, p. 66
7. Inland Lake, p. 67
8. Kilby, p. 68
9. Manning, p. 69
10. Nairn Falls, p. 70

11. Okeover Arm, p. 71
12. Porpoise Bay, p. 72
13. Porteau Cove, p. 73
14. Roberts Creek, p. 74
15. Rolley Lake, p. 75
16. Saltery Bay, p. 76
17. Sasquatch, p. 77
18. Silver Lake, p. 78
19. Skagit Valley, p. 79
20. Stawamus Chief, p. 80

Legend

1   Highway Number

20   Campground Number

Park

Water

——   Major Highway

········   Ferry Crossing

-------   U.S.–Canada Border

Scale in kilometres

0   20   40   60

Alice Lake

Location

Alice Lake is situated not far from the community of Brackendale, home to the largest population of bald eagles in North America. Visitors to this campground have a good chance of seeing these splendid birds, but eagles are not the only attraction of this extremely popular park. Alice Lake, easily accessible from Vancouver (71 kilometres away), is positioned in breathtaking mountain terrain and has every amenity campers require. The park is found on Highway 99—the Sea to Sky Highway—13 kilometres north of Squamish, which has all services.

Facilities

Situated in a forest of western hemlock are 108 large private shady camping spots suitable for all camping vehicles; 55 camping spots have electrical hook-ups and ice is sold. The campground is equipped with two shower buildings, flush and pit toilets and a sani-station. Many facilities are wheelchair-accessible, and reservations during the summer months are a must.

Recreational activities

There is never a dull moment here as the 396-hectare park has an abundance of activities to keep campers busy. One of the biggest attractions is a series of 10 walking and hiking trails, ranging in length from half a kilometre to a day's hard walking. One of the most popular is the Four Lakes Trail, which takes hikers around the four warm-water lakes that dominate the area. Swimming, canoeing and fishing for rainbow trout and Dolly Varden are popular pursuits, and large grassy areas provide venues for ball games. The two excellent lakeside beaches are perfect for children, and there's a safe swimming area.

Additional information

Alice Lake is a very popular campground even during the week, and it is frequently full during the peak summer months of July and August, so if you arrive without a reservation during these times, be sure you have other options available. In 2008, a small concession stand opened in the day-use area selling drinks, ice cream, chips, sand toys and many other things. A great addition to the park and useful for familities, the stand is open daily during July and August.

BIRKENHEAD LAKE

Location

Six kilometres long, Birkenhead Lake is surrounded by breathtaking snow-capped Coast Mountains and blessed with clear beautiful waters. The 9,755-hectare park is located only a three-hour drive (210 kilometres) from Vancouver and is reached by taking Highway 99 to Pemberton, then turning off at Mount Currie to head toward D'Arcy. Just before D'Arcy, a 17-kilometre gravel road leads to the campground. Gas and restaurants are located in Mount Currie and Pemberton.

Facilities

Seventy-nine camping spots are available here, and all but a few are located in a beautiful wooded area with streams running adjacent to them (ideal for keeping your drinks cool on a hot summer day). There is a sani-station but no flush toilets. The only wheelchair-accessible part of the park is a trail near the beach. The only other disadvantage is that some spots are near stagnant water pools, so mosquitoes can be a problem at certain times of year. Reservations are accepted.

Recreational activities

Birkenhead Lake has a lovely beach and protected swimming area, although the waters themselves, which come directly from the surrounding mountain snow, can be cold. There is a boat launch and canoe rentals are available. Fishing for kokanee and rainbow trout is reputed to be good, as is wildlife watching for moose, black bear, mountain goats and deer. Ospreys and bald eagles are often seen circling over the waters of the lake. A good trail leads along one side of the lake and is used by mountain bikers and walkers.

Additional information

The tranquil location, spectacular scenery and pleasant drive from the Lower Mainland make this my favourite provincial park for a weekend getaway from Vancouver. I have stayed here five times in different seasons. In June, the waters were so high I could not see the beach, but the hiking was excellent. In July, there were millions of flies and mosquitoes, and in late August, it was hot and perfect. When I stayed in July 2003, an enterprising couple had set up a really quaint "camper's store" in the back of their truck near the campground. Camping provides opportunities for a variety of entrepreneurs but challenges the travel writer—you never know if the same people will be in business in subsequent years. Hopefully, this couple will be.

CHILLIWACK LAKE

Location

Today it is rare to find areas of old-growth forest in BC. However, by undertaking a short walk from Chilliwack Lake, visitors can view majestic redcedar trees that are hundreds of years old. Southeast of Vancouver and situated in the magnificent Coast Mountains, this popular park was created in 1973 to protect an area of spectacular beauty and was recently extended to include the east side of the lake. The campground is 64 kilometres southeast of Chilliwack and can be reached by taking exit 104 from Highway 1 and following the signs for Cultus Lake until Cultus Lake Road. Rather than turning here, take Vedder Road across the bridge and turn right onto Chilliwack Lake Road, a paved/gravel access road leading to the lake—a distance of 40 kilometres. The nearest concentration of services is in Chilliwack; more limited provisions can be found at the Pointa Vista Store, 32 kilometres west of the park.

Facilities

One hundred and forty-six camping spots are available in the 9,258-hectare park, divided amongst Radium Loop, Greendrop Loop, Lindeman Loop and Paleface Loop. The majority of sites are large, private and well positioned (about 10 of the Paleface ones are near the lake); the remainder are close, confined and offer little privacy. Only the basic camping facilities are provided here (pit toilets, drinking water, fire pits, picnic tables). There are wheelchair-accessible pit toilets at Radium Loop.

Recreational activities

The park is a delightful place to visit if you enjoy hiking, as there are a variety of trails starting from the campground and the Post Creek parking lot. For instance, walkers can take an easy 6-kilometre-return route to the Ecological Reserve with no elevation gain, or hike 14 kilometres to Flora Lake with a climb of over 1,000 metres. Chilliwack Lake is used for waterskiing, boating and fishing for Dolly Varden, kokanee, rainbow and cutthroat trout, and is equipped with a boat launch. The water, however, can be cold for swimming. A playground for children at the Paleface Loop camping area ensures the little ones are well entertained. Of interest to walkers, horseback riders and cyclists, the Trans-Canada Trail winds through the park; see www.trailsbc.ca.

Additional information

If the campground is full, a notice will be posted on the park sign at the store on Chilliwack Lake Road, not far from the bridge. Almost 3 kilometres along a logging road that leads from the campground and follows the edge of Chilliwack Lake is the Chilliwack River Ecological Reserve. It was created in 1981 to protect a unique area of old-growth forest featuring large western redcedars and is just one of a number of ecological reserves that exist in BC, which is geographically and biologically the most diverse province in the country.

CULTUS LAKE

Location

On average, almost 30,000 family groups stay at Cultus Lake per year, making it the fourth most popular campground in the province. The 2,561-hectare park includes both the east and west side of the 5-kilometre-long Cultus Lake, from which a spectacular vista of mountains can be seen. *Cultus* means "worthless" in the Chinook language, but the lake's immense popularity suggests that many have found it anything but worthless. Cultus Lake is located 11 kilometres southwest of Chilliwack off Highway 1 on a paved access road. While Chilliwack provides all services, a number of small commercial facilities can be found adjacent to the park in the small community of Cultus Lake.

Facilities

This campground is the third largest in the province (after Manning and Golden Ears) with 281 spaces spread across four locations: Maple Bay (97), Delta Grove (52), Clear Creek (85) and Entrance Bay (47). All campsites are large and positioned well in wooded areas. There are a number of double camping spots, and 19 of the campsites at Delta Grove are close to the water's edge with their own section of beach. All amenities are found here, including flush toilets, a sani-station, showers and various accessible facilities for campers in wheelchairs. Reservations are accepted.

Recreational activities

Numerous recreational pursuits can be enjoyed. You can catch coho, chinook, chum, pink and sockeye salmon, rainbow and cutthroat trout, and Dolly Varden if the powerboaters and water skiers do not decide to disturb the tranquility of the lake. Windsurfing is possible (if the jet skiers are not out in force), as is swimming from lovely sandy beaches. There are also several hiking trails. The most popular trek is to Teapot Hill, 5 kilometres return, where a good viewpoint rewards your efforts. Some trails permit mountain bikes and horses and have recently been extended and upgraded. Unfortunately, the play area at the Entrance Bay campground had to be dismantled due to damage from 2006–07 winter storms, but close to the park there are golf courses, go-carts, canoe and Jet Ski rentals, trail rides, waterslides, laundromats, restaurants and stores.

Additional information

Although the setting and facilities here are perfect, the park can become very busy during the summer months, especially on weekends, and some-what loud if too many powerboats congregate on the lake. Cultus Lake attracts a youthful summer crowd and, in my mind, represents the most commercial side of provincial park camping and is not an aspect to which I'm particularly drawn. The best time to stay here is in the spring, when the trees are budding, wildflowers are blooming and the woodlands are alive with birds attracted to the deciduous forest.

EMORY CREEK

Location

Emory Creek is located next to Highway 1, 18 kilometres north of Hope and 6 kilometres south of Yale. This beautiful campground on the banks of the majestic Fraser River is located on the site of Emory City, which in its 1880 heyday boasted 13 streets and a population of over 500 pioneers. Two decades earlier, the same number of people worked here after coming in search of gold. If you visit today, all you'll see is a lovely serene wooded campground. A convenience store and restaurant are located opposite the campground.

Facilities

Nestled in a mixed forest area of the 15-hectare park are 34 large private camping spots suitable for every type of recreational vehicle. Some spots have views of the water. One of the most distinctive features of this campground is the "flushing thunderboxes"—from the outside, these toilets look like pit toilets but they actually flush. During my first two stays in this park, the toilets not only flushed but the washroom also contained small containers of dried flowers and air fresheners. Unfortunately, I didn't find this nice touch on my last stay in 2008. There is no sani-station, showers or wheelchair access. The transcontinental railway is adjacent to the park, and the sound of trains, while audible, can be quite soothing in the night.

Recreational activities

Although there is not a lot to do at Emory Creek, the park seems to attract the retired folks looking for a tranquil spot in which to spend a few days. There is a small trail, and visitors can fish for salmon in the Fraser, which is easily accessible from a pebbled beach. When I last visited, two grey-haired gentlemen were busy panning for gold, an activity that struck me as an extremely pleasant way to spend an afternoon. There is a small beach that's ideal for children, but swimming isn't really an option.

Additional information

Co-managed with the Yale First Nation, this provincial campground has a wonderful feeling about it. Its lack of defined or structured activities makes it particularly appealing to older campers, while the well-cared-for and unique washroom facilities are a welcome surprise to seasoned campers who often approach pit toilets with a deep dread, especially in the height of summer. The area was the site of one of the richest finds during the 1858 gold rush, before prospectors moved farther north. When Simon Fraser first travelled here in 1808, this attractive valley was inhabited by the Coast Salish people, who hunted and fished in the region. A short drive north on the Coquihalla Highway is Coquihalla Canyon Provincial Park, where visitors can walk through a series of disused railway tunnels, which were blasted through the rock in the early years of this century.

GOLDEN EARS

Location

Almost 40,000 camping parties regularly visit Golden Ears, making this large well-appointed provincial park one of the most popular campgrounds in BC. Like Cultus Lake and Manning Park, Golden Ears is close to Vancouver. Although this proximity may dissuade some campers from visiting, let me add that whenever I have stayed here—even at the height of summer—the park has never felt crowded or busy, although the campground itself can get a little noisy. Named either for the twin peaks that shine golden in the sunlight or, as some locals claim, for a nesting place for eagles, "Golden Eyries" is located 11 kilometres north of Haney off Highway 7, on a paved access road, and is an easy 45- to 60-minute drive from Vancouver. All services are available at Haney, and there are a few additional stores close to the campground and a small concession stand in the park itself during the peak summer months.

Facilities

Alouette, Gold Creek and the newer North Beach campground provide the camping options in Golden Ears, offering a combined total of 408 spaces. All have large private spots within a forested area. There are showers, flush toilets, a sani-station and wheelchair access. In the peak summer months, a security patrol operates. Reservations are accepted for all three campgrounds.

Recreational activities

The 62,540-hectare park is blessed with a number of trails suitable for both hikers and horses. Hiking options vary from 20-minute interpretive trips to overnight excursions up to the Golden Ears, and more than 20 kilometres of horse trails are available to those who love riding (horseback riding can be arranged from local facilities). Fishing for rainbow trout, coastal cutthroat, kokanee, Dolly Varden and freshwater trout is popular in Alouette Lake and Alouette River, Pitt Lake, Mike Lake and Gold Creek. Good swimming beaches are available at Alouette Lake in both the day-use and camping areas. Boating and waterskiing are permitted on the lake away from the swimming area, and canoes can be rented in the park. An adventure playground keeps young ones entertained, and interpretive programs for children and adults operate during the summer.

Additional information

The area around Alouette Lake was originally the hunting and fishing ground of the Interior Salish and Coast Salish peoples. During the early 1900s, the area was the primary site for BC's railroad logging operations, and there are stories of loggers in the 1920s felling trees up to 4 metres in diametre. A huge fire that ripped through the area in 1931 stopped the logging operations. Today, Golden Ears is characterized by a second growth of western hemlock, western redcedar and Douglas fir, but evidence of the earlier logging is everywhere.

INLAND LAKE

Location

Inland Lake is located next to 1,065-metre-high Mount Mahony, 12 kilometres north of Powell River. Turn right off Highway 101 onto Alberni Street. Go up the hill to Manson Avenue, turn left and follow Manson to Cassiar Street. Turn right onto Cassiar (which becomes Yukon Street) and continue to Haslam Street. Turn right onto Haslam and stay on it until the first junction, where you take the left fork to the campsite. Services are available in Cranberry and Powell River.

Facilities

Camping provisions at Inland Lake make this one of the choicest parks for disabled campers. It has ramps and larger toilets, and 13 kilometres of flat wheelchair-accessible trail around the lake, six piers jutting out onto the lake for easy fishing and a concrete ramp sloping into the water, plus five wheelchair-accessible cabins. The main campground is next to the day-parking area and accommodates 22 parties, with spaces for large RVs. Pit toilets, fire pits, garbage bins and picnic tables overlooking the lake are in a lightly wooded area. Pumps are used to collect lake water, which should be boiled before using. Two wheelchair-accesible cabins are located here, and three are spaced along the lakeside trail and have their own wheelchair-accessible pit toilets. Four overnight camping spots are also located around the lake.

Recreational activities

The biggest draw at this 2,763-hectare provincial park is the 13-kilometre trail circling the lake. Convenient for cyclists, people in wheelchairs or those with strollers, it has kilometre markers placed along it and wooden carvings of local pioneers, animals and other subjects. You can take two paths from the trail: one to Lost Lake then on to Haywire Bay on Powell Lake, the other directly to Powell Lake. Or you can hike along the shoreline and then cross a small bridge to Anthony Island (which has three walk-in campsites). Inland Lake is great for canoeing and kayaking; although powerboats are permitted, they are limited to 10-horsepower engines. For fishers, the 349-hectare lake contains trout, and fishing is said to be best starting in April. Loons, eagles, ducks, ravens, grouse, blue jays and hummingbirds can be seen, and sometimes beavers, otters and bears. The lake water is calm, clear and warm—ideal for swimming.

Additional information

This campground and lake are wonderful. During our last visit, on a day that started with rainy skies, we set off on our hike in waterproof gear. Halfway around the trail the skies cleared, and by the time we returned to the car, we were hot and sweaty. Three families were playing in the lake, proving it was not cold, so we got changed and revelled in the warm water. On a Labour Day weekend there was no shortage of space and few people on the trail.

KILBY

Location

Kilby is now operated by the Fraser Heritage Society but retains ties to BC Parks. This 3-hectare provincial park is situated 15 kilometres from Agassiz, one kilometre off Highway 7 at Harrison Falls on the Fraser River. From the highway, follow the signs that will lead you onto School Road and then Kilby Road, which leads into the park. Services can be found along the highway or at Harrison Mills, Agassiz and Harrison Hot Springs.

Facilities

Twenty-two large campsites on the river provide excellent spots from which to watch the Fraser meander on its course—unless the river level is very high, as it was in June 1996 when the campground had to be closed because it was under water. There are flush and pit toilets and water, but no sani-station, showers or wheelchair accessibility. I visited in 2008 and found Kilby to be a little run-down and not on par with other provincial parks, so my advice to anyone wanting to camp for more than one night would be to go somewhere else. It is also quite expensive to stay here: $25.00 per night in 2008.

Recreational activities

This campground is ideally located for those who want to explore the surrounding communities of Mission, Agassiz, Chilliwack and Harrison Hot Springs. It also provides its own attractions in the form of a wide sandy beach and a river for boating, waterskiing and swimming. As the campground is positioned near both the Fraser and Harrison rivers, a variety of fishing spots in the immediate vicinity are available, where anglers can try their luck for cutthroat and Dolly Varden. There is a boat launch in the day-use area, and because the campground is a designated BC "Wildlife Watch" area, birdwatching is quite good.

Additional information

One of the biggest attractions here is the Kilby General Store Museum, which is part of the adjacent 2-hectare historical site. The two-storey general store was built in 1904 and operated by the same family up until 1976. Guides dressed in period costume provide fascinating details of the development of the area at the turn of the century. The museum also boasts a gift shop and an excellent tearoom that serves traditional tea and scones. Both children and adults will find it is easy to pass the hours in the museum, reading and learning about the Fraser River's colourful past. Specifically, the photographs of huge sturgeon caught in the Fraser River should not be missed. The historic site also includes a small working farm (with pigs, goats and hens—a delight for children) and an orchard, in addition to a number of buildings that have been faithfully restored. For hours and fees, check the Kilby Historic Site website: www.kilby.ca.

MANNING

Location

Manning hosts the second most popular provincial campgrounds (after Golden Ears). Within three hours of Vancouver (224 kilometres away) and covering over 65,000 hectares of the Cascade Mountains, this is a fantastic area for recreational use. The western park entrance is 26 kilometres east of Hope and the eastern park entrance is 52 kilometres west of Princeton, both off Highway 3, which runs through the park. Accommodation, gas, food and other commercial facilities are located in the park.

Facilities

In addition to wilderness camping, there are four vehicle-accessible campgrounds with a total of 355 spots: Hampton (99), Mule Deer (49), Coldspring (64) and Lightning Lake (143). Lightning Lake has showers and flush toilets, and all of its 143 campsites are included in the reservation system of BC Parks. It's a great place for children. The other three campgrounds operate on a first-come, first-served basis. All spaces are large and set among trees, offering privacy, although some campsites are close to the road and Coldspring is a little sparse on vegetation due to a recent attack of pine beetle. There is a sani-station located at the park's visitor centre.

Recreational activities

Manning Park offers an abundance of things to do and see. Upon arriving, visitors should go to the visitor centre located a kilometre east of Manning Park Lodge to pick up a detailed map of the area. The centre also has human and natural history displays of the park and area. Manning is a hiker's paradise; extensive trail systems meander through the mountains to alpine meadows, waterfalls and rivers, and there are also self-guided interpretive trails. Eight trails are mountain-bike accessible, and there are also 11 trails open to horseback riding. Anglers can fish in the Similkameen and Sumallo rivers for Dolly Varden, rainbow and cutthroat trout, and also in Lightning and Strike lakes. Lightning Lake has a beach with a swimming area, a boat launch and good canoeing (rowboats, canoes and kayaks can be rented in the day-use area; the hourly charge in 2008 was $15.00). Powerboats are not permitted anywhere in the park, a rule that ensures a peaceful stay.

Additional information

Manning Park is named after E.C. Manning, chief forester of British Columbia from 1936 to 1941. In recent years, the park has suffered from devastation from the mountain pine beetle. The north end of the Pacific Crest Trail also lies in the park. Almost 4,000 kilometres in length, it's a six-month trek to follow it all the way to Mexico. Fortunately, Manning provides a number of delightful shorter hiking options: for an easy 45-minute trail, try the Canyon Trail (2 kilometres); for a slightly longer walk, the Lightning Lake Loop (9 kilometres) is appealing. The Lightning Lake Chain Trail is 24 kilometres round-trip, but there's no elevation gain.

NAIRN FALLS

Location

One year I stayed here in July, when the temperature was in the high 20s, so I really appreciated the shady canopy this wooded campground offers. Just 3 kilometres south of Pemberton off Highway 99, and considerably less popular than Alice Lake, its nearest big neighbour to the south, this is an exquisite laid-back provincial park. Services are conveniently located at Pemberton or at Whistler, 32 kilometres to the south.

Facilities

Ninety-four spacious forested camping spots are available (the 40 reservable ones are the best ones as they overlook the canyon, but the others are not bad). All sites will accommodate the largest recreational vehicle. Facilities include drinking water, fire pits, picnic tables, pit toilets and a sani-station. Since 2000, Nairn Falls has accepted reservations.

Recreational activities

Travellers regularly use Nairn Falls as a picnic spot. An easy trail (3 kilometres round-trip) leads to the falls, which tumble down 60 metres into a beautiful canyon of Douglas fir, cedar, and hemlock. The park contains other trails, but when I visited, signage left a lot to be desired and some trails were washed out. Fishing is possible in Green River, while a short drive/walk from the park on Highway 99 toward Pemberton One Mile Lake is popular for swimming—a real luxury on a hot summer's day. The shady peaceful campground is perfect for reading and relaxing, and Nairn Falls gives the impression of offering an almost sophisticated camping experience for those who want to escape from life's pressures.

Additional information

When I stayed here, my calm camping environment was occasionally disturbed by the noise of powerboats ascending the rapids to take groups of visitors whitewater rafting. Excursions of this nature can be organized in Pemberton and Whistler. Nairn Falls is a good location from which to explore Whistler (and is also considerably cheaper than staying right at the year-round resort). The lack of recreational pursuits may put some people off; there is little to do in the park itself for those with young families, although the pretty lake just to the north of Nairn Falls has a small beach, despite there being a lot of reeds in the water. For the majority of people, though, Nairn Falls is a haven.

OKEOVER ARM

Location
In recent years, the waters and islands of this area have become known as a kayaker's dream. Consequently, Okeover Arm Provincial Park is a kayaker's campground. At the end of the Sunshine Coast Road (Highway 101), overlooking Okeover Arm on the eastern side of the Malaspina Peninsula, this small campground is ideal for campers who plan to kayak in Desolation Sound Marine Park. The park is located 19 kilometres north of Powell River, 5 kilometres on a paved road from Lund. Powell River provides all services, but the small community of Lund 9 kilometres away has a store and accommodation.

Facilities
Okeover Arm was upgraded in 1997 to ensure more camping spots were available for both vehicles and tents. There are now 14 vehicle-accessible camping spaces and 4 tent-only sites; some have tent pads and a few have views of the water. Only the basic amenities are available here (pit toilets, drinking water, fire pits, picnic tables). The pit toilets here are wheelchair-accessible.

Recreational activities
The main recreational activities here are walking in a lightly forested area, swimming, canoeing, kayaking and boating; there is a boat launch adjacent to the park. As mentioned, the campground is an ideal base for those who wish to explore Desolation Sound Marine Park, BC's largest marine park with more than 60 kilometres of shoreline, several islands and a multitude of bays and coves.

Additional information
Lund was originally settled in 1895 by two brothers from Sweden and is named after the Swedish city. The renovated hotel, which dates back to the turn of the century, is the hub of the community.

When I drove into Lund, I had planned to spend a few hours exploring the community but found it could be done in a few minutes, although there are a couple of coffee shops and restaurants where you can people-watch.

PORPOISE BAY

Location

Reaching this 61-hectare park from the Lower Mainland requires a lovely excursion on BC Ferries to the Sunshine Coast. Take the ferry from Horseshoe Bay to Langdale, then Highway 101 to just north of Sechelt, where a 5-kilometre paved road leads to the campground. Services can be found in Sechelt, where the wide selection of restaurants, bakeries and coffee bars offers a great alternative to campground food.

Facilities

Campers here want for nothing. Porpoise Bay has flush and pit toilets, showers, a sani-station, good wheelchair access and it accepts reservations. There are 84 large camping spots, including a few double sites, set amongst a second-growth forest of Douglas fir, western redcedar, western hemlock and alder. Campfires at individual campsites are prohibited here, but group campfires are encouraged, so this integral part of the camping experience is not lost altogether. Reservations are accepted.

Recreational activities

This popular park and campground offers a wide sandy beach and a protected swimming area, making it ideal for family camping. A large number of grassy areas great for ball games are a feature here, and there are small trails, one of which leads to Angus Creek, a salmon-spawning waterway for chum and coho. The park is a base for kayakers who wish to explore the many coves and inlets of the surrounding area. At low tide it is really pleasant to beachcomb; wander through the rock pools and turn over the rocks looking for the marine life. My children adored fishing with nets for "toe biters" and small crabs.

Additional information

Porpoise Bay is near Sechelt Inlet's Provincial Marine Recreational Area, which includes eight wilderness campsites located amongst the sheltered waters of Sechelt Inlet—a paddler's delight. The area is also rich in marine life. I last stayed at Porpoise Bay in June, when only half the camping spots were taken. The water was somewhat cold for swimming, but the tranquility was wonderful. I had reserved a space but need not have bothered, as the park does not get really busy except on weekends until July and August, when reservations are a must.

PORTEAU COVE

Location

The views from this campground off the fantastic Sea to Sky Highway (Highway 99) are stunning if the weather is good, and for this reason alone every attempt should be made to stop here. Although almost impossible to see from the road, Porteau Cove is an enchanting roadside campground with an astounding vista of Howe Sound, the most southerly fjord in North America. Thirty-eight kilometres north of Vancouver and a little over 8 kilometres south of Britannia Beach, Porteau Cove is a haven for campers and daytrippers. Britannia Beach has food; gas and other provisions are available in Squamish. A small concession has been set up at the entrance to the campground, but supplies are limited.

Facilities

The campground has 44 vehicle camping spots and 16 walk-in sites and all the amenities (showers, flush toilets, sani-station, wheelchair access and reservations). Some spots overlook the water's edge with views of the mountains on Vancouver Island, and while the sites are not as large as those in other provincial parks, they are private thanks to the surrounding Sitka spruce trees. Electrical hook-ups are available in all drive-in sites for an additional fee. The campground is set away from the road, so traffic noise is not a problem, but the railway runs close by and a number of trains pass during the day and night (if you're in a tent, it feels like the train is passing right over your head).

Recreational activities

One of the biggest attractions of this location is scuba diving. There are man-made reefs and two ships have been sunk in the nearby waters to attract marine life and create a destination for diving enthusiasts. They also provide entertainment for those of us who just want to watch funny rubber-clad individuals plunge into the cool waters. Away from the diving area it is possible to swim in the waters of Howe Sound. When I last camped here I used Porteau Cove as my base but swam and sunbathed at Alice Lake, less than a 20-minute drive north. There are two public boat launches, but you can only fish outside of the park's boundaries.

Additional information

The park is an extremely popular campground and picnic spot for people travelling along the highway. The mining museum at Britannia Beach is well worth a visit if you have time. Visitors are given hard hats and taken on a tour that includes a rail trip underground and a demonstration of past mining machinery. Britannia Beach also has a large number of arts and craft shops and cafés to visit. Slightly farther north, check out the Squamish Adventure Centre—you'll recognize it by the huge sculpture of a logger—a must for any visitor to the area.

ROBERTS CREEK

Location

If you want to spend your time relaxing, beachcombing and staring out to sea to look for whales, stop at Roberts Creek. With fantastic views of the Strait of Georgia and beyond to the mountains of Vancouver Island, this campground is found 14 kilometres west of Gibsons on Highway 101. From the Lower Mainland, visitors take a beautiful ferry ride from Horseshoe Bay to Langdale. Services are available at Gibsons or Sechelt, 12 kilometres to the north.

Facilities

Camping facilities at this 40-hectare park are situated in a lightly forested area of second-growth Douglas fir and western redcedar. There are 21 spaces with wheelchair-accessible pit toilets and a sani-station but no showers or flush toilets. The campground is quite near the main road, and traffic noise may be a problem for some people. The day-use area is a short drive from the campground.

Recreational activities

Beachcombing is a favourite activity here. At low tide a cobblestone beach reveals sea stars, mussels, oysters and an array of other marine life. From the beach it is also possible to see whales, seals and sea lions, but don't count on it—they were somewhat elusive when I visited. Although the waters tend to be cold, some people enjoy swimming and fishing.

Additional information

The area of coastline between Langdale and Lund is called the Sunshine Coast because of its warm summers and mild winters. Annual precipitation here is almost 170 millimetres less than in Vancouver, making the Sunshine Coast a desirable place to live. Roberts Creek campground is located on one of the busiest sections of the area. The park was established in 1947 and the campground in 1954. The community of Gibsons to the south is famous because the TV series *The Beachcombers* was filmed here. It also has a small maritime museum. To the north, Sechelt has a number of great bakeries and cafés—don't stop here if you are on a diet, but if you're not, it's a nice little community to wander through.

Rolley Lake

Location

Some parks are criticized for being too big, some for being too small. In my opinion, 115-hectare Rolley Lake is the perfect size. It is also easily accessible from Vancouver, has a delightful setting, boasts a number of recreational activities and is well equipped. It is located 23 kilometres northwest of Mission (70 kilometres east of Vancouver). Although well signposted from Highway 7, the location is a little hard to find. In Maple Ridge, turn off Highway 7 north at 287th onto the Dewdney Trunk Road, turn right onto Bell Road, then make a left turn toward the park. The road is paved all the way. Maple Ridge and Mission both have comprehensive services.

Facilities

This popular campground has 64 spacious units set in a woodland area of western hemlock and mature vine maple, offering privacy and shade. The facilities are among the best provided by BC Parks and include showers, a sani-station, flush toilets and good wheelchair access. Reservations are accepted.

Recreational activities

Rolley Lake Provincial Park provides a relaxing environment for campers. The lake is surrounded by forest, and, because powerboats are prohibited, it is a peaceful place to relax, canoe, swim and fish (the lake is stocked with coastal cutthroat trout and rainbow trout). There are a couple of short walks: one leads to a waterfall, while another leads around the lake, includes a section of boardwalk and takes about 60 minutes to complete. Children can have fun in the play area. Rolley Lake is also a good place for observing bird life, and there is a wildlife-viewing site for BC Wildlife Watch.

Additional information

Rolley Lake, which takes its name from Fanny and James Rolley, who settled here in 1888, has played an active part in the logging industry of BC. In the early part of the 20th century, the lake stored shingle bolts destined for a mill located at Ruskin, 5 kilometres away. In the 1930s, when all the old-growth forest had gone, it became home to a small Japanese-Canadian logging operation harvesting Douglas fir. BC Parks acquired it in 1961, and today it provides a tranquil environment for those who wish to escape the main centres of population. The only problems with this idyllic setting are the mosquitoes, which can be troublesome at times. During my first visit to Rolley Lake, the beach was littered with Canada goose droppings, but on a subsequent visit in 2008, it was clean.

SALTERY BAY

Location

Saltery Bay Provincial Park is located about 27 kilometres south of Powell River on the north shore of Jervis Inlet. Visitors must take two delightful short ferry rides, one from Horseshoe Bay to Langdale, the other from Earls Cove to Saltery Bay. The land and sea route from the Lower Mainland and the ocean-view scenery at Saltery Bay make this camping excursion a real delight. The campground is just 1 kilometre

north of the ferry terminal, and Powell River has all services 30 kilometres north but there is also a store at Black Point 6 kilometres away.

Facilities

This 69-hectare park has 42 large private camping spots in an evergreen forest. The campground is wheelchair-accessible and has a sani-station, but only pit toilets and no showers. Reservations are accepted.

Recreational activities

You can see Canada's first underwater statue at Saltery Bay, but remember to bring all the correct diving gear! In addition to the superb ocean-view scenery, the shallow offshore waters of the park are the biggest attraction here. Scuba divers are enticed to the area by the variety of marine life, underwater coves and shipwrecks (there is also access for divers with disabilities). To the delight of many divers, a 3-metre bronze mermaid has been sunk at Mermaid Cove. For those who do not dive, the park offers beaches for swimming and sunbathing in the day-use area. There is also a 2-kilometre hiking trail to Little Saltery Falls, the chance to see killer whales, seals and sea lions, who occasionally bask in the area, and salmon fishing from April to October.

Additional information

Saltery Bay is named after the fish saltery that was located here at the turn of the century; prior to that time, First Nations inhabited the area. This popular diving area has been featured in *National Geographic* and is an excellent spot from which to explore the Sunshine Coast. Even if you do not want to dive, this is a quaint campground and the journey to it is delightful.

SASQUATCH

Location

With four pristine lakes, including the freshwater fjord of massive Harrison Lake, and 1,217 hectares of land, it is easy to see why this park is popular. The park offers a vast expanse of beautiful mountain scenery to explore. Sasquatch is located 6 kilometres north of Harrison Hot Springs off Highway 7. All services are found at Harrison.

Facilities

The 177 camping spots here are set in an area of second-growth deciduous forest and are divided between Hicks Lake (71 spots, some close to the lake) and the campgrounds of Lakeside (42 spaces and my favourite) and Bench (63 spaces), which are nearer to Deer Lake. Lakeside has some wonderful spots with access directly onto the lake, while the spaces at Bench are heavily shaded. There are flush and pit toilets and a sani-station but no showers. The park accepts reservations but is not wheelchair-accessible.

Recreational activities

The four lakes (Harrison, Hicks, Deer and Trout) vary in size—and in the recreational pursuits they offer. Harrison and Hicks lakes allow powerboats, and at Deer Lake only boats powered with electric motors are permitted. Trout Lake prohibits powerboats completely and is therefore the best choice for canoeing and kayaking. Trout fishing in all the lakes is reputed to be excellent. A number of trails lead around the park. Two beach locations ensure sun-worshipping opportunities: one is at the southern end of Hicks Lake and the other is by the group-camping area, where you can swim over to two small forested islands to explore. A play area for children is located at the Lakeside campground, and the day-use area on Harrison Lake has tons of picnic tables, plus sunbathing and swimming opportunities. Canoe rentals are also offered at Hicks Lake and the cost in 2008 was $15.00 per hour. Famous for its mineral pools, the nearby town of Harrison Hot Springs holds a sandcastle-building contest in September and an arts festival in July.

Additional information

The name "Sasquatch" is an English corruption of the Coast Salish word *sasqac*. The sasquatch is a mythical creature believed to possess a certain type of spirit that should be avoided—a sort of Bigfoot. Local Native people still report sightings of the sasquatch around Harrison River, so be warned! This area is spectacular in the fall when the colours are at their height; fall is also a good time to visit Harrison Hot Springs, which can become very busy during the peak summer months. This really is a great place to take the kids, but even for those without little ones, a lot of fun can be had at Sasquatch.

SILVER LAKE

Location

Confession time: I do not much care for this campground. When I visited (on my way to Skagit Valley—a far superior campground), groups of teenagers from Hope were loud and boisterous and consequently shaped my impression. The relatively small lakeside campground is located 12 kilometres from Hope off Highway 1, the last 6 kilometres on a good gravel road. All services are available at Hope.

Facilities

There are 25 sites at this 77-hectare park; some are little more than pull-ins at the side of the road, but the surrounding Fraser Valley scenery is great. Not surprisingly, only the basic facilities exist (drinking water, pit toilets, picnic tables, and fire pits). There are wheelchair-accessible pit toilets.

Recreational activities

One of the other problems I have with Silver Lake is that there is little to do here, in stark contrast to its neighbour Skagit Valley. It is possible to swim in the lake and fish for trout. A small 1-kilometre-long trail follows the water's edge, and there is a gravel boat launch. The town of Hope is an interesting place for a wander, as there are a number of carved wooden sculptures in the downtown and a number of restaurants and eateries.

Additional information

I cannot tell a lie: I would not want to camp here. Although the scenery is stunning and the campground's proximity to Hope is attractive, my advice to campers is to choose Skagit Valley—or, if you cannot face the gravel road, head to Emory Creek, or even to the Alaska Highway! Anywhere is better than Silver Lake—unless, of course, you are 18 years old, have a four-wheel-drive monster truck, love loud music and want to hang out with like-minded people.

SKAGIT VALLEY

Location

Encompassing around 28,000 hectares, this park is in the Northern Cascades. West of Hope, a gravel road leads 32 kilometres to Skagit Valley, but the main camping area is an additional 26 kilometres on bumpy gravel. Once at Ross Lake (the main campground), the scenery is awesome. The nearest services are back at Hope, so stock up before making the journey.

Facilities

Two campgrounds offer 131 sites: 43 are set among the trees at Silvertip, adjacent to the Skagit River near the park's entrance, and the remaining 88 are more out in the open at Ross Lake, where some sites are near the water's edge. There is no sani-station or wheelchair access, and facilities are basic (drinking water, fire pits, picnic tables, pit toilets).

Recreational activities

At Silvertip, trails lead along the Skagit River, and Ross Lake has hiking trails in the immediate vicinity, but there are more than 50 kilometres of hiking trails in the park itself. Swimming, canoeing and kayaking are possible from Ross Lake's sandy beach, and the lake is surrounded by fantastic snow-covered mountains. There is a boat launch at the Ross Lake campground, which also has an adventure playground for children and a large grassy field. While not suitable for canoeing or kayaying, the Skagit River is one of the best fly-fishing streams in North America and the most productive stream in the Lower Mainland. Fishing for Dolly Varden, char, eastern brook trout and cutthroat trout is good. Wildlife here includes deer, black bears, cougars, coyotes, minks and raccoons; there is also a wide array of birds.

Additional information

Over 20 years ago, a public protest saved the valley from being flooded by a Seattle hydro company. Today, the water level at Ross Lake is controlled by a hydro dam in Washington State and is subject to fluctuations. As I bounced along the 58 kilometres of gravel road, I cursed the fact that the park entrance is so far from the campground. But then I beheld the mountain scenery that surrounds the lake and suddenly the journey was worth it. Unfortunately, for me, the words "Skagit Valley" and "mosquitoes" are synonymous, but had I visited when these insects were not biting, it would probably rank as one of my top 10 campgrounds, but I did not stay the night due to the blood-suckers that were out in force that July day. However, it appears others have had the same experience, so be forewarned.

STAWAMUS CHIEF

Location
Right next to Shannon Falls Provincial Park, this campground takes its name from the majestic piece of rock under which it is situated, and the primary reason for camping here is to scale it. The park is located on Highway 99, 5 kilometres south of Squamish, where all services are available.

Facilities
There are 47 walk-in sites and 15 drive-in sites—the latter unsuitable for larger RVs as they are very close together. Because the campground is relatively new, the ground vegetation is sparse, making the camping spots under the trees look quite dark and sad. Pit toilets and water are available but not fire pits because campfires are prohibited here (there is a shared shelter for cooking should you bring a stove).

Recreational activities
If you're a climber this is the place to be; however, others may not find it so appealing. When I visited, the world-class climbing destination was dominated by skinny Lycra-clad individuals setting out to climb "the Chief," which is the second-largest granite monolith on Earth. Generally, the 700-metre-high rock is closed to climbers from March 15 to July 31 to protect the nesting peregrine falcons. For those who do not wish to climb, it is also possible to hike up the rock, but be warned: this excursion is not for the faint of heart and a sign at the outset reads "unsuitable for dogs." Upon reaching the top a few years ago, I discovered another small rock climb was required, after which it was necessary to walk a narrow pathway with dramatic crevices on either side. I turned back, believing this hike was not just difficult for dogs, but also for many two-legged individuals! However, there are other easier hiking trails and less than 2 kilometres away is Shannon Falls Provincial Park, which is a great place for a picnic and a stroll to a platform for viewing BC's third-highest waterfall. The restaurant across the road also provides good views of the 335-metre falls. The railway museum at Squamish and the mining museum at Britannia Beach are also well worth a visit.

Additional information
This is not a picturesque campground as the views are minimal and the spaces small. There is also the distant sound of traffic. But if your passion is climbing, camp here and you will inevitably meet like-minded people. For all others, my advice is to stay at nearby Porteau Cove, Alice Lake or Nairn Falls.

THOMPSON OKANAGAN

The Thompson Okanagan region includes a huge central area of land reaching from the U.S. border in the south to the Canadian Rockies in the north. Pack the sunscreen if your plans include a trip to the southern portion, as summertime temperatures here are often the hottest in the province. This region features miles of orchards and vineyards, crystal-clear lakes, warm-hearted communities and undulating countryside that gives way to beautiful mountains in the north. The southern Okanagan region incorporates Highway 3 from the Kettle Valley to Princeton, Highway 33, Highway 97, Highway 5A south of Aspen Grove to Princeton and Highway 6. Farther north, three of the province's most spectacular provincial parks can be found: Mount Robson is named after its majestic mountain, the highest in the Canadian Rockies; Wells Gray is BC's fourth-largest park and is known as "the waterfall park"; and Shuswap Lake has over 1,000 kilometres of waterways and many sandy beaches. The northern region encompasses campgrounds accessible from Highway 16 from the border of Alberta to Route 5, Highway 5, Highway 5A, Highway 1 as far as Lytton and the northern section of Highway 23. With such diversity, there is something for every camper in this area of BC.

Fish and swim in the Similkameen river at Bromley Rock Provincial Park.

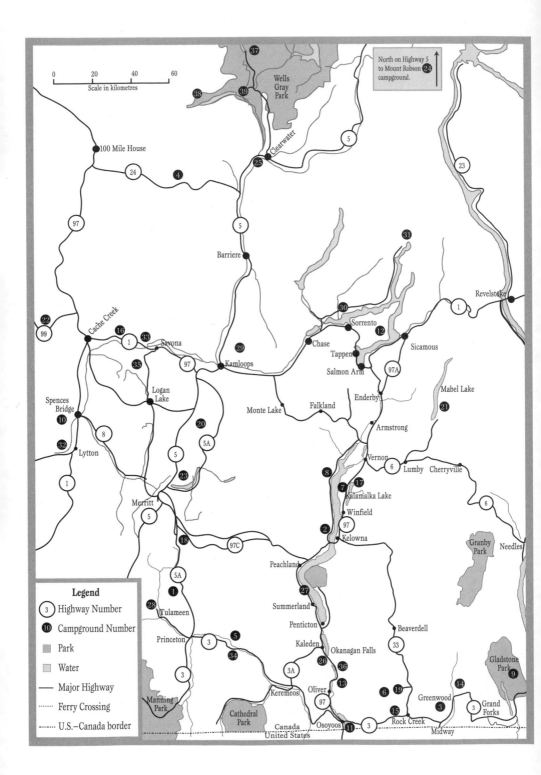

Campgrounds in the Okanagan are very busy in peak summer months, so book ahead to avoid disappointment.

Thompson Okanagan

ALLISON LAKE

Location
On the relatively quiet Highway 5A at the southern end of Allison Lake there is an enchanting little 23-hectare park, perfect for those with time on their hands. Services can be found at Princeton, 28 kilometres south.

Facilities
Twenty-four large well-positioned camping spaces are found in a lovely forested area of mature Douglas fir. The sites are suitable for every type of vehicle, and although some are quite close to the road, there is not a lot of traffic. All the basic amenitites exist (fire pits, drinking water, picnic tables, pit toilets).

Recreational activities
The primary recreational activities here centre on beautiful Allison Lake and include swimming (although there are quite a few reeds), fishing (the lake is stocked with blackwater rainbow trout), canoeing and kayaking. A single-width gravel boat launch is located in the day-use area. Aspen trees border the lake, and the area is particularly attractive during the fall when the trees turn golden and red, presenting fantastic photography opportunities.

Additional information
This is one of the better roadside campgrounds used primarily for overnight camping. Highway 5A between Kamloops and Princeton is a lovely quiet route, suitable for appreciating the scenery of the Okanagan. And for those who have the time, it is a far more pleasant way to travel than the busy Coquihalla Highway. The route is 118 kilometres longer than the main highway but avoids the long steep hills of the Coquihalla. Be prepared for little development and a scenic drive if heading south from the campground as the road follows Allison Creek to Princeton. The area is rich in mining history; information is available from the visitor centres in Princeton and Merritt.

BEAR CREEK

Location
Go to sleep to the sound of tree frogs at this popular 178-hectare park. Bear Creek exhibits a variety of geological features, including sandy beaches and spectacular canyons and waterfalls. These features are supplemented with a diversity of vegetation, which encourages wildlife populations. The park is situated to the north of the Okanagan, 9 kilometres west of Kelowna (where all services are found) on the western side of Okanagan Lake, off Highway 97 on paved Westside Road.

Facilities
Bear Creek provides 122 camping spots and every type of camping service, including flush and pit toilets, a sani-station, showers and wheelchair access. Sites accommodate all recreational vehicles, and there are a number of double spots. Some of the more desirable spots overlook Lambly ("Bear") Creek, where campers can be lulled to sleep by the sound of the trickling waters (not recommended for those with weak bladders). The park administrators operate a small concession selling ice cream, juice, pop and some groceries. Reservations are accepted.

Recreational activities
This stunning location facilitates a variety of recreational pursuits. The beach is over 400 metres in length, ideal for swimming and sunbathing. The lake has rainbow trout, whitefish and kokanee, as well as boating potential. There is a boat launch. In addition to a number of smaller interpretive trails, over 15 kilometres of well-maintained hiking trails exist, some of which lead to views of the lake and canyon. Remember to pack your camera, as there are excellent photographic opportunities. Children can enjoy an adventure playground, and there is also a horseshoe pit. Bear Creek is home to an array of wildlife, including swallows, hawks and owls. Tree frogs can be heard in the spring, and rattlesnakes live in the vicinity but are rarely seen. There is also an amphitheatre where interpretive programs are conducted during the summer.

Additional information
In the early fall, kokanee can be seen spawning in the lower reaches of the creek. This park is extremely popular in the summer months and is particularly appealing for those with children. I strongly advise making a reservation if you hope to camp in July or August.

BOUNDARY CREEK

Location

If you are debating whether to spend the night at Boundary Creek or at another location, my advice would be to choose the alternative. Though it does have the advantage of being the only campground in the immediate area and is conveniently situated 4 kilometres west of Greenwood (where all services are found), this 2-hectare park has little to recommend it.

Facilities

The 18 camping spots of this roadside campground are quite large, but the lack of dense vegetation makes them open and without privacy. The campsites adjacent to the creek are somewhat more private, as cottonwood trees line the banks of the creek itself. All the basic facilities offered by BC Parks are available (picnic tables, flush and pit toilets, drinking water, fire pits), but there is no wheelchair accessibility. As the campground is close to the main road, it can be quite noisy.

Recreational activities

This is very much an overnight campground and therefore offers little recreational activity. It is possible to catch rainbow and brook trout in the creek. The mining industry developed the area adjacent to the campground. A nearby slag heap and crumbling stack are evidence of the BC Copper Company's smelter, which employed over 400 men during its years of operation in the first part of the 20th century. The historic town of Greenwood contains some beautiful turn-of-the-century buildings, including a courthouse and post office, and is a pleasant place to stroll around. We visited in 2008 with a seven-year-old and a nine-year-old and found a great playpark at the eastern end of the town.

Additional information

Out of necessity, I stayed at Boundary Creek in late September one year. The proximity to the road coupled with the openness of the sites themselves mark this as one of BC Parks' less desirable spots; however, it does have the advantage of being the only campground in the immediate area. I visited Greenwood during the late afternoon and enjoyed it, so I went back in the evening, only to find it extremely quiet. Despite its claim to be Canada's smallest city, little occurs in Greenwood after 6:00 p.m.

BRIDGE LAKE

Location

This area, known as the "Interlakes District," is an angler's paradise, as hundreds of lakes offer fishing for eastern brook and lake trout, burbot and kokanee. Covering a modest 11 hectares, Bridge Lake Provincial Park was established by BC Parks in 1957, and there are two main ways to reach it. The first entails turning off Highway 97 east of 93 Mile House onto Highway 24 (the campground is 51 kilometres east of 100 Mile House); the second is to turn off Highway 5 at Little Fort and travel west on Highway 24. Full services are available at 100 Mile House.

Facilities

Thirteen vehicle-accessible and three walk-in campsites are available at the south end of the lake. The sites are large, set amongst trees and have views of the lake. Facilities are basic and consist of picnic tables, fire pits, drinking water and pit toilets. There is no sani-station.

Recreational activities

Activities at this location include fishing for burbot, lake and rainbow trout, boating (there is a boat launch) and swimming. The lake is also ideal for canoeing and kayaking. A small hiking trail skirts the lakeside, and there is an archaeological site in the park itself.

Additional information

Recently a number of resorts have developed in the area, and these now offer holiday excursions. The easy access from two main highways means that this campground is a convenient stop-off for the traveller during the busy peak months of July and August. The location seems to be particularly popular with anglers.

BROMLEY ROCK

Location

Set astride a rock bluff on the Similkameen River, 21 kilometres east of Princeton on Highway 3, is the riverside campground of 149-hectare Bromley Rock Provincial Park. By staying here, campers trace the footsteps of the early pioneers who came in search of gold and other minerals. Services are located in Princeton (21 kilometres west) or Hedley (15 kilometres east).

Facilities

The campground has 17 spots set in a forested area on the Similkameen River. All the basics are here (fire pits, drinking water, picnic tables, pit toilets), and two of the pit toilets are wheelchair-accessible. The campground is located near the road so there is the noise of traffic, as Highway 3 is quite busy.

Recreational activities

The river offers swimming in delightful cool swimming holes, and there is fishing potential. Be careful when swimming, though, as the current is strong. When I visited, local young male adventurers were "tubing" downstream to Stemwinder Provincial Park, a popular activity not recommended for the uninitiated. Just outside the park, hiking trails lead to fantastic views of the Similkameen Valley. The nearby town of Princeton was named in 1860 to commemorate the visit of the Prince of Wales that year. Princeton has a pioneer museum with displays of clothing, mining items and furnishings. Artifacts from the Salish people and Chinese immigrants, who played a major role in the early development of mining and the railway, are also on display.

Additional information

This campground is only 14 kilometres from Stemwinder Provincial Park, which is slightly larger in capacity and may provide an alternative should Bromley Rock be full. Bromley Rock is a great place to stop for a picnic even if you do not want to camp. Salish and Shuswap people inhabited the area originally, and they have left traces of their existence. More recently, the area was explored by miners and trappers. Anyone travelling west along Highway 3 should make time to visit the nearby Grist Mill and Gardens at Keremeos. Even if you do not have time to tour this BC Heritage site, just call in for coffee and the wonderful home cooking.

CONKLE LAKE

Location

If you are looking for a backcountry retreat to get away from the crowds, and you can endure a bumpy road and navigate around herds of cows, this is the place for you. The campground is in a beautiful location amidst the Okanagan Highlands, but BC Parks warns that the access route along twisting gravel roads is not suitable for large motorhomes or towed trailers. Consequently, those travelling in these types of vehicles may wish to choose another spot. The park can be reached by gravel access roads from three points: from Highway 33 at Westbridge, you can reach the park by driving for 16 kilometres on a gravel road; from Highway 3, 6 kilometres east of Bridesville, a 26-kilometre gravel road leads to the site; and from Highway 97 at Okanagan Falls, a 35-kilometre gravel road can be taken. Services are available at Westbridge and at the junction of highways 3 and 33.

Facilities

There are 34 private camping spots located in a lightly forested area of western larch, lodgepole pine, alder and willow on the northwest corner of the 3-kilometre-long lake. Some spots overlook the lake. Only the basic facilities are provided by BC Parks (pit toilets, picnic tables, pump water, cooking pits). There is no sani-station.

Recreational activities

Secluded Conkle Lake has a beautiful beach, where you can sunbathe, swim or fish for rainbow trout. A steep dropoff, however, means non-swimmers and children should be cautious. There is a boat launch, but the park has a motorboat size restriction. A number of hiking trails lead from the campground, one of which goes halfway around the lake. The 1.7-kilometre Falls Trail includes a beautiful multi-tiered waterfall. For rainy days, a covered picnic shelter is available.

Additional information

The park is named after an early settler to the Kettle Valley, W.H. Conkle. The fact that this park is relatively difficult to access by the RV population may suggest it is a campground only for four-wheel-drivers and their passengers to enjoy. When I visited, there were quite a few large recreational vehicles that had obviously managed the routes and whose owners were enjoying the beautiful Okanagan scenery. However, the roads should not be attempted by those with low-loaders or long vehicles because of the number of tight switchbacks.

ELLISON

Location

If diving is your game, then Ellison Provincial Park should be your aim. In addition to the diving opportunities it provides, Ellison is an excellent spot for a family vacation, perfect if you have children to entertain. Set on the northeastern shore of Okanagan Lake and encompassing 200 hectares between the Thompson Plateau and the Monashee Mountains, the park is reached from Highway 97 by heading south for 16 kilometres on 25th Avenue from Vernon's main intersection. All services are available in Vernon.

Facilities

The park has 71 spacious, well-appointed sites set in a natural forest of Douglas fir and ponderosa pine and is suitable for every size of recreational vehicle. There are wheelchair-accessible flush toilets, pit toilets and a sani-station. When we stayed in 2008, two yurts were available for rent for $65.00 a night, reservable through www.discovercamping.ca. Each one accommodates up to four people, but you must supply your own bedding.

Recreational activities

Ellison Provincial Park is home to Canada's only freshwater dive park, located at Otter Bay. A number of objects and artifacts have been sunk here to attract fish and create a diving haven for the rubber-clad enthusiasts who explore the dark cold waters. If diving is not your passion, there is a wide array of other activities to enjoy, including 6 kilometres of hiking trails that take visitors to many of the park's natural features and viewpoints. (Watch out for porcupines, often seen on the popular Ellison Trail.) Two protected beach areas ideal for swimming and sunbathing are equipped with changing facilities and an outdoor shower. A little farther away is a third beach, which allows dogs. Fishers can try their luck for large carp, burbot, kokanee and trout, and while there is no boat launch in the park, one is located 6 kilometres to the north. A number of the camping spaces overlook the playground and are ideal if you have young children. There is also an almost manicured green field, which many golf courses would be envious of, for ball games.

Additional information

Ellison is in the heart of the fruit-growing region of the province, and orchards, ranches and farms dominate the area, as they have since the 1800s. This park provides an excellent base from which to explore the North Okanagan and savour the produce of the region.

Fintry

Location
This is a wonderful provincial park to explore. It has so many facets and is one of my favourites in the area. Ideally situated for exploring the Okanagan and found in one of the region's few remaining natural areas, Fintry started to register campers in 1996. The park is on the northwest side of Okanagan Lake, 32 kilometres north of Kelowna and 37 kilometres south of Vernon. It is clearly signposted from Highway 97 and accessed by 8 kilometres of paved road. Services are available in Kelowna and Vernon.

Facilities
Camping facilities here include flush toilets and showers. Camping spots are in a large open area. Some are shaded by pine trees, and others have views of the lake. A hundred camping spots are available and reservations are accepted. There is also one yurt available for rent for $65.00 a night. It can accommodate up to four people—but you must supply your own bedding. The yurt is reservable by phone only by calling 1-800-689-9025.

Recreational activities
Close to the campground is a beautiful 2-kilometre sandy beach, ideal for swimming, sunbathing and family activities. For paddlers and boaters, there is a paved boat launch and a floating dock in the park. Fishing in the warm waters of Okanagan Lake can be rewarding, and hiking the Shorts Creek Canyon Trail provides opportunities to view white-tailed deer, bighorn sheep and a variety of birds. BC Parks warns that caution should be exercised on sections of the trails; in places it is quite narrow and near steep cliffs. I last visited this park in 2007 and was amazed at the newly renovated Manor House, which was full of stuffed animals and artifacts from international hunting trips. It's one of the best small museums in BC that I've seen, and my children loved it. The Friends of Fintry Society has a good website with a calendar of park events and list of things to do at www.fintry.ca.

Additional information
The park is a heritage site occupying the former Fintry Estate. Its history dates to the last century, when fur dealers traded with the Native inhabitants of the area. In 1909, James Cameron, originally from Scotland, purchased the land and called it Fintry. He built many of the buildings that can be toured today, including the manor house and farm buildings. Fintry has the advantage of being located in a popular area of BC, but being a relatively new camping haven, it has yet to be fully exploited by the camping public.

GLADSTONE (TEXAS CREEK)

Location

Gladstone (formerly Texas Creek) Provincial Park is located at the north end of Christina Lake, 20 kilometres northeast of Grand Forks. To reach the campground, take Highway 3, then turn onto East Lake Drive and drive for 4 kilometres on a paved road. Residents of Christina Lake boast that the waters here are the warmest in BC; however, Wasa Lake and Osoyoos Lake residents make the same claim. Whatever the truth, Christina Lake is an immensely popular recreational place where all services can be found.

Facilities

Sixty-three large camping spots are set in an open pine forest in this 39,387-hectare provincial park. Facilities include the basics: fire pits, drinking water, picnic tables, pit toilets. Some park facilities are wheelchair-accessible and reservations are accepted.

Recreational activities

Nineteen kilometres long, but only 55 metres deep, Christina Lake supplies a wealth of leisure pursuits, including swimming from delightful secluded pocket beaches and boating and fishing in the clear waters. There is a boat launch. Gladstone has 48 kilometres of trails, including one that leads north along the lakeshore and another that heads to Deer Point Lookout (26 kilometres return); details of all trails can be found on the park's notice board. The nearby popular holiday centre also has golf courses and country clubs to enjoy.

Additional information

For years I avoided staying here, as I found the community of Christina Lake very busy and commercialized and envisaged the campground having similar traits. How wrong I was! This is a wonderful quiet camping spot where very lucky campers gain sites overlooking the water. I spent a gorgeous summer night here and cursed my previous preconceptions about the place, which were grounded in the knowledge that the population of Christina Lake swells from 1,000 to 6,000 in the summer months. More recently the community of Christina Lake has grown even more, but the campground away from the centre of population provides a tranquil camping experience.

GOLDPAN

Location

Watch out for river rafters and gold prospectors if you plan to sojourn here. Goldpan is a 5-hectare roadside provincial park conveniently located on Highway 1, 10 kilometres south of Spences Bridge, where services are located. There is also a restaurant just down the road.

Facilities

There are just 14 camping spots available here beside the mighty Thompson River. Facilities are basic (drinking water, fire pits, picnic tables, pit toilets). Railway trucks and the noise of road traffic can be heard from the campground.

Recreational activities

Goldpan's main draw is fishing, and the park attracts steelhead anglers, especially

in October, November and December. Because the Thompson is very fast-moving, swimming in the river is not recommended, but it is popular for kayaking and river rafting. We picnicked here in July 2006, and during our brief visit witnessed six different whitewater-rafting excursions glide past our beach spot. The area is heavily used during the peak summer months by commercial river-rafting companies looking for a resting place for their downriver trips. As one would surmise, gold panning can be undertaken here. Ospreys also frequent the area—so keep looking up.

Additional information

Spences Bridge, named after Thomas Spence, who built the original bridge in 1865, is where the Thompson and Nicola rivers meet. This area has been fished for hundreds of years by the Thompson First Nation, whose people continue to fish here today, as indeed do many others. For those who want a taste of adventure by whitewater rafting, the area is ideal. Be warned: in summertime the area is prone to very high temperatures (often the highest in the country) so remember the sunscreen. The campground was established in 1956 and is primarily a one-night stop for travellers on Highway 1. Having camped here again in 2004, I confirmed my feeling that this park serves well as a picnic spot for breaking the journey on Highway 1, rather than an ideal place to camp. Skihist Provincial Park, a short drive south, is far superior and not as noisy, and it also offers much-needed shade.

Haynes Point

Location

It is a great shame that this popular campground is not larger. For the longest time, whenever I attempted to stay in this idyllic setting, it was full. I finally succeeded in September 2002 and got the last remaining space, even at that supposedly quiet time of the year. Haynes Point is located at the southern end of the Okanagan River Valley, in the rain shadow of the Cascade Mountains on Osoyoos Lake, just 2 kilometres from Osoyoos on Highway 97.

Facilities

It is little wonder that Haynes Point is a popular retreat, as all of the 41 camping spots are located on a narrow sandspit with over half of them having direct access to the beach. There are both flush toilets and pit toilets, and one flush toilet is wheelchair-accessible, but no sani-station or showers. Reservations are accepted but only for a maximum of seven nights.

Recreational activities

The deep Okanagan River Valley, formed by glacial erosion, receives less than 35 centimetres of rain per annum and is located at the northern end of the Great-Basin Desert. The lake is reputed to be the warmest in the country, making it a magnet for swimming, boating (there is a boat launch) and for rainbow trout and bass fishing. The fish are huge here and can easily be seen from a trail in the park. Haynes Point's trails have recently been upgraded and extended. The warm climate and lack of precipitation promote desert-loving plants such as ponderosa pine, bear cacti, sagebrush and greasewood, which in turn provide a habitat for a wide array of bird, animal and reptile life (including species unique to this area of BC, such as the spadefoot toad, burrowing owl and desert night snake).

Additional information

This 38-hectare park is named after Judge John Carmichael Haynes, who came to Osoyoos in 1866 and became a renowned legal authority and landowner. Native people have lived, hunted and fished in the area; two archaeological sites in the park provide evidence of this long history. Haynes Point is an extremely popular location during the peak summer months. It can be extremely hot in the summer, but the area's climate ensures a pleasant stay for those who visit in the spring and fall. Some of the Okanagan's finest vineyards and fruit farms are found in this region. From May to November, fresh fruit and vegetable stands at the side of the highway provide produce for campers to enjoy around an open fire. Besides the high summer temperatures, the only disadvantage to this campground is that at certain times it can be a little noisy, as the sound of traffic and music is easily audible from the town of Osoyoos across the water.

HERALD

Location

A variety of flora and fauna and easy access to the calm waters of Shuswap Lake are just two of the many attributes of Herald Provincial Park. The vegetation is attributable to the park's distinctive position amid steep uplands and flat deltas. It includes Douglas fir, juniper, dryland shrubs, redcedar, hemlock, cottonwood, aspen and paper birch. A naturalist's delight, Herald is found on the Salmon Arm of Shuswap Lake, 14 kilometres east of Tappen off Highway 1. Services are available at Tappen.

Facilities

On the calm lakeside are 119 beautiful wooded camping spaces with all the services required for a comfortable camping experience, including showers, flush and pit toilets and a sani-station. Some facilities are wheelchair-accessible. The campsites are at three locations: Reineker, Bastion Mountain and Homestead. Reineker's 36 sites are closer to the water, Bastion's 15 sites are larger and more secluded, while the 68 sites at Homestead don't have much shade. Reservations are accepted.

Recreational activities

Shuswap Lake is a relatively warm lake and therefore a delightful place to swim. The park has sand and fine-gravel beaches ideal for sunbathing. Fishing and boating are pursuits enjoyed by many, and there is a boat launch in the day-use area (1 kilometre from the campground). There are also a number of trails in the park, including a 20-minute one that leads through an area of cedar growth to the beautiful Margaret Falls. Reineker Creek runs through the park near the campground, and evidence of Shuswap Nation pit houses is visible west of the creek. Birding is reputed to be fantastic, as more than 70 species frequent the park.

Additional information

The lake is named after the Shuswap First Nation, who recognized it as a bountiful hunting and fishing ground. Cliff faces around the lake display pictographs (rock paintings) that provide evidence of humankind's long residency in the region. Although the lake is named after the area's first inhabitants, the park takes its name from the Herald family, who were early settlers of the area. The remains of the family's farm buildings can still be seen today. Herald Provincial Park is very popular with both locals and tourists as it offers every facility yet is not tremendously large. It's a delightful place to camp. The sani-station here has the best view of any sani-station in the province, so even this most mundane camping chore becomes a delight.

INKANEEP

Location

Inkaneep Provincial Park is an ideal spot from which to experience the excellent local fruit and wine; however, the campground here offers little else: it's primarily geared to overnight camping. On the shores of the Okanagan River, this 21-hectare park is 6 kilometres north of Oliver on Highway 97. Services are found in Oliver, or at the gas station at the junction of Highway 97 and the turnoff to the campground. The park was established in 1956 and plays a role in protecting old cottonwood trees.

Facilities

Inkaneep offers seven camping spots, more suitable for tents than RVs, set in a shady oasis of cottonwood trees on the edge of the Okanagan River. Only the basic facilities are available here (pit toilets, picnic tables, drinking water, cooking pits). The campground is very close to a group of houses, and in this respect it is quite suburban.

Recreational activities

From this campground it is possible to fish in the Okanagan River and to canoe (although it is quite a trek from the campground to the water). The arid desert habitat around the park is home to many species of wildlife; consequently, one of the main activities here is birdwatching. A small path through old-growth cottonwood trees leads from the campground to a small dike on the Okanagan River, where there are birdwatching opportunities. The area is home to black-headed grosbeaks, northern orioles, yellow warblers, blue-listed Lewis' woodpeckers and warbling vireos. An ecological reserve is also located nearby.

Additional information

The town of Oliver was established in 1921 under a land grant by then-BC premier John Oliver as a settlement for veterans from the First World War. Now it is known for housing some of the best wineries in the country, which can be toured by visitors. Be sure to make time to explore the local caves and perhaps purchase a bottle of wine for savouring around the campfire. Just south of Oliver is a "pocket desert." When I first visited in 1999, it was somewhat difficult to find, as there were no signposts. However, in 2001 it was designated as a provincial park and now has lovely broad walls with interpretive signs and information. The area supports subtropical flora and fauna, such as cactus, horned lizards, rattlesnakes and burrowing owls. Remember to take along drinking water, as it can be very hot.

Jewel Lake

Location

Somewhat off the beaten track, Jewel Lake provides a getaway-from-it-all camping experience, and if campers are keen on fishing, then this place could be heaven. Found 12 kilometres east of Greenwood off Highway 3, the park is accessed by travelling toward Jewel Lake Resort. All services are available at Greenwood, but the resort also has some provisions and boat rentals.

Facilities

There are 26 vehicle-accessible spots here, and the basic facilities (drinking water, picnic tables, fire pits and pit toilets); the pit toilets are wheelchair-accessible. All sites are in a heavily forested area of Douglas fir, hemlock, birch and larch and are not suitable for larger RVs.

Recreational activities

Like so many out-of-the-way places in the province, Jewel Lake is primarily a location for fishing. Stocked with brook and rainbow trout from the Summerland Trout Hatchery, the 3-kilometre-long lake attracts anglers by the score. Fly-fishing is also popular. There is a car-top boat-launch location, and boats can be rented at Jewel Lake Resort. Motors are restricted to 10 horsepower, making canoeing a delightful alternative. Swimming is also possible. The historical town of Greenwood has a number of interesting buildings, but be warned that everything seems to close early—even at the height of summer.

Additional information

Now for my confession: I have not personally visited this campground in my 20 years of camping in BC. But when undertaking the research on this location and speaking to people who have, the words "fish" and "mosquito" always punctuate their sentences. Sometimes there are good reasons why even the most dedicated travel writers should gain their information second-hand.

JOHNSTONE CREEK

Location

Established in 1956 for day use only, this small 38-hectare roadside provincial park started offering camping recently. It is located near Bridesville on Highway 3, about 5 kilometres west of Rock Creek and 45 kilometres from the town of Osoyoos, where all services are available.

Facilities

Situated in an area of Douglas fir, pine, and aspen are 16 campsites a little distance away from the road. The trees make a good sound barrier, so noise from traffic is not a huge issue. The spots seem to be evenly split between those that are quite open with only a few shrubs dividing them and those with more privacy, thanks to the trees. There are four pit toilets, picnic tables, fire pits and drinking water. I stayed here in the springtime, so the smell of blooming spring vegetation was an added bonus.

Recreational activities

A pleasant waterfall where the waters of Johnstone Creek and Rock Creek converge is the main attraction here. There are also good photography opportunities at Rock Creek Canyon. According to BC Parks information, white-tailed deer and woodpeckers are often seen in the park. There is very limited hiking and fishing potential in the immediate vicinity, as the campground is geared to the overnight camper.

Additional information

On the drive from Osoyoos to Johnstone Creek, look out for huge sculptures of bald eagles, moose, pumas, ravens, deer and even a Yeti, which make for great photo opportunities. For those interested in prospecting for gold, a visit to the ghost town Camp McKinney is a must. Situated 11.5 kilometres northwest of Highway 3 on Mount Baldy Road are the ruins of a mining town, which yielded more than 80,000 ounces of gold between 1887 and 1903. A stop at the Osoyoos Visitor Centre provides more details. For those who plan to camp in the area longer than one night (and have a vehicle that can take the terrain), Conkle Lake is the preferred option; for others, Johnstone Creek is a superior roadside campground.

Juniper Beach

Location
Situated 19 kilometres east of Cache Creek on Highway 1, Juniper Beach is distinct from many other provincial parks because of its dry desert setting. Services are available at Cache Creek or at Kamloops (53 kilometres to the west).

Facilities
On the banks of the Thompson River, 30 camping spots are yours for the taking. The vegetation consists of sagebush, prickly pear cactus, juniper and cottonwoods. Although the camping spots accommodate every type of recreational vehicle, they are somewhat open. A special area has been designated just for tents, and some of the vehicle sites have the advantage of being close to the water. The campground is wheelchair-accessible and has pit toilets, a sani-station, electrical hookups and pay-to-use showers. Located a fair distance from the road, the campsites are not affected by the noise of road traffic, but two railway lines are close by. This is not the place to stay if you hate trains, as there is considerable rail traffic. When I stayed here, there were quite a few trains to lull me to sleep.

Recreational activities
Juniper Beach provides one of the few access points to the Thompson River between Savona and Spences Bridge. The easy river access makes this provincial park a pleasant place to stay and fish, and picnics on the shoreline are a delight. BC Parks says this is a good place to view sockeye salmon and to witness the summer migration of chinook and coho, although when I stayed here, there was no evidence of fish, either in the river or being caught by the patient anglers. A large natural pool separated from the river is perfect for swimming when the river's not too high, and canoeing and kayaking are also possible. There are lots of prickly pear cactus plants so be careful if you're camping with little children.

Additional information
This campground is located in the desert area of the Thompson–Nicola region and so looks quite barren compared to BC parks in more fertile regions. Do not expect to find much shade here on a hot summer day! I came here from the waterlogged Alice Lake campground and really appreciated the fantastic hot dry climate.

KEKULI BAY

Location

This is one of BC Parks' newest additions, but unlike many other recent arrivals, it is not small in capacity. Although only 57 hectares in size, it has space for 70 camping parties, and all sites have fantastic views of the lake. It is located on a gorgeous bay on the west side of Kalamalka Lake, 2 kilometres from Highway 97 and 11 kilometres south of Vernon, where services are available.

Facilities

Kekuli has flush and pit toilets, drinking water, showers and all the other amenities. The toilets and showers are wheelchair-accessible. Traffic noise may be an issue for some, and a railway line, though not much used, is also close to the campground. The lack of shade in the campsites also makes for very hot camping from mid-June to September. Reservations are accepted.

Recreational activities

The boat launch at this location is reported to be the best on Kalamalka Lake. Kayaking and canoeing are also pleasant here. With a sandy beach close by, those who don't want to ride on the waters can certainly have fun splashing in them. A small trail circles the campground, and there is a great kids' play area. If the weather isn't accommodating, a host of activities awaits in the town of Vernon. Kalamalka Lake Provincial Park, just north of Kekuli, provides a habitat for a variety of birds and wildlife (including rattlesnakes), while the high rodent population at Kekuli Bay ensures a healthy population of birds of prey, including ospreys and vultures. Yellow-bellied marmots run around the campground and are great fun for preschoolers to watch. The campground is the closest one to Predator Ridge golf course, which reputably has some of the best greens in the Okanagan.

Additional information

Kekuli Bay Provincial Park takes its name from semi-subterranean homes built by the Interior Salish First Nation. I visited this campground for the first time in June 2002 and loved the views but hated the intense heat and lack of shade. I cannot imagine staying here in the height of the summer without an air-conditioned RV. Trees have been planted, though, so in a few years' time there will be shade. Until then, my advice for summer campers is to stay at Okanagan Lake instead.

Kentucky–Alleyne

Location

Campers from the Lower Mainland looking for a weekend getaway cannot go wrong in choosing Kentucky–Alleyne, a real gem of a park situated 38 kilometres south of Merritt. To reach the campground, turn off Highway 5A just south of the Okanagan Connector and follow the marked 6-kilometre paved road; from the east, follow the signs from the Coquihalla for 11 kilometres. Services are available in Merritt.

Facilities

The 144-hectare park has 58 camping spots. Although most spots do not have the advantage of vegetation to afford privacy, they are well spaced and suitable for every type of recreational vehicle, and some are right on the lake. Facilities are basic (pit toilets, fire pits, picnic tables, drinking water).

Recreational activities

This is a stunningly beautiful area consisting of undulating glacial hills and grasslands surrounded by forests of pine and fir in the heart of cattle country. Lakes are re-stocked annually so there is good fishing potential for rainbow trout, and I love the way there are two "ponds" between them restricted to "children only" fishing. There is a boat launch and canoeing is a delight here, as is swimming. In 2004, when we were camping with our children, our four-year-old went running to the children's pond, straight through mud that resembled sand, and sank in it almost up to his waist. So, be warned of sand that is actually mud, especially if you have little ones! A number of trails take visitors around the lakes to different areas of the park where it is possible to see beaver lodges. As the campground is spread out, cycling on the many gravel roads and trails is an enjoyable activity for all ages; however, there are a number of private roads displaying NO TRESPASSING signs.

Additional information

I love this park. Although the camping spots themselves are not stunning, the size of the camping area, the many dirt trails and roads around the park and the glacial topography make Kentucky–Alleyne a pleasant place to explore. The sunsets are gorgeous—it is magical to cook dinner on an open fire while watching the beautiful red sunset over the water, as ospreys circle above. We stayed here in 2003, when my husband and I escaped without our children for a few days, camping with just our tent, some alcohol and a plastic bag of sandwiches. The BC Parks attendant, on collecting our fee and seeing our meagre provisions, asked if this was my first camping trip ever . . .

KETTLE RIVER RECREATION AREA

Location

Between 1860 and 1864, this region was worked by more than 500 miners, who scoured the gravel for gold. Today, it provides a more tranquil setting for camping enthusiasts and is characterized by old-growth cottonwood and ponderosa pine trees. Named after the river that runs through it, Kettle River Recreation Area is located 5 kilometres north of Rock Creek on Highway 33. Services (pub, gas, store, accommodation) are located at Rock Creek, and they have improved tremendously over the last 10 years.

Facilities

At a bend on the west bank of the river are 87 well-spaced camping spots nestled in an area of ponderosa pine and birchgrass, with sites suitable for every size of recreational vehicle. In addition to the basic facilities offered, there is a sani-station, flush toilets and pit toilets. Site 38 is completely wheelchair-accessible. Reservations are accepted.

Recreational activities

The Kettle Valley Railway discontinued its service in the early 1970s, and the track between Midway and Penticton was removed in 1980. The abandoned route runs through the park and is an excellent hiking and biking trail (see www.kettlevalleyrailway.ca). There is also fishing, swimming and canoeing in the park; tubing is another river-based activity popular with locals and regular campers. On the eastern banks of the river, remains of gold and silver mines can be seen—evidence of the pioneers who travelled and worked in the area at the turn of the century. Excellent opportunities exist for the photographer and artist in this locale, and many people resurrect the past by having a go at panning for gold.

Additional information

For those who decide not to cook, there is an interesting collection of eateries at Rock Creek, including a pub and some good breakfast cafés. Rock Creek dates back to 1857, when a prospector called Charles Dietz started a gold rush here. There were never large quantities of gold found, only copper. During the winter the area is popular with cross-country skiers and snowshoers. This is a lovely place to stop and relax, and break your journey along Highway 1.

LAC LE JEUNE

Location

If you are looking for a base from which to explore the region, this 213-hectare lakeside provincial park, easily accessible from Kamloops and Merritt, is an excellent bet. It is situated just off the Coquihalla Highway, 37 kilometres south of Kamloops and 47 kilometres north of Merritt, and a full range of services can be found at these locations, and at Logan Lake, 26 kilometres away.

Facilities

Set among a forest of pinegrass and lodgepole pines at the cool elevation of 1,280 metres are 144 large well-positioned wheelchair-accessible campsites. A few of these spots have the added advantage of being close to the lake. There are flush toilets and a sani-station in the day-use area. Reservations are accepted for 60 percent of the spaces. In addition to firewood, the park also sells ice.

Recreational activities

Lac Le Jeune is equipped with a boat launch (powerboats are limited to a speed of 20 kilometres per hour), and swimming is possible in a protected swimming area. All the literature on the park states that Lac Le Jeune is famous for "fighting rainbow trout," so go win a battle! There is also an adventure playground, a horseshoe pit and interpretive programs in the summer. The Gus Johnson Trail rings the lake and is an easy 8-kilometre hike, and there is also a trail connecting the park to the adjacent Stake/McConnell Lakes Park, which has 160 kilometres of trails for hiking, mountain biking during the summer and cross-country skiing in the winter. Walloper Lake Provincial Park, a short drive from here off Highway 5, has only wilderness camping, but it does offer canoe and boat rentals and access to the beautiful waters of the area.

Additional information

During the hot dry days of summer, this campground offers a welcome respite from the heat, as it is at a higher elevation than Thompson Valley to the north and Nicola Valley in the south. Lac Le Jeune is an excellent base from which to explore the towns of Merritt, Kamloops and Logan Lake. When I visited, we took a short 20-minute trail to a trout-spawning stream that the camp host had told us about. My only criticism of this park is the lack of information boards or maps detailing the trails in the area. Hopefully, this will have been addressed by the time you visit.

Mabel Lake

Location

Mabel Lake is perfect for those who want to appreciate the Okanagan from a cooler vantage point. Somewhat off the beaten track, it is a lovely 182-hectare provincial park between the Thompson Plateau to the west and the Monashee Mountains to the east. Temperatures here tend to be cooler than in many other areas of the Okanagan, providing a pleasant respite from the summer heat. The campground is 60 kilometres northeast from Vernon. Travel east on Highway 6 to Lumby, then take a paved road for 36 kilometres followed by 1 kilometre on gravel. Services are available at Lumby; there is also a small marine store by the campground, which sells candy, milk, propane and other supplies.

Facilities

You can camp here at one of two campgrounds: Monashee or Trinity. Together, they provide a total of 81 well-situated spaces in a wooded setting, some with great views of the lake. Monashee's sites are smaller but more private. There is a sani-station but no flush toilets or showers. Some park facilities are wheelchair-accessible.

Recreational activities

A 2,100-metre shoreline that includes two lovely beaches (and a pet beach) with safe swimming areas provides access to the waters of 35-kilometre-long Mabel Lake. Fishing is good both from the shore and in the deeper waters where anglers hope to catch rainbow trout, Dolly Varden, lake trout, kokanee and chinook salmon. Waterskiing and boating are popular, and the nearby marina offers boat rentals. The area is attractive to canoeists, who paddle down the Shuswap River just south of the park. For those who like to see more unusual wildlife, painted turtles can be observed in Taylor Creek. The park also has a one-hour interpretive trail, tons of grassy areas and a kids' playground. When our children were three and five, we really enjoyed staying here.

Additional information

The surrounding area offers interesting alternatives to the recreational activities found in the park. The road between Lumby and Mabel Lake takes travellers through the distinctive landscape of ranches and farmland—quite beautiful and somewhat "un-Okanaganish." Wilsey Dam has a picnic spot with trails leading to the awe-inspiring Shuswap Falls. I adore this park and highly recommend it. The 36-kilometre approach road is a lovely drive, and the reward at the end is well worth the effort. Bears and deer are often seen in the vicinity. My only note of caution: there can be mosquitoes.

MARBLE CANYON

Location

Established in 1956, 355-hectare Marble Canyon Provincial Park is popular with rock climbers, who are attracted to the area for its rugged terrain. It is not difficult to see why mountaineers and others choose to visit this park nestled on a lakeside below towering limestone cliffs and amid the beautiful scenery of Marble Canyon. The campground is found by travelling 40 kilometres northwest of Cache Creek on Highway 99. It is about 35 kilometres northeast of Lillooet. Services are available at Cache Creek or Lillooet or at the Butterfly Creek Store, 2 kilometres from the campground.

Facilities

There are 30 relatively small gravel campsites with little privacy, some directly overlooking the lake and some with tent pads. The services provided are limited to the basics (pit toilets, picnic tables, drinking water, fire pits).

Recreational activities

Leisure activities include fishing, swimming, rock-climbing, kayaking and canoeing. Only electric motors are permitted on the lake and there is no boat launch. A trail along the side of the lake leads to a waterfall and is an easy 30-minute trek. There are two archaeological sites where First Nations pictographs have been found. The park was established in 1956, but in April 2001 Pavilion Lake was added to the park to preserve unique freshwater stromatolite features (fossilized remains of microorganisms considered to be among some of the oldest life forms on Earth). People interested in fauna and flora will find the vegetation and the bird and animal life here fascinating.

Additional information

Reaching this campground is a beautiful and scenic drive. Close to Lillooet, travellers see some of the ginseng farms for which BC is known, easily spotted by looking for vast expanses of black plastic. At the junction of Highway 97 and Highway 99, the historic 1861 Hat Creek Ranch, an original stopping place on the Cariboo Wagon Road, offers guided tours. The area is noted for its rock formations, scenery and the beautiful lake. The disadvantage to camping here is the campsite's proximity to the road; although the route is not tremendously busy, campers may be kept awake by the sound of traffic. When I stayed here in 1995, noise was not a problem, and we enjoyed an evening meal cooked at the lakeside, as our campsite was on the water's edge. I found a marked difference in 2004, when there seemed to be a lot more traffic from around 6:00 a.m. onward. Wasps can also be a problem but they have not bothered me on the four separate occasions I have camped there. As always, black bears inhabit the vicinity.

MONCK

Location

With fantastic views of the Nicola Valley south of Kamloops, and within easy reach of Merritt, the nearest large settlement, this 92-hectare park has a great deal to offer. Monck Provincial Park is reached by taking Highway 5A to Nicola then following a paved road to the campground, situated 22 kilometres north of Merritt (where all services are available).

Facilities

With the exception of showers, this 120-space campground has all the necessary requirements for camping, including a sani-station and wheelchair-accessible flush toilets. The cheery camping spots, set among a lightly forested area of ponderosa pine and fir on the north side of Nicola Lake, are suitable for every type of recreational vehicle. Most have views of the water. Reservations are accepted.

Recreational activities

Monck Provincial Park is an ideal family vacation spot. There is a playground and a sandy beach leading to the beautiful waters of Nicola Lake, where a cordoned-off swimming area and two change houses are provided. The beach shelves quickly, so you do need to use caution. Fishing for kokanee is reputed to be excellent, and 25 species of fish, including rainbow trout, can be caught in the waters. There is a concrete boat launch to facilitate boating and sailing pursuits. A number of trails lead from the campground through a forest to various vantage points. First Nations pit house depressions can also be found here, and a walk along an old road to Second Beach leads to a fine example of Native rock paintings (pictographs). Interpretive programs are offered during the summer.

Additional information

The Nicola Valley is surrounded by green fields and rich marshland. Originally settled by ranchers, the area is now home to Canada's largest working cattle ranch, the Douglas Lake Ranch, which offers horseback riding and ranch tours. The land that now includes Monck was donated by Major Charles Sidney Goldman in honour of his son, Lieutenant-Commander "Pen" Monck, a British Second World War soldier who changed his name to Monck to improve his chances of survival should he be captured by the Germans. Goldman moved to the Nicola Valley in 1919, purchased 6,550 acres of land, and built up a cattle ranch with over 5,000 head. It's a good location for family camping.

Mount Robson

Location

Mount Robson Provincial Park provides a camping experience that should not be missed. Mount Robson, "the monarch of the Canadian Rockies," is the highest peak in the Rockies at almost 4,000 metres. In 1913, a special act was passed by the BC legislature to preserve this 224,866-hectare area of exceptional beauty for all to encounter and enjoy. The park is about four hours north of Kamloops and is easily accessed from the Yellowhead Highway (Highway 5). Services, such as gas, food and a store, are located in the park itself at Mount Robson Motor Village.

Facilities

There are three wheelchair-accessible campgrounds in the park, and two of them are located at the western end: Robson Meadows has 125 spots and Robson River has 19 spots. Both have flush toilets and showers, and Robson Meadows also has a sani-station. The third campground is Lucerne, 10 kilometres west of the Alberta border, which has 36 spots on Yellowhead Lake. Most sites are large, private and situated well in the evergreen forest, but Robson River is my favourite campground: it's smaller than Robson Meadows but has all amenities and is adjacent to services. All three campgrounds are open from mid-May to the end of September. Robson Meadows accepts reservations.

Recreational activities

The spectacular scenery, which consists of lakes, waterfalls, rivers, glaciers and mountains, makes this a paradise for hikers, climbers, canoeists and anyone who loves the outdoors. There are over 200 kilometres of hiking trails within the park, one of the most popular being the Valley of the Thousand Waterfalls, which takes explorers past the fantastic azure brightness of Berg Lake and on to views of Tumbling Glacier's spectacular waterfalls. I believe this to be one of the best hikes in BC. Boat launches are available at Moose Lake and Yellowhead Lake, but fishing tends to be poor, as the glacial waters yield small populations of fish. The Mount Robson Visitor Centre at the Mount Robson Viewpoint has details of all the park's activities, and staff there can advise on the weather and camping conditions.

Additional information

The Shuswap First Nation calls Mount Robson *Yuh-hai-has-hun*, meaning "Mountain of the Spiral Road." It is unclear whether the park is named after Colin Robertson, a Hudson's Bay Company factor and later member of Parliament, who sent Iroquois fur hunters to the area in 1820, or John Robson, premier of BC from 1889–92. This is one of my favourite BC parks, as there is so much to do and the scenery is so breathtaking. When you're arranging a holiday tour of British Columbia, Mount Robson is a lovely destination to include on your itinerary, but do plan to spend at least three nights in order to even begin to appreciate its true beauty.

NORTH THOMPSON RIVER

Location

The most amazing feature of this 126-hectare provincial park is the meeting of two distinctly individual water systems. North Thompson River is located where the Thompson and Clearwater rivers meet, 5 kilometres south of the town of Clearwater, just off Highway 5. Clearwater has services such as gas, propane, food and accommodation, as well as a number of commercial tour operations.

Facilities

The campground is on the banks of the Thompson River in a mixed forest of Douglas fir, pine, cedar and spruce. There are 61 camping spots in total, the more desirable ones being closer to the river but these site are not suitable if you have young children as the riverbank is steep. Some park facilities are wheelchair-accessible and there is also a sani-station. A railway line runs close by, so expect the noise of trains.

Recreational activities

A number of short trails lead through the campground. All take less than 30 minutes to complete. A small wading and swimming area is located on a back eddy where the Clearwater River flows into the North Thompson. BC Parks cautions that during the flood season of June and July, currents can be powerful. Canoeing, kayaking and fishing for rainbow trout and chinook salmon are also possible here. In addition to the recreational activities available in the park itself, there is the fantastic "poggy playground" for kids, which is one of the best playgrounds I've seen anywhere—and I've seen more than my fair share of these! The nearby community of Clearwater has bikes and canoes for rent, horseback trail rides and rafting trips. Nearby Dutch Lake has swimming.

Additional information

From a viewpoint in the park you can take in the vista of the distinctive green waters of the Clearwater River meeting those of the muddy brown Thompson. It was once the site of a Shuswap Nation encampment, and there are two archaeological sites in the park. The campground is very sedate and peaceful, ideal for the older RV crowd and for family camping, and is a good spot from which to explore Wells Gray Provincial Park. That park's visitor centre in Clearwater is worth a visit: my kids liked the life-sized moose outside and there is excellent tourist information inside.

OKANAGAN FALLS

Location

Native legend recalls how the waters here once fell with "a voice like thunder" and the spray was as white as a cherry blossom. Today, development has ensured that visitors cannot experience the original natural beauty of the falls, but instead there is a lovely provincial park. Okanagan Falls is found at the community that bears its name, which is off Highway 97, south of Skaha Lake, 20 kilometres south of Penticton. All services can be found in "OK Falls" and in Penticton.

Facilities

The picturesque campground with 25 camping spots is set amongst a forest of deciduous trees just above the Okanagan River. It has an extremely neat and tidy feel about it, and when I last visited, in June 2008, all the spots were taken by large RVs whose owners seemed as if they'd been there for years. The campground is wheelchair-accessible and provides flush and pit toilets, but no sani-station or showers.

Recreational activities

Like the two other provincial parks in the immediate vicinity (Vaseux Lake and Inkaneep), the area is rich in bird and animal life and therefore makes a good location for nature study and photography. A species of small sonar-equipped bats is found here, in addition to a wealth of other birds and animals. Fishing is possible in the Okanagan River, and the park has horseshoe pits. Christie Memorial Provincial Park, which has 200 metres of beach and good swimming, is located just north of Okanagan Falls. The area is rich in grapevines, and visitors can tour the local wineries. The community of Okanagan Falls has an excellent ice cream store and fudge shop, which campground research has required me to evaluate in depth in 1998, 2000, 2002 and 2008; I suggest you do the same.

Additional information

Anyone looking for spectacular waterfalls will be disappointed, as the falls here have been reduced to rapids due to rock blasting for water control in the area. The museum at Okanagan Falls is housed in a restored 1909 prefabricated building that was ordered from a catalogue, shipped in pieces and assembled here. It contains artifacts and memorabilia of the pioneer Bassett family. I really have the impression that this is a campground geared to the retired RV owner who wants to put down roots for weeks and do little other than sit in the shade, listen to the river and pass the time with fellow campers. It's a campground geared more to adults that to children.

Okanagan Lake

Location

Okanagan Lake Provincial Park is the most popular camping location in the Okanagan. Like Haynes Point and Bear Creek, 98-hectare Okanagan Lake is very busy in the peak summer months of July and August. This park has fantastic panoramic views of the mountains and lake and is located 11 kilometres north of Summerland and 24 kilometres from Penticton. Services are available in these communities, but there is a fruit stand close to the park

entrance and the south park gatehouse sells ice, frozen treats, cold drinks and some groceries.

Facilities

The park has 168 vehicle/tent campsites: 80 in the north campground and 88 in the south campground, some with views of the lake. I prefer the camping spots in the north campground, which are better spaced and less confined than those in the south. Both are set in an unusual forest area and have showers and flush and pit toilets. The south campground shower building is wheelchair-accessible. Reservations are accepted for both campgrounds.

Recreational activities

With over a kilometre of beach (some of it pebbly), Okanagan Lake Provincial Park is a paradise for swimmers, sunbathers, anglers and water-sports enthusiasts. There is a boat launch at the south campground and the lake is popular for windsurfing and sailing. For those who prefer other activities, there are interpretive programs in the summer and a number of small hiking trails to explore. One of the unique features of the park is an arboretum of more than 10,000 exotic trees, including Russian olive, Chinese elm, Norway, Manitoba and silver maples and red, blue and mountain ash. This woodland enhances the birdlife, so keep your eyes peeled for hummingbirds, larks and woodpeckers, which can be easily seen. Fantastic photography opportunities abound.

Additional information

Due to its popularity, you may well be disappointed if you arrive at this campground without a reservation in the peak summer months. Summerland's Kettle Valley Steam Railway operates a quaint steam train during the summer months. Each year this attraction employs wonderful volunteers and enthusiastic employees, dressed in period costume, who provide tons of information for the tourist (www.kettlevalleyrail.org).

OTTER LAKE

Location
BC Parks suggests that 51-hectare Otter Lake is ideal for "old-fashioned camping," a provincial park where campers can find privacy in a natural setting. This park is 33 kilometres northwest of Princeton off Highway 5A. From Princeton, drive to Coalmont and Tulameen on Coalmont Road, then to Otter Lake, which is well marked with signs. The park can also be accessed from Highway 97C by turning at Aspen Grove (which is Highway 5A) and following the signs. Services are available in the small towns of Coalmont and Tulameen.

Facilities
Otter Lake boasts 45 beautifully spaced, large camping spots on the northwest shore of the lake, some with views of the water. Large trees provide much-needed shade in an area of the province that can become very hot in the summer. Some park facilities are wheelchair-accessible and there are flush and pit toilets but no sani-station or showers. Reservations are accepted.

Recreational activities
Five-kilometre-long Otter Lake provides the main venue for recreational activities, which include fishing for rainbow trout, swimming from a warm beach in the day-use area (5 kilometres from the campground) and boating (two boat launches are provided). There is also a horseshoe pit. The surrounding area is home to a variety of animals, including otters, beavers, red squirrels, mountain goats, cougars and grizzly bears—but don't expect to see them all on your first visit! A few kilometres away, the now disused Kettle Valley Railway, part of the Trans-Canada Trail linking Princeton and Merritt, offers a fantastic mountain bike or hiking route amid some spectacular scenery. Bikes can be rented in Tulameen.

Additional information
Otter Lake is an ideal base from which to explore the mining history of the Tulameen region. The town of Tulameen (the name is a First Nations word that means "red earth" in the Nlaka'pamux [Thompson] language) is located 5 kilometres south of the campground and was first used by First Nations for hunting and fishing and then explored by gold miners in the last century. The Hudson's Bay Company used a road that passed through Tulameen and labelled the settlement *encampment des femmes*, as it was populated primarily by women waiting for their men to return from trapping and hunting. The town of Coalmont, also south of the park, sprang to life during the gold rush; in 1925 it produced 100,000 tonnes of coal, making it the region's largest producer. By 1940, the mine was exhausted, and most residents moved away. Today, Coalmont contains a café, a general store and a hotel dating back to 1912 (you won't be able to miss the hotel—it's painted bright pink).

PAUL LAKE

Location

Provincial parks near populated areas often offer the best amenities for family camping, whether you're staying in a tent or an RV. Paul Lake is one such park. Residents of Kamloops and visitors are regular patrons of this popular provincial park, conveniently located 24 kilometres northeast of Kamloops. Access Paul Lake by turning off Highway 5 and following a well-maintained twisting road across a meadow landscape for 17 kilometres. Gas and food are available at the turnoff from Highway 5; all other needs can be accommodated in Kamloops.

Facilities

The 670-hectare park has 90 large well-maintained private camping spots suitable for every type of recreational vehicle, making the park popular with RVers. The campground is set in a lightly forested area of Douglas fir and aspen and there is a sani-station and flush and pit toilets; some park facitities are wheelchair-accessible.

Recreational activities

The lake provides a host of activities, including swimming in a protected area from a 400-metre sandy beach, boating (with canoes and paddleboats available for rent) and good fishing since Paul Lake is stocked with rainbow trout. Over 7 kilometres of trails lead from the campground and a pleasant hike, with over 900 metres in elevation gain, leads up Gibraltar Rock (the last section is the steepest). The park is particularly appealing to people with young children; it has a playground, horseshoe pits and wide grassy areas, plus a maze of paved roads connecting the camping facilities that ensures fun for young cyclists and rollerbladers. In 1996, 268 hectares were added to the park to protect the habitat of ospreys, falcons, bald eagles, coyotes and mule deer. The area is popular with the birdwatching community.

Additional information

At certain times of the year the park is blessed with an array of beautiful wildflowers. (Remember, visitors are forbidden to pick vegetation in the provincial parks.) For good views of the vicinity, campers with stamina are advised to climb Gibraltar Rock. The park's proximity to Kamloops means it is often filled to capacity but reservations are not accepted. For some reason, though, I find this park to have little atmosphere and not as much character as most others. In some respects, it appears too ordered and regimented, almost clinical. This is a purely personal observation and clearly not one shared by everyone, for when I visited, a number of campers, especially family groups, seemed to be well established. I just find it to be one of BC's more formal parks.

SHUSWAP LAKE

Location

For people who love water-based activities, Shuswap Lake, with over 1,000 kilometres of waterways, is a real magnet. The provincial park is conveniently located 90 kilometres east of Kamloops on Highway 1 at Squilax. A 20-kilometre paved road leads to the campground. Some supplies can be found at a store adjacent to the entrance of the park, while more comprehensive supplies are found in Sorrento, 35 kilometres away.

Facilities

Because Shuswap Lake is one of BC's largest provincial parks, the facilities offered here are comprehensive. There are 272 camping spots suitable for every type of recreational vehicle, flush and pit toilets, a sani-station, showers and full access for those in wheelchairs. Reservations accepted and BC Parks describes Shuswap Lake as operating "at capacity" from mid-July to Labour Day. Those who arrive without a reservation are assigned a camping spot at the entrance of the park, so there is no opportunity to "cruise" the campground to find the most desirable spot.

Recreational activities

Shuswap Lake is perfect for water sports like paddling, waterskiing and windsurfing, and the 1-kilometre-long beach has a designated swimming area. There is also a boat launch, and 2 kilometres offshore is Copper Island, which has a 2.8-kilometre hiking trail and lookout. Anglers can fish in the lake for 19 different species. Another popular recreational pursuit here is cycling, as there are over 11 kilometres of paved road in the 149-hectare park itself, plus trails that permit bikes. To entertain the entire family there is an adventure play area and a nature house with summertime interpretive programs, and this facility now rents kayaks in July and August. Other commercial recreational activities (boat rentals and go-carts, for example) are easily accessible in the North Shuswap and surrounding area.

Additional information

The park was established in 1956 and named after the First Nations people of Shuswap, whose artifacts were found here. Although there is no overnight boat mooring at Shuswap Lake, the nearby Shuswap Lake Provincial Marine Park offers this option, as well as six developed and eight undeveloped camping locations along all four arms of the lake. As already noted, this area is extremely popular during the summer months and may not be to everyone's taste at that time, as it presents the more commercial side of camping in BC parks. For those who want to experience the delights of the lake from a quieter vantage point, Herald and Silver Beach provincial parks are tranquil alternatives.

SILVER BEACH

Location

Campers who wish to enjoy the waters but not the crowds of Shuswap Lake should head for Silver Beach. This somewhat remote provincial park is located 65 kilometres from Scotch Creek. Turn off Highway 1 just east of Squilax and take the paved road to Scotch Creek. The road to the park from Scotch Creek is only partially paved (expect approximately 42 kilometres on gravel). Gas and limited provisions are available near the campground.

Facilities

Silver Beach has 35 vehicle/tent campsites located in a forest of Douglas fir and aspen at the head of the Seymour Arm of Shuswap Lake. The campground offers the basic amenities (pit toilets, picnic tables, drinking water, fire pits).

Recreational activities

As this quiet campground is at the northern end of Shuswap Lake, all activities involving the lake can be enjoyed here: swimming at a delightful sandy beach, fishing (for trout, among others), boating, canoeing, windsurfing, waterskiing, etc. In August and September, it is possible to view sockeye salmon spawning in the Seymour River, which runs into the lake near the campground. Wildfowl observation is good, and there is also a short trail along the top of the beach.

Additional information

The remains of Ogden, an old gold rush town of the late 19th century, can be seen here if you are prepared to navigate a somewhat overgrown trail. An old graveyard and archaeological sites are also in the park. With its beautiful sandy beaches, the Silver Beach area is popular with sailors and houseboaters exploring the lake, so expect to share your tranquility with more than just your fellow dry-land campers.

Houseboating is a very popular activity on the four arms of Shuswap Lake: at the height of the season, as many as 350 houseboats can be navigating its waters. Silver Beach provides a quieter and less commercialized view of Shuswap Lake than Shuswap Lake Provincial Park but does not have all the facilities the larger park offers.

SKIHIST

Location

Anyone stopping here will be rewarded with brilliant views of the Thompson Canyon, but be sure to remember the sunscreen, as Skihist is situated in an area prone to very high summer temperatures. This quaint 33-hectare provincial park is found 8 kilometres east of Lytton on Highway 1. Services are available in Lytton.

Facilities

Fifty-eight well-positioned quiet camping spots (including four walk-in ones for tents only) are available, set in a lightly forested area high above the Thompson and Fraser rivers with great views of the Coast Mountain Range. The park has both pit and flush toilets and a sani-station, and wheelchair accessibility (there is one wheelchair-accessible pit toilet). There is also a large day-use area, which is a popular resting place in the summer.

Recreational activities

Recreational activities in the park including picking saskatoon berries, which are plentiful at a certain time of year, taking photographs, admiring the fantastic views and looking for the elk that have been introduced to the area. The campground is a good base for those who wish to try whitewater rafting; trips are easily arranged through commercial businesses in Lytton and Spences Bridge. Hiking is possible from the trailhead in the campground. The trail leads to Gladwin Lookout; this 90-minute hike rewards hikers with excellent views of the mountains. The route includes portions of the Cariboo Gold Rush Trail. Remember to take along lots of water, as this area can be very hot in the summer.

Additional information

Skihist Provincial Park includes part of the old Cariboo Wagon Road used by the early pioneers of the province. Its main attraction must be the fantastic views of the Thompson Canyon, where water gushing over thousands of years has cut into the pre-glacial valley floor. (The fact that the park has flush toilets is another attraction!) Lytton, at the junction of the Fraser and Thompson rivers, claims to be Canada's official "hot spot," although its northern neighbour, Lillooet, disputes this claim. As neither community has a weather station, the debate continues, but be prepared for some hot days if visiting Skihist in the peak summer months.

STEELHEAD

Location

Set in an almost desert environment, Steelhead, which began operating in 1997, really is the baby of provincial parks. The 37-hectare park is located on the site of one of the oldest homesteads in the Interior, which was also a ferry stop and a stagecoach depot. Steelhead is an excellent base for exploring the city of Kamloops, Kamloops Lake, the mighty Thompson River and the surrounding plateau scenery. The campground itself is rather spartan and is found 40 kilometres west of Kamloops on Highway 1 just west of Savona, which has food, gas and supplies.

Facilities

The campground is situated at the outflow of Kamloops Lake. Forty-four camping spots are available, all quite open, but half of them overlook the lake. There are flush toilets, showers and wheelchair-accessible pit toilets. Steelhead is also one of the very few BC parks with water and electricity hookups (10 sites). In addition to firewood, ice can be purchased onsite.

Recreational activities

Campers can enjoy swimming from a good beach and canoeing in Kamloops Lake. There is also fishing here and in the many plateau lakes in the region. There is only a cartop boat launch in the park, but Savona has a public boat launch a short drive away. Naturalists will appreciate the wildlife in the area, which includes deer, elk and mountain sheep, plus migratory waterfowl, shorebirds and songbirds. The city of Kamloops is only a short drive away and is the major centre of the region. Just south of the campground is the community of Logan Lake, where fascinating tours of the Highland Valley Copper Mine can be taken.

Additional information

BC Parks should be sincerely thanked for establishing a number of additional campgrounds in the High Country Region just over a decade ago. Steelhead is the most developed; other recent additions are Momich, Tunkwa and Roche Lake, but they have only primitive camping facilities. All used to be forestry campsites, but BC Parks became responsible for their administration in 1997. On a personal note, I do not find the Steelhead campground very appealing, probably due to the lack of vegetation and the near-desert surroundings. I prefer Juniper Beach, just down the road, which is more spacious and offers better views. If staying in this region, be prepared for some very high temperatures, and remember to put on the sunscreen.

STEMWINDER

Location

Between 1904 and 1955, $47 million in gold was extracted from the mountains adjacent to 4-hectare Stemwinder Provincial Park, and rumour has it that there is still some left. So what are you waiting for? *There's gold in them thar hills!* The park's small roadside campground is very much geared toward overnight stops and is located 35 kilometres east of Princeton on Highway 3, next to Hedley. Services are available in Hedley and at a store adjacent to the campground.

Facilities

The campground offers 26 spots on the banks of the Similkameen River. Only the basic amenities are available (drinking water, pit toilets, picnic tables, fire pits). One of the pit toilets is wheelchair-accessible. A number of the camping spots are quite close to the road, so expect the noise of traffic.

Recreational activities

Because this campground is geared toward overnight camping, there are limited recreational activities. The waters of the Similkameen River can be fished but are fast-flowing. Caution must be taken by those who wish to swim; only strong swimmers should consider it. A number of people try "tubing" from this location, and you can try your luck at panning for gold, an activity that started here at the turn of the century. Be careful to avoid the poison ivy found along the riverbank. If you drive 25 minutes along Highway 3, the Grist Mill and Gardens at Keremeos cannot be too highly recommended. It's a BC Heritage site illustrating the last remaining pioneer flour mill dating back to 1881. When I visited, a man on a penny farthing cycled around the wonderful gardens. My children delighted in feeding chickens and collecting eggs, and the tearoom served delicious pastries and desserts. Well worth a visit.

Additional information

When visiting this area, it is worth turning off Highway 3 to explore the museum, the back roads and the older architecture in Hedley. The quaint Similkameen community dates to the early 1900s, when the Nickel Plate Mine, one of BC's first hardrock mining operations, was established 1,200 metres above the town. The mine operated from 1904 to 1956, extracting gold, silver and copper. The remnants of the Mascot Mine's buildings can be seen perched on a cliff high above the town, and tours are offered. These are not suitable for children and involve quite a bit of climbing, so you have to be fit, but they provide an excellent insight into BC's past.

TUNKWA

Location

Tunkwa Provincial Park covers a massive 5,100 hectares of land not far from Logan Lake, a town established in 1970 for the 1,000 employees of the Highland Valley Copper Mining Corporation. The park is situated 16 kilometres north of the town, off Highway 5, but can also be accessed off Highway 1 at Savona and also from the Coquihalla Highway. All access roads are good gravel routes. The nearest services are at Logan Lake; Kamloops is 40 kilometres away.

Facilities

Tunkwa, Leighton and Leighton North are the three campgrounds here, offering a total of 275 spaces, some with excellent views of the lake. The vast majority are informal "cluster" sites that allow up to four groups to camp together; 55 sites are of the kind traditionally found in BC Parks. Only the basic amenities are available (pit toilets, picnic tables, fire pits and drinking water). Reservations are not accepted.

Recreational activities

Trout fishing is popular not only at this location but also in the multitude of lakes in the vicinity. Tunkwa and Leighton lakes are known for their excellent trout fishing, with Tunkwa voted one of the top 10 provincial rainbow-trout locations (I have a firm mental image of the individuals involved in this research!). There is a boat launch at each lake, but it is also possible to swim, canoe and kayak here. Logan Lake has a nine-hole golf course, and tours of the copper mine can be arranged. Horseback riding is available at a few of the corrals in the area and is an excellent way to experience the rugged landscape. BC Parks says that wild horses can be seen grazing in meadows adjacent to Tunkwa Lake. Be advised that ATV use is also popular here, so noise can be a problem.

Additional information

Formerly the site of a forestry campground, the park was initially established to protect an area of fragile grassland and wetland. It is popular in winter for ice fishing, snowmobiling and cross-country skiing, but in the summer it is really a venue for the fishing community. Like other parks in this area of the province, it can become extremely hot during the peak summer months, so come prepared.

VASEUX LAKE

Location
Vaseux is French for "silty," and this shallow weedy lake is one of Canada's foremost birding areas and a real magnet for ornithologists. Between Highway 97 and the lake sits 12-hectare Vaseux Lake Provincial Park, located just 4 kilometres south of Okanagan Falls and 25 kilometres south of Penticton.

Facilities
Surrounded by cliffs, this 12-spot roadside campground contains all the basic amenities found in BC Parks (pit toilets, picnic tables, drinking water, fire pits) and is wheelchair-accessible. There is no sani-station. As the highway is close to the campground, noise from traffic is audible and constant, but the advantage is that camping spots are right on the lake.

Recreational activities
A variety of grasses, weeds and willow vegetation provide a home for birds and animals, so this area attracts ornithologists and wildlife enthusiasts. Waterfowl and birds calling the park home include trumpeter swans, widgeons, Canada geese, wood ducks, blue-winged teal, chuckar partridge, wrens, swifts, woodpeckers and dippers. California bighorn sheep inhabit the cliffs near the park, and smaller mammals in the area include beavers, muskrats, deer, mice, rattlesnakes and turtles. Vaseux Lake is excellent for fishing in both winter and summer and yields largemouth bass, rainbow trout and carp. The park also has a beach for sunbathing and swimming. There is no boat launch and powerboats are prohibited, but canoeing and kayaking are permitted on the lake.

Additional information
Just north of the park is the Canadian Wildlife Service wildlife sanctuary, in addition to two wildlife management units operated by the federal and provincial governments. If you are an ornithologist, Vaseux Lake really is the place to be as over 160 species of birds can be seen. The park is also a popular location for winter sports, such as ice fishing and ice-skating.

WELLS GRAY

Location

BC Parks calls Wells Gray a "vast, untamed and primitive wilderness." The 540,000-hectare park displays a landscape formed by volcanoes and water and contains two large river systems, five huge lakes, numerous small lakes, streams, waterways, rapids and waterfalls. The main entrance to Wells Gray is 40 kilometres from the community of Clearwater on a paved access road. The road from Helmcken Falls to Clearwater Lake is gravel. The park can also be reached by travelling 88 kilometres on a secondary road from 100 Mile House, and there is also access from Blue River. Services are located at Clearwater and 100 Mile House.

Facilities

In addition to numerous wilderness camping spots, Wells Gray has three vehicle-accessible campgrounds. Two of them are accessed from the Clearwater approach road: Pyramid has 50 campsites while Clearwater Lake/Falls Creek has 80 campsites, divided between two campgrounds. Reached from the 100 Mile House entrance off Highway 97, the Mahood Lake campground has 34 splendid huge sites. Clearwater Lake/Falls Creek has a sani-station and some park facilities and trails are wheelchair-accessible. There are also two log cabins for rent at Clearwater Lake.

Recreational activities

How do I even begin to describe one of the best provincial parks in BC? There are hundreds of things to see and do at Wells Gray, BC's fourth-largest provincial park. Fortunately, BC Parks publishes informative leaflets on all the recreational activities, and this information is a must for anyone wanting to gain maximum benefit from a holiday. Numerous trails run through the park and lead to waterfalls and creeks; some of the trails are open to mountain bikes. Boat launches are provided at Mahood and Clearwater lakes, and canoeing and kayaking are very popular in the park (especially on Murtle Lake, which prohibits powerboats). Fishing is reputed to be good in Canim River, Mahood Lake, Murtle Lake and the Murtle River, and the best swimming is at Mahood Lake. It is impossible to count the number of waterfalls in the park, but two of the

best known are Helmcken Falls (three times higher than Niagara Falls) and Dawson Falls. Down the road at the former Spahats Creek campground is the magnificent Spahats Creek Falls. From a lookout, visitors can view the 122-metre-deep canyon carved by Spahats Creek to the 61-metre falls that cascade down the volcanic precipice to the Clearwater River below. Be sure to bring a camera, as I think these falls are more spectacular than the more popular Helmcken and Dawson falls.

Additional information

This massive provincial park is named after the Honourable Arthur Wellesley Gray, minister of lands for BC from 1933 to 1941. A travel information centre at the junction of Highway 5 and Clearwater Valley Road has all the information you need to know about the park and has a wonderful huge moose outside that makes for a good photograph. This area of the North Thompson is becoming increasingly popular with outdoorspeople, who come to explore the hectares upon hectares of undisturbed forest, abundance of lakes, rivers and streams, fantastic mountain scenery, kilometres of trails and moderate summertime temperatures.

Kikomun Creek Provincial Park is beautiful and varied; it is home to a large collection of western painted turtles. (BC Parks photo)

Illecillewaet campground is one of the camping areas in spectacular Glacier National Park. (Parks Canada/Rob Buchanan photo)

BC ROCKIES

Just mentioning the famous Canadian Rockies conjures images of high snow-capped mountains, icefields, glaciers, huge lakes, fertile valleys, rushing rivers and dramatic waterfalls. When you travel in this region of BC, you won't be disappointed—you will see all these splendid features and more. Despite its great beauty, this part of the province is not densely populated. This chapter provides details of the national and provincial parks situated in the Rockies/Kootenay area of the province accessible from highways 1, 93/95, 95, 3, 3A, 31 and 6. There are few large camping spots here; instead, the accommodation tends to consist of campgrounds with fewer than 100 camping spots but nestled in some of the most breathtaking scenery you'll ever see.

Spectacular alpine meadows, glaciers and waterfalls await visitors to Yoho National Park.

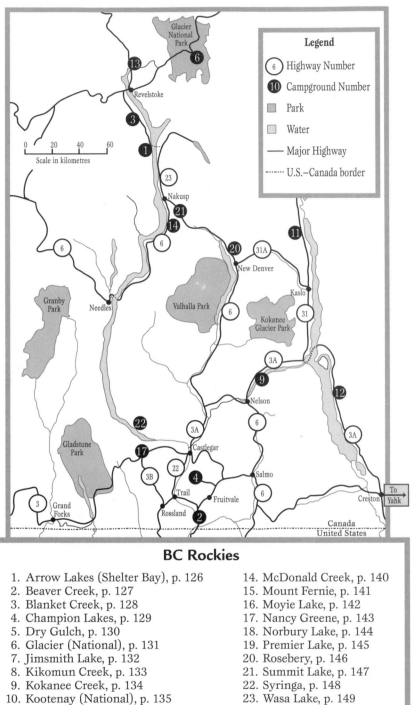

BC Rockies

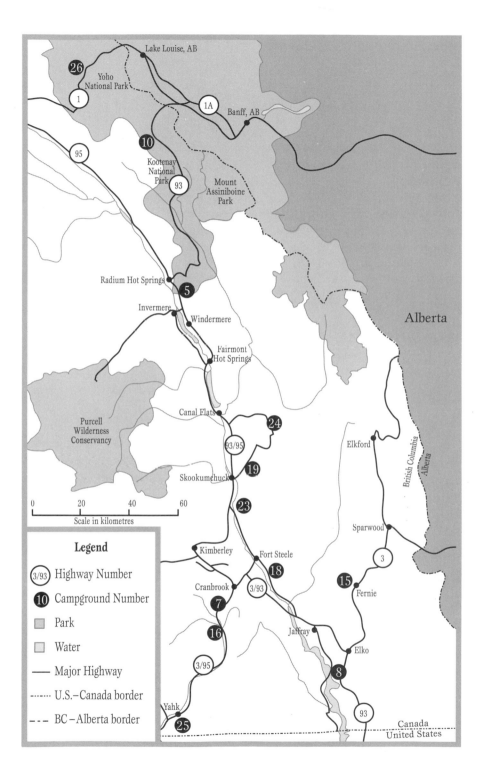

ARROW LAKES (SHELTER BAY)

Location

Pack the camera and marvel at the sunsets from the quaint little roadside campground located on the western side of Upper Arrow Lake. The park is reached by taking Arrow Park Ferry from Galena Bay, just south of Nakusp, or by travelling 50 kilometres on Highway 23 south of Revelstoke (which has all services).

Facilities

Seventeen camping spots are positioned quite close together and, as there is no vegetation, they afford little privacy. Some do, however, overlook the lake, providing beautiful views of the water and the landscape beyond. Only the basic amenities found in BC parks are available (pit toilets, picnic tables, drinking water, fire pits). Those who prefer flush toilets and sinks can find them a short walk away at the Shelter Bay ferry terminal.

Recreational activities

This campground is primarily for overnighters. The lake is excellent for swimming (though the water is not that warm) and fishing for rainbow trout, Dolly Varden and kokanee. There is a boat launch, and it is possible to canoe and kayak from the park.

Additional information

This is a pleasant place to stop because of its proximity to the lake and for the views of the rugged Selkirk Mountains that reach over 3,000 metres. Although the campground is near the road, traffic ceases around 9:30 p.m. when the ferries stop, so the location is very peaceful at nighttime. The five-minute ferry ride from Shelter Bay to Galena Bay is free and provides a beautiful break from driving to enjoy the scenery. I stayed here in August, and the campground was barely half full. With no traffic noise and a beautiful lake in which to bathe, this is definitely one of the better roadside camping spots.

BEAVER CREEK

Location

Beaver Creek is a new addition to *Camping British Columbia* and is a Category C provincial park, jointly administered with the local Kiwanis Club. As a result, the services provided may differ slightly from other BC Parks. The park is found on the eastern side of the Columbia River, close to Trail Airport (which isn't very busy so noise shouldn't be a problem). Access is from Highway 22A, 10 kilometres from Trail where all services are located. The nearest local store is 4 kilometres north of the park at Waneta Junction.

Facilities

This 81-hectare park's campground has 19 vehicle-accessible semi-shaded camping spots beautifully situated along the Columbia River. The campground only has pit toilets, but, unusually for this type of park, there is also a shower building with flush toilets, which are wheelchair-accessible.

Recreational activities

The popular day-use area has a huge picnic shelter, as well as a grassy area for ball games, a softball area, a concrete basketball court (very unusual for a BC park!) and bocce ball. There is also boat launch in the park, but it is only recommended for four-wheel-drive vehicles. Because of the Columbia River's very swift currents, BC Parks recommends it only to experienced and able canoeists and kayakers. Fishing is possible for walleye and whitefish. A hiking trail popular with locals meanders along the banks of the river at the south of the campground and there is a play park for children.

Additional information

The park is very popular with day-trippers from the Kootenays, and I have the impression this is very much a locals' campground. The campground host lives at the entrance to the campground to collect fees and ensure everyone remains a happy camper. For those with children to entertain and who want to leave the campground for a few hours, there is a great outdoor pool and waterslide on Highway 38 just before Rossland when approaching from Trail. The gold mine in Rossland is also well worth a visit and has something for every age group.

BLANKET CREEK

Location
In its former life, Blanket Creek was a busy homestead, and it is easy to see why the original pioneers chose to settle here. Created in 1982, this delightful 318-hectare provincial park is located at the point where Blanket Creek enters the Columbia River, 25 kilometres south of Revelstoke on Highway 23. The nearest services are available at Revelstoke.

Facilities
Blanket Creek has 63 large well-positioned camping spots for every size of vehicle, set in a lightly forested area and all with spectacular views of the Monashee Mountains. Some of the better spaces are adjacent to meadow areas. There are flush and pit toilets and a sani-station at the park's entrance. Reservations are accepted.

Recreational activities
In the day-use area of Blanket Creek, a large beach-rimmed lagoon ideal for swimming has been constructed and a trail leads from the campground to the pool. There is a playground here and a dog beach a 10-minute walk away. A five-minute walk along Old South Road takes campers to the beautiful 12-metre-high Sutherland Falls. Fishing in both the creek and Upper Arrow Lake can yield Dolly Varden, rainbow trout and kokanee, and in the fall, kokanee can be seen spawning in the mouth of the creek. The nearby town of Revelstoke is a lovely place to visit, offering a golf course, railway museum, piano museum and local history museum, as well as a number of cobbled streets and turn-of-the-century buildings to explore. Nakusp Hot Springs are also worth a visit.

Additional information
The site contains the remains of the Domke homestead, one of the few properties unaffected by the flooding of the Arrow Reservoir. The original log home dating back to the 1920s is still standing, but many of the other brick buildings have been dismantled. The land was abandoned in the late 1960s when the Hugh Keenleyside Dam near Castlegar was completed and the Arrow Reservoir was flooded. Blanket Creek supplies a pleasant quiet camping experience suitable for every age group. I stayed here one year in early June and the place was deserted, the weather good and the lake warm. This campground is suitable for every age group.

CHAMPION LAKES

Location

Situated in the Selkirk Mountains east of Trail at an elevation of 1,067 metres, this chain of three lakes set in a 1,426-hectare provincial park provides a taste of the true Kootenay experience. Champion Lakes is an 18-kilometre drive from Fruitvale and is reached by turning off Highway 3B after 6 kilometres and taking a paved road. There are services at Fruitvale and at Trail, a 30-minute drive away.

Facilities

The facilities at this 95-spot campsite include drinking water, a sani-station and flush and pit toilets. There is also a large day-use area with wheelchair-accessible flush toilets. The campground itself is located between Second and Third lakes, with trails leading to the water. All spots are large, shady and private, set in a forest of Douglas fir, pine and spruce. Reservations are accepted.

Recreational activities

Described as a canoeist's dream, this park supplies a ribbon of lakes and portages and offers brilliant paddling potential. Development is concentrated around Third Lake, which has a boat launch, playground, picnic area and change house, but Second Lake also has a rustic gravel boat launch. All three lakes prohibit powerboats. There are two good beaches so swimming is a popular pastime here, and there is a buoyed swimming area for kids. Another popular pursuit is angling for rainbow trout, which are stocked in the lakes. Onshore, more than 6 kilometres of hiking and walking trails lead from the campground: the Third Lake Trail is a 1.5-kilometre trek and is a popular stroll between the Main and Campers beaches on Third Lake, while the Second Lake Trail is about 2.5 kilometres long and has sections of boardwalk and good views.

Additional information

The trio of lakes is named after James W. Champion, who was an early settler and orchardist in the area. First Champion Lake is about 1,500 metres long, and Second and Third are each about 800 metres long. The park's location between the Coastal and Dry Biotic zones results in a diversity of plant species, as well as more unusual animals such as beavers, porcupines, minks and muskrats. Painted turtles also frequent the lake. If canoeing is your passion, you should definitely include Champion Lakes on your list of prime paddling locations. Families are also big winners here, as there is a wonderful beach and the waters are relatively warm. We stayed here in 2005 when Syringa Provincial Park was full. My children were in the water until 8 o'clock at night and I marvelled at at the way the beach was free of goose poop. We loved it so much that we returned in 2006 and 2007. Another wonderful BC provincial park.

DRY GULCH

Location

If hot springs are your passion, you'll love Dry Gulch. This beautiful little campground is less than 5 kilometres south of Radium Hot Springs, at the foot of Redstreak Mountain amid steep-sided gullies eroded by glaciers. All amenities can be found at Radium Hot Springs, just a short drive away. The campground is one kilometre from Highway 93.

Facilities

Dry Gulch Provincial Park consists of 26 campsites set in a lightly forested area of Douglas fir and ponderosa pine. It's one of the better small campgrounds: all sites are large, private and able to handle every type of recreational vehicle; some have tent pads. There are flush and pit toilets but no sani-station or showers. The park is wheelchair-accessible and there are wheelchair-accessible flush toilets. The campground is located just far enough from the main road that traffic noise is not a problem.

Recreational activities

Bighorn sheep are often observed on the grassland behind the campground, but one of the biggest attractions of staying here is your proximity to the world-famous Radium Hot Springs, which are located in Kootenay National Park. Prior to their formal development in 1911, the springs had been used for centuries by the Interior and Plains First Nations. Dry Gulch is an excellent quiet campground for enjoying the mineral waters. In addition to the springs, the resort has a café and shop. Other recreational activities in the vicinity include golf courses and the towns of Invermere (where there is a boat launch) and Radium. There's also easy access to the Panorama Ridge Resort, which is a great place to hike, golf and take children.

Additional information

As this 29-hectare park is adjacent to Kootenay National Park on the west slope of the Continental Divide, the campground is often used as an overspill location when the national park campgrounds are full. In addition to the hot springs, Kootenay National Park has more than 200 kilometres of hiking trails and features alpine meadows, snowfields, lakes and mountains.

Glacier (National)

Location

A region of spectacular high-mountain scenery shaped by avalanches and snow, Glacier National Park is found in the Northern Selkirk range of the Columbia Mountains, 49 kilometres east of Revelstoke on Highway 1. The park is aptly named: nearly 12 percent of its total 136,500-hectare area comprises more than 400 active glaciers and icefields. Adjacent to the Rogers Pass Information Centre in the park are a gas station, hotel, café and shop.

Facilities

Glacier has three campgrounds a short drive from the park's western entrance, all fairly close together: Loop Brook (20 spots), Illecillewaet (60 spots) and Mount Sir Donald (15 spots). The first two campgrounds have flush toilets, kitchen shelters and food lockers, while Donald is more primitive and campfires are not permitted. There are no showers or sani-station. 2008 fees ranged from $15.70 to $21.50, and there was an $8.80 fee to have a fire.

Recreational activities

Anyone visiting this park should stop at the snowshed-shaped visitor centre, which has displays of natural and human history, as well as videos illustrating various aspects of the park, its early relationship with the railroad and subsequent development. Park staff are always willing to provide advice on Glacier's numerous attractions and can gear suggestions to your preferences and timelines. Interpretive programs are offered in the summer months. Twenty-one hiking trails zigzag across 140 kilometres of park and include the Abandoned Rails Interpretive Trail, which starts at the information centre. Renowned for climbing and mountaineering opportunities, the park also offers potential for canoeing, horseback riding and fishing for whitefish, Dolly Varden and trout in the Illecillewaet River. Fishing in national parks is governed by a number of regulations and requires purchasing a permit (in 2008, the cost was $9.80/day; $34.30/year).

Additional information

A daily entrance fee is charged by national parks even if you are staying overnight (in 2008, fees were $7.80/adult, $3.90/child, $19.60/family; or you can purchase an annual pass good for all national parks). Even if you do not intend to stay at Glacier, stop and visit the information centre and learn about the history of Rogers Pass, chosen for the railroad by railway engineer Major A.B. Rogers in 1882. By 1885, railway construction had been completed. In 1956, the Trans-Canada Highway was surveyed through the area, and the road linking the Illecillewaet River to the Beaver River was completed in 1962. Videos and displays give testimony to how hazardous and challenging this construction process was. Today, experts constantly monitor the snow conditions, and there is an avalanche control program. Further information is available on the park's website: www.pc.gc.ca/glacier.

Jimsmith Lake

Location

It's easy to see why this park is popular with both visitors and locals. Although Jimsmith Lake is relatively small (14 hectares), it is well situated at the western end of the Rocky Mountain Trench and surrounded by a forest of Douglas fir, spruce, western larch, aspen, and lodgepole and ponderosa pine. The campground is reached by taking Highway 3/95 south from Cranbrook then heading west on a paved road. All services are available in Cranbrook, which is just 5 kilometres away.

Facilities

Twenty-eight large private well-spaced campsites suitable for every type of vehicle are available here (as long as you can navigate a gravel road with a few potholes). The park has all the basic amenities (drinking water, fire pits, picnic tables, pit toilets) and a couple of sites have views of the lake. There is no sani-station.

Recreational activities

Campers can enjoy a lovely sandy developed swimming beach, grassy picnic area, canoeing and kayaking and fishing for rainbow trout and largemouth bass. Powerboats are not allowed and the 13-hectare park is frequently used for picnics and day trips by locals who relish the tranquility it offers. The nearby town of Cranbrook houses the Canadian Museum of Rail Travel, where trains from an earlier era are shown and tea can be taken. Cranbrook also boasts a self-guided heritage tour that highlights buildings dating from 1898 to 1929. Sixteen kilometres from Cranbrook is the heritage town of Fort Steele, where more than 60 buildings from the turn of the century have been restored to recreate a bygone era.

Additional information

This 14-hectare park is a popular destination in the wintertime for ice fishing, ice-skating, cross-country skiing, sledding and tobogganing. The economy of Cranbrook has been built on mining, fishing and the railway. It is the largest town in the region (population 21,000) and has five provincial parks all within a 30-minute drive. Jimsmith Lake has a very "local" feel about it, and the campground offers a rather urban (although pleasant) camping experience. When I last visited the park, there were several groups of teenagers in the day-use area, which made me presume this area was used well into the evening. Fortunately, the day-use area is located far enough away from the campsites that noise from adolescents is not a problem.

KIKOMUN CREEK

Location

Sometimes the human influence on the geography of an area is beneficial. Such is the case at Kikomun Creek Provincial Park in the southern part of the Rocky Mountain Trench by Lake Koocanusa. This man-made lake was created by the construction of Libby Dam on the Kootenay River in Montana. The park is reached by turning off Highway 3 at Elko and travelling 8 kilometres west, or by turning off at Jaffray and travelling 16 kilometres south. Jaffray has a store/gas station, coffee shop and pub, and there is a marina 4 kilometres from the campground selling gas, propane and food. A small concession stand also operates in the park during the peak season.

Facilities

Located in two campgrounds are 105 sites that can accommodate every type of recreational vehicle. There are flush and pit toilets, a sani-station, showers and some park facilities are wheelchair-accessible. Surveyor campground has the shower building and the best location while camping at Kalispell Trail is somewhat regimented, but these sites are closer to the boat launch and Koocanusa Reservoir. Reservations are accepted.

Recreational activities

Fishing in this park is varied and good. The smaller lakes (especially Hidden Lake and Surveyors Lake) offer potential for catching bass, eastern brook, rainbow trout and Dolly Varden, while the 144-kilometre-long Koocanusa Reservoir has cutthroat trout and Rocky Mountain whitefish (and a boat launch). Powerboats are not permitted on the smaller lakes, thus ensuring a peaceful time for paddlers, and canoes can be rented in the park. There are two beaches, and picnic areas are found at Surveyors Lake. Hiking trails around the smaller lakes (30 to 90 minutes) offer opportunities to see elk, deer, badgers and ospreys. Old roads and railway beds give hikers and bikers easy access to the 682-hectare park. For young campers, there is an adventure playground, and interpretive programs are offered.

Additional information

Kikomun Creek Provincial Park houses one of the largest populations of painted turtles in BC, so-called because of the bright pattern underneath their shells. The turtles can easily be seen soaking up the sun. Kikomun Creek is a beautiful and varied place, ideal for a family vacation. It reminds me of an English country estate because of its size and the many roads that meander through the park.

KOKANEE CREEK

Location
It is difficult to imagine anyone not enjoying a visit to Kokanee Creek—especially if you have children—as this popular provincial park has a wealth of activities for campers of all ages. The 260-hectare park is situated amidst the beautiful scenery of the Slocan Range of the Selkirk Mountains on the west arm of Kootenay Lake, 19 kilometres east of Nelson on Highway 3A. Services are conveniently located in Nelson or Balfour (15 kilometres away).

Facilities
Kokanee Creek has 168 wooded camping spots in two locations, Sandspit and Redfish, off paved lanes and suitable for every size of vehicle. Redfish is closer to the road, making Sandspit my personal preference. The site is home to the West Kootenay Visitor Centre, so the facilities here are good and include flush toilets, showers and a sani-station. Sandspit also has a wheelchair-accessible campsite, flush toilet and shower stall. Reservations are accepted.

Recreational activities
You can easily spend a week at Kokanee Creek campground. There is a wealth of things to see and do, both in the park itself and in the immediate vicinity. Activities linked with the water include swimming from wide sandy beaches, boating, waterskiing and windsurfing. The fishing is reported to be excellent for both rainbow trout and kokanee, and the park has a boat launch. There is a large children's play area, a visitor centre that has exhibits of natural and human history and hosts interpretive programs, and there are a number of trails. The nearby town of Nelson boasts the largest concentration of heritage buildings in BC, and farther north on Highway 3, visitors can explore the Cody Caves near Kaslo or relax in Ainsworth Hot Springs' therapeutic mineral pools.

Additional information
The spawning channel and visitor centre here make this a truly educational place to visit. The word *kokanee* means "red fish" in the Kootenay First Nation language and is the name given to the landlocked salmon that spawn here in large numbers (the average is 2,000–4,000, but the number has been as high as 20,000). When I first stayed here, it was late August and the spawning was at its peak. At dusk, bald eagles and ospreys can be seen diving for salmon, and although it is sad that a few of these fish who have come so far with the sole thought of spawning will meet their demise so close to their destination, the spectacle is straight from a *National Geographic* television program. The salmon, together with the many other activities and the beautiful location, make this provincial park well worth a visit in August or September. In June, the wild roses are in full bloom, and the colours spectacular. This campground must be considered one of the best in BC.

KOOTENAY (NATIONAL)

Location

Along with Banff, Yoho and Jasper, Kootenay National Park was designated a World Heritage Site in 1985 when UNESCO officially recognized the beauty and significance of the Rocky Mountain landscape. The only national park to contain both glaciers and cacti, Kootenay National Park is found on Highway 93 1 kilometre north of Radium Hot Springs (west park entrance) and straddles over 90 kilometres of the highway as it heads north. Services are located in Radium.

Facilities

In addition to backcountry camping options, Kootenay National Park has about 400 campsites, spread over three campgrounds offering wheelchair-accessible campsites and washrooms. The largest campground, and my preference, is Redstreak, which is within easy walking distance of the village of Radium and the hot springs pools. Redstreak has 242 spots set in a lightly forested area: 50 are fully serviced sites, 38 sites have power only and 154 are unserviced. There are showers, flush toilets and a sani-station here, plus recycling bins and food storage. Redstreak is the only campground that accepts reservations, which are made through www.pccamping.ca or by calling 1-877-RESERVE. Much smaller in size, Marble Canyon is a "high-altitude" campground, located 86 kilometres

north of Radium, near the park's information centre. Set in a dense subalpine forest, Marble Canyon is the quietest of the three campgrounds and has 61 sites, with flush toilets, kitchen shelters with stoves, recycling bins, food storage and a sani-station. At the time of writing, Kootenay's third campground, McLeod Meadows, was closed indefinitely because no running water was available. When open, this campground located on the Kootenay River, 27 kilometres north of Radium Hot Springs, offers 98 shady spots— some close to the water's edge, some quite small—and there are flush toilets, kitchen shelters, recycling bins, food storage and a sani-station. In 2008, fees ranged from $21.50 to $38.20. Campfires are permitted and firewood is provided but a permit must first be purchased ($8.80 in 2008).

Recreational activities

One of the park's biggest attractions is, of course, Radium Hot Springs, which are the largest in Canada. Valued for centuries for their rich healing powers, they are within easy access of Redstreak campground and are open year-round (in the summer from 9:00 a.m. until 11:00 p.m.). In 2008, admission fees for the pools were $6.30 per adult and $5.40 per child/senior, or $19.10 per family, and swimsuits, towels and lockers are also available for rent. But there are hundreds of other things to do in this 140,600-hectare park. Wildlife is readily observable (including bighorn sheep, elk, moose, coyotes, wolves and more than 179 species of birds), and there are a number of walking and hiking trails, covering over 200 kilometres. One of the more impressive shorter trails is Marble Canyon, a 30-minute walk that takes visitors into an ice-carved limestone and dolomite canyon; interpretive boards detail the canyon's 500-million-year development. It's an easy hike for old and young alike—my two-year-old managed it without assistance. Other recreational pursuits include horseback riding, mountaineering, canoeing and rafting down the Kootenay and Vermillion rivers, and mountain biking on certain fire roads. Fishing in national parks is governed by a number of regulations and requires purchasing a permit (in 2008, the cost was $9.80/day; $34.30/annual), but since most of Kootenay's streams and rivers are glacier fed, the waters are too cold to yield high fish populations. In addition, a great range of interpretive programs is offered nightly at Redstreak Campground, which also has a playground.

Additional information

A daily entrance fee is charged by national parks even if you are staying overnight (in 2008, fees were $7.80/adult, $3.90/child, $19.60/family; or you can purchase an annual pass good for all national parks). The Banff–Windermere Highway, which runs through the park, was built in 1922 and was the first road constructed through the Canadian Rockies. It is a very pleasant drive, with 11 different picnic locations, and you can often spot animal life while travelling. Kootenay has its own website: www.pc.gc.ca/kootenay.

KOOTENAY LAKE

Location

Kootenay Lake Provincial Park has two beautiful quiet campgrounds located on the west side of Kootenay Lake, north of Kaslo on Highway 31, in the heart of Kootenay country. There is little to distract the camper other than mountain scenery and bald eagles flying overhead. Services can be found in Kaslo, a 30-minute drive south.

Facilities

Thirty-two campsites are available at two locations: Davis Creek offers 18 sites and Lost Ledge has 14. Some sites are very close to the lake and afford fantastic views of the Purcell Mountains. There is no sani-station and the facilities are the basic ones found in BC Parks (pit toilets, drinking water, fire pits and picnic tables). There is a wheelchair-accessible campsite and pit toilet at Lost Ledge.

Recreational activities

Leisure pursuits include swimming (but take it from one who knows—the water here is very cold), boating (there is a boat launch at Lost Ledge) and fishing for kokanee, bull and rainbow trout. In addition, the quaint town of Kaslo is well worth a visit. In Kaslo, you can rent canoes, kayaks and bikes to explore the lake and surrounding area. To the south, Ainsworth Hot Springs provides a relaxing afternoon activity.

Additional information

The campgrounds are located on a very quiet section of Highway 31. When I stayed, I cycled north to Duncan Dam then on to Howser, which has a small café. The highway follows the lake and has excellent views. There is another provincial park children and adults will adore located a short distance from Kootenay Lake: Cody Caves has no camping facilities and is located in the Selkirk Mountains just above Ainsworth Hot Springs, 11 kilometres down a good forest road off Highway 31. Visitors to this provincial park are treated to a full array of spectacular cave formations, including stalagmites, stalactites, waterfalls, draperies, rimstone dams and soda straws, and you must wear protective clothing and hard hats (the necessary equipment is provided) when taking the highly informative tours offered by BC Parks.

LOCKHART BEACH

Location

This quaint lakefront provincial park, established in 1939, covers just 3 hectares and is therefore one of the smallest in the province. It's located on the east side of the south arm of Kootenay Lake, 19 kilometres south of Crawford Bay. Food and lodging are available at Crawford Bay; more comprehensive services are located at Creston, an hour's drive south (40 kilometres).

Facilities

The campground, primarily for overnight stops, has 18 camping spots across the road from the lake and they are suitable for every type of camper. It features the basics (pit toilets, pump water, fire pits, and picnic tables). There is no sani-station or access for those in wheelchairs, and campers are advised to boil their drinking water for at least five minutes. Traffic noise from the road is audible, but a couple of sites are close to the creek, where you'll hear the babble of water instead.

Recreational activities

The park has a lovely quiet beach area where you can swim or fish for rainbow trout and Dolly Varden. A trail leads from the park and through a forest of Douglas fir, redcedar and ponderosa pine along Lockhart Creek. You can catch rainbow trout in the creek. It takes about three hours to hike the trail, which has an elevation gain of 800 metres.

Additional information

Highway 3A from Creston to Kootenay Bay is a lovely drive that takes tourists past small stores, galleries and an amazing circular glass house that a retired funeral director constructed out of 500,000 square embalming-fluid bottles. Definitely the only one in Canada, if not the world, the house is 7 kilometres south of the campground. At Kootenay Bay, travellers can take the Kootenay Lake Ferry—the world's longest free ferry ride—across the lake to Balfour. If you take the *Osprey*, you will be able to experience the excellent little café onboard. Be sure you're hungry when you embark: the breakfast is very good, as is watching the lake go by as you eat. This boat trip offers excellent photography opportunities and is recommended to everyone holidaying in the area. Lockhart Beach is definitely one of the better roadside campgrounds.

MARTHA CREEK

Location

The views from this 71-hectare park, which overlooks the Revelstoke Reservoir, stretch on to the Monashee Mountain Range and provide fantastic photography opportunities. In June, a blanket of colourful wildflowers covers the campground. For these reasons alone, Martha Creek is a delightful place to sojourn and located just 20 kilometres north of Revelstoke on Highway 23. All services are available in Revelstoke.

Facilities

Located on an old river terrace on the western shore of Revelstoke Reservoir, Martha Creek has 25 paved campsites, many with access directly onto the beach, although some are quite close to each other. There are flush and pit toilets but no sani-station. There is one wheelchair-accessible campsite.

Recreational activities

A swimming beach is located near the campground, and you can fish in the Revelstoke Reservoir for rainbow and bull trout (there's a boat launch at the southern end of the park). An enchanting 7-kilometre hiking trail leads walkers through wildflowers, cedar and hemlock and on to flowering meadows and alpine lakes within the Sleeker Mountains. There is a children's playground and a large grassy field with a volleyball net. The historic town of Revelstoke has been restored over the last few years and is an appealing place for shopping and wandering. In the summertime the bandstand in the town's plaza has evening entertainment for visitors. I spent a lovely August evening dancing to a local band as the sun went down—just the sort of light exercise needed before retiring to the tent or RV.

Additional information

When staying in this vicinity, you must visit the Revelstoke Dam, one of North America's largest and most modern hydroelectric developments, located five minutes from Revelstoke on the road to Martha Creek. Mica Dam, two hours north of Revelstoke on Highway 23, is also worth a visit. Both offer fascinating tours of their facilities and interesting programs on how and why they were constructed. In 1999, as we travelled toward Revelstoke over Robson Pass with the rain pouring, I called in to the hotel to inquire about a room for the night: $125.00 plus tax! We travelled on to Martha Creek, and the skies cleared and the sun shone. We spent much, much less to camp in a field full of wildflowers and wonderful smells! In 2003, we returned and discovered Canyon Hot Springs, about 20 kilometres east of Revelstoke on Highway 1. Here there are two wonderful hot mineral pools where you can soak in therapeutic waters while surrounded by mountains. Recently renovated and worth a visit.

McDonald Creek

Location

Ten kilometres south of Nakusp on Highway 6, this 468-hectare provincial park occupies land on both the eastern and western shores of Upper Arrow Lake. Camping facilities are situated adjacent to the highway on the eastern side of the lake. It's a perfect location for an evening's beach barbecue or lunchtime picnic. All services are found in Nakusp.

Facilities

Forty-six relatively private campsites are available in a lightly forested area, some overlooking the lake. Facilities are confined to the basics (drinking water, fire pits, picnic tables and pit toilets). Reservations are accepted.

Recreational activities

Massive Arrow Lake is the central source of activity. You can swim, sunbathe, sail and fish for kokanee, bull and rainbow trout. The water levels in the lake fluctuate: in June, there is mud, but a sandy beach is revealed in July and August. A boat launch is available in the park. The nearby town of Nakusp is renowned for its hot springs, located north of the town, 12 kilometres down a gravel road. The pools are high in the Selkirk Mountains: one is 38°C, the other 41°C. The views from these outdoor pools to the Selkirk Mountains are quite spectacular, and if you visit at the right time you could have this facility all to yourself. A 20-minute drive farther north of Nakusp on Highway 23 is Halcyon Hot Springs Resort. The original world-famous hotel was destroyed by fire in 1955 but rebuilt in 1999. Today, the timber-frame day lodge offers a licensed restaurant, two mineral hot pools and a heated swimming pool, all situated on a steep hillside next to Upper Arrow Lake.

Additional information

Arrow Lake, like Kootenay Lake, holds Gerrard trout, the world's largest rainbow trout. When I visited, I had to stay at the overspill site, but even so I had a wonderful time cooking dinner by the lakeside on a hibachi and watching the sun go down. Although it was full, the campground did not appear crowded, and it has a good ambience. As with other communities in the Kootenays, the economy of Nakusp has depended on the logging industry since 1910 and, notwithstanding some diversification, remains so today. Evidence of the logging industry is never far away from the traveller vacationing in the Kootenays.

Mount Fernie

Location
Rich in First Nations legends of unrequited love, broken promises and catastrophes, this 259-hectare park in the shadow of Mount Fernie has been described as the eastern gateway to the Kootenays. It is located 3 kilometres south of Fernie on Highway 3. Services are provided at Fernie.

Facilities
The campground has 40 sites set amongst a parkland of diverse vegetation including western larch, Douglas fir, black cottonwood, trembling aspen, western redcedar and spruce. Campsites here can accommodate all sizes of RVs. There are flush and pit toilets but no sani-station or showers. Reservations are accepted.

Recreational activities
The main attraction of this park is a 3-kilometre interpretive trail that winds its way through the park and takes visitors to picturesque Lizard Creek and waterfalls. The walk from the parking lot to the falls also makes a pleasant short trip for those people not intending to spend the night here. The trail continues on past the falls, but when I was last here that trail was badly signposted and no maps were available, so I couldn't explore it to the extent I would have liked. Hopefully, BC Parks will have updated the signposting when you visit. The park has areas of old-growth forest, and there are wildlife-viewing opportunities: you may see black bears, elk or deer, which are common here. The town of Fernie, just 3 kilometres from the park, has a historical museum, buildings dating back to 1904, a historical walking tour and a cultural centre and restaurant on the site of the former Canadian Pacific Railway station. Mountain biking is popular in the area, and there are lots of trails at Fernie Alpine Resort, but this activity not permitted within Mount Fernie Provincial Park.

Additional information
Fernie is named after William Fernie, who was instrumental in the development of coal mining in the area. Legend has it that William Fernie found out about the coal deposits from the Tobacco Plains people by promising to marry one of their young women. After gaining this information, he rejected her, thereby provoking her father to place a curse on the name "Fernie." The town subsequently suffered calamities: a mine explosion killed 128 men in 1902; there were two fires in 1904 and 1908, the latter leaving 6,000 people homeless; and several floods. In 1964, Chief Red Eagle of the Tobacco Plains Nation lifted the curse. Some people still believe that on summer nights the ghost of the First Nations woman, led by her father, rides across Hosmer Mountain in search of William Fernie.

Moyie Lake

Location
A restful relaxing time awaits campers at this beautiful 90-hectare provincial park. Adjacent to the eastern fringe of the Purcell Mountains near the northern end of Moyie Lake, the campground is a wonderful retreat, especially for folks with young children. Moyie got its name from the French word *mouillé*, which means "wet." Established in 1959, the park is 20 kilometres south of Cranbrook (where all services are available) and 5 kilometres north of the community of Moyie on Highway 3/95.

Facilities
The 111 camping spots are all large and private but do not have views of the water. The campground has a sani-station, plus flush toilets and showers (including facilities exclusively for those in wheelchairs). The only downside here is that there's a railroad near the campground, which may cause problems for light sleepers. Reservations are accepted.

Recreational activities
A wealth of activities can be enjoyed at Moyie Lake. Campers can hike the Meadow Interpretive Trail, which describes the forest typical to the area, or the Kettle Pond Trail (both are 2 kilometres long, 30 minutes return). Swimming is easy from a protected swimming area, and there are 1,300 metres of beach. For anglers, the lake contains ling cod, kokanee, burbot, rainbow trout and eastern brook trout. A boat launch is available and windsurfing is possible, weather permitting. Children can be kept busy at the adventure playground. For those who enjoy mountain biking, a half-day trip up a gravel road to Mineral Lake, formally a forestry recreational site, is a fun excursion.

Additional information
Moyie Lake is a delightful place to set up camp and an ideal place to spend time in if you have a young family. But the campground is not just for those with children: for campers who decide not to cook, the pub situated about 10 minutes south of the campground on Highway 3 is worth a visit, and the nearby town of Cranbrook supplies all services should you have forgotten any basic camping items. When I last stayed here, the only drawback was the three jet skiers who shattered the calm of the afternoon and made me appreciate the lakes on which powerboats are prohibited. My advice to those who prefer a smaller quieter experience is to try Jimsmith Lake instead.

NANCY GREENE

Location

This lovely 203-hectare park is by all accounts just as popular in the winter-time as it is in the summer. Named after Canada's world-famous Olympic skier Nancy Greene, who came from the Rossland–Trail area, this provincial park is nestled in the Rossland Range of the Monashee Mountains, 29 kilometres north of Rossland on Highway 3, at the intersection of Highway 3B. Services can be found at either Rossland or Castlegar; both communities are about a half-hour drive from the campground.

Facilities

There are 14 formal campsites here, primarily geared to tenters and smaller recreational vehicles. These sites are not great, being closely packed and ad-jacent to the car park. Larger RVs are allowed to camp in the parking lot. All the basic facilities exist (pit toilets, picnic tables, pump water, fire pits). There is no sani-station or wheelchair access. Noise from traffic is audible, but the road is not tremendously busy, especially at night.

Recreational activities

The park itself and the adjacent recreational area of the same name contain the subalpine Nancy Greene Lake, and there's a lovely beach area, where you can swim, fish for rainbow trout or sail (powerboats are not allowed). A self-guided, 5-kilometre nature trail leads around the lake, and the recreational area offers more than 20 kilometres of hiking trails. The area is popular in the winter for both downhill and cross-country skiing. The park has a covered picnic shelter and an old log cabin with wood-burning stove.

Additional information

The picturesque town of Rossland dates back to the turn of the century. More recently, it has gained a reputation for mountain biking. Just outside Rossland is the Le Roi gold mine, where visitors are taken underground to become acquainted with the life and work of a hardrock miner. Be-tween 1900 and 1916, the Le Roi mine produced 50 percent of BC's gold and swelled the population of Rossland to 7,000 before its de-mise in the 1920s. The mine is a great place to visit and tour, as is the adjacent museum. Both Trail and Rossland are delightful com-munities to spend time in.

Norbury Lake

Location

Norbury Lake is nestled in the Hughes Range of the Rocky Mountains and supplies excellent views of the Steeples—a distinctive feature of the Hughes Range and also of the Purcell Mountains. The 97-hectare provincial park is easily found 13 kilometres southeast of Fort Steele on a paved road from Highway 93/95. Services are available at Fort Steele. The campground is approximately 1 kilometre away from the day-use area at Peckham's Lake.

Facilities

This is a secluded location, with 46 gravel camping spots set amongst a lightly forested area of Douglas fir, lodgepole pine, ponderosa pine and western larch. The number of trees decreased considerably in June 1998 when a strong wind blew through the area, causing the campground to close for more than two weeks (fortunately two families camping at the time were not hurt). Facilities are restricted to the basics (pump water, fire pit, picnic tables, pit toilets). There is no sani-station or wheelchair access.

Recreational activities

Recreational pursuits within the park include fishing for rainbow trout in Peckham's Lake, swimming and boating (there is a boat launch but powerboats are prohibited). Two trails are available to lead explorers through a diverse area of lightly forested landscape where it is possible to see elk, deer and Rocky Mountain bighorn sheep. Norbury Lake is close to the historic town of Fort Steele, a fascinating example of turn-of-the-century life in Canada and a real delight to visit. In 1961, the provincial government recognized Fort Steele as being of historical significance, and the reconstruction that started then continues today. A perfect example of a pioneer town, Fort Steele contains some 60 buildings, including an original North West Mounted Police camp, excellent bakery, restaurant, theatre and museum.

Additional information

Norbury Lake is named after F. Paget Norbury, a magistrate who served in Fort Steele in the late 19th century. This park is the site of the Kootenai First Nation's ceremonial grounds. An informative display giving details of their culture is found at Peckham's Lake entrance.

Not far from Logan Lake, Tunkwa is a great place to camp if you like trout-fishing. (BC Parks photo)

Camp at Liard River Hot Springs and you won't have to pay extra to access the two hot pools located in the park. (BC Parks photo)

A short drive from Victoria, Goldstream has a number of hiking and walking routes—and scenic places to perch and take in the surroundings. (BC Parks photo)

See loons, red-necked grebes, ruffed grouse and beavers at Tyhee Lake, which has an interpretive nature trail and a marsh-viewing platform. (BC Parks photo)

Margaret Falls is the jewel of Herald Provincial Park; the park also has access to Shuswap Lake. (BC Parks photo)

Park your RV for the night at Lockhart Beach, one of the province's better roadside campgrounds. (Trevor Julier photo)

Family-friendly Kokanee Creek takes its name from the tributary that runs through the park. (BC Parks photo)

Monck's campsites on the north side of Nicola Lake are suitable for all types of recreational vehicles. (BC Parks photo)

Step back in time to the 1920s at Kilby Provincial Park, which includes a historic site with a restored general store and farm buildings.

Jimsmith Lake has a lovely swimming beach, and there is no noise from powerboats—they're not allowed. (Trevor Julier photo)

Camp at Yoho and pretend you're in the Swiss Alps. (Trevor Julier photo)

A group campfire on the beach at Sidney Spit Marine Park. (Parks Canada/Josh McCulloch photo)

Montague Harbour has a glass-bottomed nature hut with hands-on kids' activities.

Oceanside campgrounds are perfect for beachcombers.

Some spots at Porteau Cove overlook the water's edge, with views of the mountains on Vancouver Island.

Gordon Bay is located in one of the warmest valleys on Vancouver Island, so you may want to take a dip in Lake Cowichan if you're camping here in the summer. (BC Parks photo)

Island campgrounds, such as the one on Newcastle Island, are special places—and they usually have good beach access. (BC Parks photo)

Kayaking is a popular activity at many provincial parks, including Chilliwack Lake. (BC Parks photo)

Alice Lake is an excellent choice for group camping.

Lakeside campgrounds are perfect for canoeists. (BC Parks photo)

Yahk Provincial Park may be located in a relatively noncommercialized area of BC, but you can still get ice cream nearby.

You never know what you'll see at the side of the road when you're driving to a campground.

Many campgrounds, including Lac Le Jeune, have playgrounds for children.
(BC Parks photo)

Climbing to the top of Stawamus Chief, the world's second-largest granite monolith, is strenuous and challenging, but the view is worth it. (BC Parks photo)

The historic town of Fort Steele is just 13 kilometres north of the campground at Norbury Lake.

If the campground doesn't have flush toilets, you'll have to use a "thunderbox" (pit toilet) instead.

With its huge network of trails, Wells Gray Provincial Park is a hiker's dream. (BC Parks photo)

A popular activity at riverside Bromley Rock is tubing downstream to Stemwinder Provincial Park. (BC Parks photo)

Shuswap Lake is ideal for water sports. (BC Parks photo)

Interpretive programs are offered by many of the larger campgrounds, including Mount Robson. (BC Parks photo)

In the heart of the Slocan Valley, Summit Lake is one of the newest provincial park campgrounds. (BC Parks photo)

Wildlife-viewing opportunities are plentiful in BC's provincial and national parks.

Okanagan Falls Provincial Park is located at the northern edge of the Great-Basin Desert.

The campground at Okanagan Falls has some nice sunny campsites.

Wasa Lake has the reputation of having some of the warmest water in the east Kootenays.

Camp lakeside at Kentucky–Alleyne, a gem of a park located just south of Merritt.
(Trevor Julier photo)

Pitch your tent practically on the beach at Sidney Spit, part of the Gulf Islands National Park Reserve since 2003. (Parks Canada/Josh McCulloch photo)

Some of the campsites at Syringa overlook Lower Arrow Lake.

The campground at Rolley Lake is set in a wooded area, which offers campers privacy and shade. (BC Parks photo)

PREMIER LAKE

Location

Long ago, the K'tunaxa First Nation camped, hunted and fished in this area. Today, visitors are attracted to the region for the splendid views. Premier Lake is in the Hughes Range of the Rockies, about 45 kilometres northeast of Kimberley. It is reached by turning off Highway 93/95 at Skookumchuck (which is a Chinook word meaning "strong or turbulent water") and travelling 9 kilometres on a paved road and 5 kilometres on a gravel road. (Watch for logging trucks, which frequently travel along this route.) A gas station, shop and restaurant are available at Skookumchuck.

Facilities

Set amongst Douglas fir, western larch, cottonwood and aspen trees are 56 campsites suitable for all vehicles, some with tent pads and some adjacent to a bubbling creek. Facilities are the basics (pump water, fire pits, picnic tables, pit toilets). Some facilities in the park (including a pit toilet and picnic site) are wheelchair-accessible. An unusual manually operated solar-heated shower is available here; plastic shower bags are supplied by the park but their supply has been a bit haphazard. Reservations are accepted and advised.

Recreational activities

Seven lakes—Premier, Canuck, Yankee, Turtle, Quartz and the two Cat's Eye lakes—exist in this 662-hectare park, which has gained a reputation as a good spot to fish for eastern brook trout and Gerrard rainbow trout. A short walk from the campground there is a spawning and viewing area together with an interpretive display to explain enhancement procedures, including how eggs are collected for the Kootenay Trout Hatchery. Forty percent of rainbow trout eggs required for the provincial egg hatchery system come from here and are distributed to over 350 lakes and streams in the province. Premier Lake has a boat launch and swimming is available. The park also contains a number of trails that cover a variety of distances and take between 20 minutes and five hours to complete. For children, there is an adventure playground.

Additional information

The area is rich in wildlife—watch for elk roaming on the cleared hills near the highway. Premier Lake is yet another BC provincial park located amidst spectacular breathtaking scenery. It is a little off the beaten track and offers a very adult camping experience. I last stayed in August 2007 when the campground was very busy. A gorgeous location but the camping spaces are quite tightly packed.

Rosebery

Location

Rosebery Provincial Park has undoubtedly one of the better campgrounds dedicated primarily to one-night stops. The scenery here is lovely: visitors can gaze across Slocan Lake to the majestic Valhalla mountains. The 32-hectare park is situated on Highway 6, 6 kilometres south of Rosebery between Nakusp and New Denver, where services are available.

Facilities

Campers can take their pick of 36 large private shady camping spots suitable for every type of recreational vehicle. Some overlook the rushing Wilson Creek, while others are closer to the road (although the road is not busy at night). There is no sani-station or wheelchair access, and the facilities are basic (pit toilets, drinking water, fire pits and picnic tables).

Recreational activities

There are few activities to pursue in the park itself. Wilson Creek runs through the park and has a short trail leading along its edge. Fishing for rainbow trout is possible. By crossing nearby Slocan Lake you can explore and hike the much larger Valhalla Provincial Park. There are also a number of private golf courses in the area. New Denver is a delightful place to wander around, and a number of lovely coffee shops have recently sprung up to entice tourists to linger. This turn-of-the-century community has some wonderful buildings that are currently being restored to their former glory.

Additional information

Located directly across Slocan Lake from Rosebery is Valhalla Provincial Park. This is a region of dramatic and diverse wilderness that includes lakes, alpine meadows and the impressive New Denver glacier. Despite limited road access, the park offers 50,000 hectares of beautiful unspoiled land to explore. Observant sailors heading toward Valhalla can spot pictographs painted by the forefathers of the Arrowhead First Nation on the western shoreline of Slocan Lake.

SUMMIT LAKE

Location

Although this tiny 6-hectare provincial park was established in 1964, the campground only opened in 2001, making it one of BC's newest provincial park campgrounds. Situated at the southwestern corner of Summit Lake, it is one of only two campgrounds in the Slocan Valley (Rosebery is the other) and therefore a much-needed addition to the area. It can be found on Highway 6 between New Denver and Nakusp. The nearest services are at Nakusp, 18 kilometres north.

Facilities

Summit Lake is one of the better roadside campgrounds. Some of the 35 vehicle-accessible sites are quite closely packed together, but a number have wonderful views of the lake and are set in a lightly forested area of hemlock and cedar. Although the campground is quite near the road, noise is not much of a problem, as traffic is not heavy. There are flush and pit toilets, drinking water and fire pits, as well as a picnic shelter with a wood stove. Reservations are not accepted.

Recreational activities

When my family visited in September 2003, the biggest attraction for us was skimming stones on the fantastically calm waters of Summit Lake. The lake has 100 metres of pebbly beach and is quite warm and attractive for swimming. There is a small trail that meanders from the day-use area to the campground. The campground has a boat launch, and canoeing and kayaking are popular pastimes. Fishing is also reputed to be good, as the lake is stocked with over 10,000 rainbow trout annually (do you ever wonder whose job it is to count them?), and the local fly-fishing championships are held here. New Denver and Nakusp are pleasant places to wander through and stop for coffee in, and you'll find the wonderful Nakusp Hot Springs to the north of Nakusp.

Additional information

This park could easily have been named Toad Provincial Park. It houses an important breeding ground and migration habitat for western toads. Information boards in the park describe these primarily nocturnal creatures. In the fall, thousands of toads emerge from the lake and head for the adjacent forest to hibernate. Other wildlife includes eagles, kingfishers, hawks, bears and mountain goats. Summit Lake is a delightful addition to the campgrounds of the province.

SYRINGA

Location

On a creek on the eastern side of Lower Arrow Lake, Syringa Provincial Park covers 4,417 hectares below the Norns Range of the Columbia Mountains. The lake, on the Columbia River, resulted from the construction of the Keenleyside Dam. The campground is reached by turning off Highway 3A just north of Castlegar and travelling 19 kilometres on a paved road. All services are available in Castlegar, a 25-minute drive away, while a nearby marina and store offer more limited supplies.

Facilities

Sixty-one large private spots, some overlooking the water and others adjacent to a grassy meadow, are available in a forest of redcedar, western hemlock and ponderosa pine. In addition to the basic facilities, Syringa has a sani-station and flush and pit toilets and wheelchair access (including wheelchair-accessible flush toilets). Reservations are accepted.

Recreational activities

Syringa boasts a fantastic rocky beach from which to view the Columbia Mountains and Monashee Range. Though water levels fluctuate, all forms of aquatic activity are possible, including swimming, boating, waterskiing (the park provides the only public boat launch in the area, but be warned—the waters can be rough when there is a wind) and fishing for kokanee salmon and rainbow trout. For those who prefer non-water-based pursuits, a number of trails lead from the park for walking and mountain biking. The 2.7-kilometre Yellow Pine Trail is a particularly pleasant 45-minute interpretive trail. There is also an adventure playground and a beautiful grassy area by the beach that's perfect for ball games. When I stayed here, I got chatting with parks staff Pam and Debbie, who told me that the mosquitoes were never a problem here, as the wind tends to keep them away—information well worth having.

Additional information

The park is named after the syringa (a.k.a. mock orange), a regional white-flowered shrub that blooms in early spring. Nearby Castlegar is rich in Doukhobor history; a heritage museum near the airport details this culture and is worth a visit. Although the paved road ends at the park, an unpaved road carries on to an area known as Deer Park, where there is an attractive waterfall. My children really love this park—it's one of their favourites, along with Alice Lake.

Wasa Lake

Location
This gem of a provincial park provides a comprehensive range of facilities and activities. The campground, one of the largest in the region, lies at the northern end of Wasa Lake, a glacier-formed kettle lake, reputed to be one of the warmest in the east Kootenays, if not the province. Wasa Lake Provincial Park is situated 40 kilometres north of Cranbrook on Highway 93/95. The community of Wasa, 1 kilometre away, has stores, a gas station, restaurants, laundry facilities and a neighbourhood pub.

Facilities
With the Rocky Mountains to the east and the Purcells to the west, the views from the Wasa Lake campground are staggering. There are 104 well-appointed camping spots set among pine and aspen trees, which can accommodate every type of recreational vehicle. There are flush and pit toilets and a sani-station but no showers. The flush toilets (and some other park facilities) are wheelchair-accessible. Reservations are accepted.

Recreational activities
The lake supplies a wealth of recreational activities with four excellent beaches providing access to warm waters. There is a boat launch, and fishing for largemouth bass is a favourite pursuit. A self-guided 2.7-kilometre nature trail, which takes about an hour to complete, gives details of the flora and fauna of the area. The Lazy Lake Bike Loop is 33-kilometre mountain-bike ride leading from Wasa Lake to Lazy Lake and back. There is also an adventure playground for children. Beyond the park, the historic town of Fort Steele is only 18 kilometres to the south; likewise, the "Bavarian" community of Kimberley, Canada's highest city, is within easy reach. Here visitors can marvel at the world's largest operating cuckoo clock, stop at gingerbread-fronted stores or play a round of golf.

Additional information
Each year on the Sunday of the August long weekend, a sand-sculpture contest is held at Camper's Beach, the main beach on the lake. The park contains a variety of vegetation, including an area of endangered grasslands. A few years ago Wasa had a bad reputation for mosquitoes, which arrived the second week of July and stayed until the end of August (like most of the tourists), but when we stayed in August 2008 they were not an issue. The local population is keen to preserve Wasa as a family camping location. A few years ago they constructed the Wasa Lions Way—an 8-kilometre paved walking/cycling/rollerblading trail encircling the lake. A BC Parks representative informed me that two grandmothers in Wasa had recently purchased rollerblades, so keep an eye out for the rolling grannies.

WHITESWAN LAKE

Location
Driving to Whiteswan Lake can be an adventure in itself. Huge logging trucks frequent the gravel road, and in places it narrows to one lane, necessitating excellent driving skills. The journey is well worth the effort. This provincial park is located on a plateau in the Kootenay Range of the Rocky Mountains east of Canal Flats, which has a store and restaurant. Both Alces and Whiteswan lakes are contained in the 1,994-hectare park, which has some fantastic views of the surrounding mountains. The campground is reached by turning off Highway 93/95 and travelling along Whiteswan Lake Road (gravel) for 18 kilometres. The nearest comprehensive services are at Invermere, 78 kilometres away.

Facilities
The park has five campgrounds, providing 114 vehicle-accessible spaces. Alces Lake (28 spots) has a sani-station and is reached after travelling 21 kilometres from the main highway; Packrat Point (16 spots) is 24 kilometres from the highway; and Inlet Creek (16 spots) is a further 4 kilometres. Located near the northeastern entrance of the park, White River (17 spots) is off White River Forest Road while Home Basin (37 spots) is off Moscow Forest Road; both are about 33 kilometres from the highway. Home Basin and Alces Lake have lakeside camping and are my personal preferences. All campgrounds offer the basic amenities (drinking water, fire pits, picnic tables and pit toilets). Home Basin has a wheelchair-accessible campsite.

Recreational activities
One of the main attractions of this location is the undeveloped Lussier Hot Springs, near the park's western boundary. The hot springs flow from the mountainside into a series of pools and, unlike the ones at Radium, Ainsworth and Fairmont, are unspoiled by commercial development. Both Whiteswan and Alces lakes provide plenty of swimming opportunities, with a beach at the north end of Whiteswan Lake. The two lakes are among the most productive fisheries in the East Kootenays, and in May and June rainbow trout can be seen spawning in Inlet and Outlet creeks. Boat launches are available at Packrat Point and Home Basin (electric motors only on Alces Lake). An 8-kilometre hiking trail takes walkers from Alces Lake to the Home Basin campground, and there are opportunities for viewing wildlife, such as golden and bald eagles, mountain goats, bighorn sheep and moose.

Additional information
Used by the K'tunaxa (Kootenai) First Nation for more than 5,000 years, this is an area rich in history. In the 1800s and 1900s, trappers and prospectors worked the region, and today logging is the prime industry—a fact you will be well aware of if you encounter a logging truck on your journey to this beautiful away-from-it-all camping location. It's a huge park not oriented toward families but is great for anglers.

YAHK

Location

This 9-hectare provincial park is found in a quiet uncommercialized area of BC, on the banks of the Moyie River. It is close to the United States border and the state of Idaho. Situated on Highway 3/95 at Yahk, 39 kilometres east of Creston, it's very much an overnight camping or picnic spot. Services can be found in Moyie, Yahk or Creston, or at the gas station just south of the campground.

Facilities

There are 26 campsites here, able to accommodate every size of recreational vehicle and set amidst a forest of Douglas fir, lodgepole pine and ponderosa pine. The basic amenities are offered (cooking pits, picnic tables, drinking water and pit toilets) and the campground is wheelchair-accessible. The campground is located close to both the railway line and road, so traffic noise may disturb some campers.

Recreational activities

Yahk is primarily for one-night camping, or for brief rest stops, as there is not a great deal to do here besides canoeing, kayaking or fishing in the Moyie River for trout. (We saw a man fly-fishing and he caught two small fish in the space of 30 minutes.) As you travel down Highway 3/95 following the Moyie River, moose and mule deer can be seen feeding, so keep your eyes peeled. The park's day-use area is an ideal picnic spot.

Additional information

Yahk was once a major supplier of railway ties to the Canadian Pacific Railway, an industry that still exists but has been in steady decline since the 1940s. Today, Yahk has a population of about 350, but it seems to be growing. When we visited in 2008, a new bakery and coffee shop had opened just south of the campground. Two Scoop Steve's ice cream bar is a must for kids. Set on a hillside overlooking the lake, the pretty community of Moyie to the south has some interesting buildings. Moyie owes its development to silver-lead mining and at one time was the richest mine of this type in the province.

YOHO (NATIONAL)

Location

Yoho is thought to be the word used by the Kootenai people to express awe, and visitors certainly will experience this emotion in Yoho, Canada's second-oldest national park. Designated by UNESCO as a World Heritage Site, and often compared to the Swiss Alps, Yoho has spectacular lakes, mountains, icefields, alpine meadows, glaciers and waterfalls. The park is found on the Trans-Canada Highway (Highway 1) between Golden and Lake Louise. The small community of Field, which is in the park, offers services. A lovely restaurant/coffeehouse that also sells camping supplies is located near the Kicking Horse campground.

Facilities

Over 250 vehicle-accessible camping spots are available to campers wanting to access the delights of Yoho, spread amongst the following campgrounds: Chancellor (59 sites), Hoodoo Creek (30 sites), Kicking Horse (92 sites), Monarch (46 sites) and Takakkaw Falls (35 sites). Chancellor is 5 kilometres from the western park boundary and provides only the basic camping facilities (pit toilets, fire pits, drinking water, picnic tables), but it is on the Kicking Horse River and has great views. There are also kitchen shelters and food storage. One kilometre down the highway, Hoodoo Creek is densely wooded and peaceful. The park's only sani-station is located here, but it was closed at the time of writing; there was also a "boil water" advisory in place. Kicking Horse is located in a lightly forested area 5 kilometres east of Field. This is the largest campground and has the most amenities. Besides the basics, there are showers, flush toilets (wheelchair-accessible), food storage, an outdoor interpretive theatre and a play area for children. Closer to Field, and within walking distance of Kicking Horse, Monarch's sites are set in a large meadow. Facilities here include wheelchair-accessible washrooms with flush toilets, food storage, a kitchen shelter with a wood-

burning stove and recycling. Takakkaw Falls is the farthest campground from Field, 17 kilometres east of the village. The campground is on Takakkaw Falls Road, off Yoho Valley Road (which has switchbacks that shouldn't be attempted if you have a long RV or are towing a trailer). You have to walk a short distance from the parking lot to access the campsites here, but a cart is available for wheeling in your supplies. The walk is worth it for the views and this campground also has the basics plus food storage, a kitchen shelter with a stove and recycling. In 2008, fees ranged from $17.60 to $27.40, and it cost $8.80 to have a campfire.

Recreational activities

Visitors to Yoho should make their first stop at the Yoho Park Information Centre located at the junction of Highway 1 and the access road into Field. Detailed maps of the vicinity can be obtained here. In a park of this size (131,300 hectares), internationally recognized for its beauty, there is a multitude of things to do. There are water-focused activities like canoeing and kayaking (canoes can be rented on Emerald Lake), rafting and fishing. Powerboats are not permitted in the park, and fishing in national parks is governed by a number of regulations and requires purchasing a permit (in 2008, fees were $9.80/day; $34.30/year).

Other ways to pass your time include mountain biking on designated trails and fire roads, mountaineering and, of course, hiking. As there are over 400 kilometres of trails, fantastic hiking opportunities abound; choose between short interpretive trails or hikes that last for days (some of the shorter ones are wheelchair-accessible). When I stayed, I hiked the Iceline Trail, which takes you to glaciers, alpine meadows, forests and mountains among some of the best scenery in the world. It is impossible to recommend this trail too highly. This trail and others have views of Takakkaw Falls, which at 254 metres is one of the highest waterfalls in North America. *Takakkaw* is a Cree word meaning "magnificent." The short 10-minute walk to these falls is also well worth undertaking. Keep an eye out for wildlife in Yoho: while driving to the start of the Iceline Trail, we saw a grizzly bear, and there are also elk, moose, coyotes and wolves in the park.

Additional information

A daily entrance fee is charged by national parks even if you are staying overnight (in 2008, fees were $7.80/adult, $3.90/child, $19.60/family; or you can purchase an annual pass good for all national parks). Yoho National Park was established in 1911. Yoho owes its development to the Canadian National Railway workers who managed to push the tracks through Kicking Horse Pass and build the first company hotel in Field. Climbers, tourists and artists came to the hotel and recognized the overpowering beauty of the area. In 1886, the Mount Steven Reserve was set aside, and this area was renamed Yoho 25 years later. Check out the park's website at www.pc.cgc.ca/yoho for a weekly report of bear sightings and tons of useful information for planning a trip to this awesome recreational area.

CARIBOO
CHILCOTIN COAST

Steeped in the history of the gold rush and covering an area of over 100,000 square kilometres, the Cariboo region has campgrounds situated off Highway 97 north of Cache Creek to Prince George. This section of road is known as the Gold Rush Trail after the pioneers who travelled it in search of the precious metal. Today, many buildings and historical markers recount the days of this original wagon road built in 1860. Campgrounds are also found on minor roads off this major route. The Cariboo is characterized by rolling hills, grasslands, over 8,000 lakes and numerous rivers stretching from the foothills of the Rockies to the Pacific coast. Recently the area has become known for its many guest ranches and for being "cowboy country," so go and ride 'em, cowboy!

Bull Canyon Provincial Park is between Williams Lake and Bella Coola.

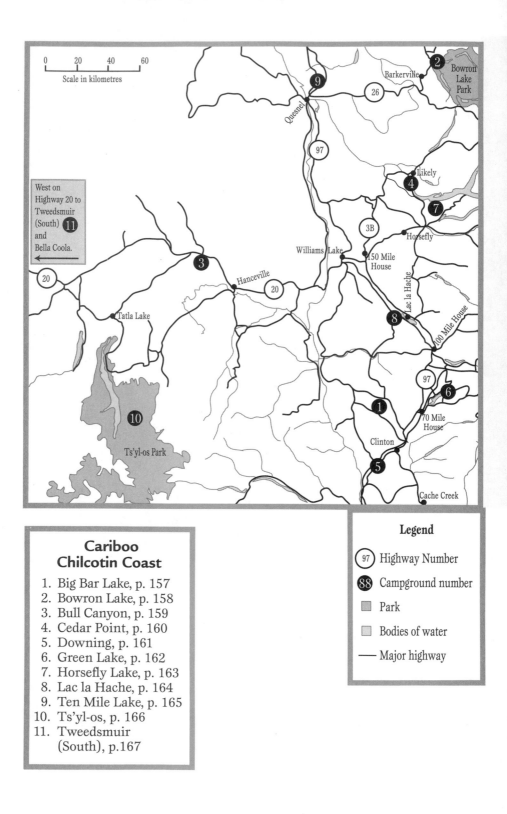

West on
Highway 20 to
Tweedsmuir
(South) **11**
and
Bella Coola.

←

Legend

97 Highway Number

88 Campground number

◻ Park

◻ Bodies of water

— Major highway

Big Bar Lake

Location
The people who once walked the land around Big Bar Lake were First Nations hunters, cowboys, cattle rustlers and gold prospectors. According to local legends, their ghosts can often be seen and heard, so be attentive when you stay here. Big Bar Lake is on the southern edge of the Fraser Plateau, a landscape formed millions of years ago by debris left by glaciers. Evidence of the ice age can be seen west of the lake, where gravel eskers remain; much of the topography owes its development to this geological period. To reach Big Bar Lake, drive 8 kilometres north of Clinton on Highway 97 and then take a gravel road west for 34 kilometres to the park itself. The nearest services can be found at 70 Mile House.

Facilities
The 332-hectare park has two campgrounds with a total of 46 spots. Lakeside's 25 sites overlook the lake, and 15 are right on the lakeshore, while the Upper campground's larger sites are located in the forest above the lake. The facilities are basic (fire pits, picnic tables, drinking water, pit toilets).

Recreational activities
A naturalist's delight, this area is characterized by forests of lodgepole pine and spruce providing an excellent habitat for wildlife, including mule deer, black bears (which we saw while travelling here), cougars, lynx, marmots and snowshoe hares. Easy access to the lake and a boat launch means boating and fishing are possible, and the lake is stocked annually with rainbow trout. Big Bar Lake is a gorgeous body of water that is also ideal for swimming: crystal-clear water, quite warm and no reeds. Waterskiing is not permitted and there is a speed limit for boats. A 3.5-kilometre trail provides excellent waterfowl and birdwatching, which is facilitated by a water-control structure built by Ducks Unlimited to encourage nesting. Longer hikes are also possible. There is a children's playground in the day-use area.

Additional information
Big Bar Lake Provincial Park is in an area of rolling hills originally settled by the Salish First Nation. Today, it's known as ranch country, and trail rides can be arranged through the numerous guest ranches located in the area. These ranches operate year-round and also offer riding lessons, pack trips, gold-panning excursions and skiing. The fact that snowshoe hares are found around Big Bar Lake should forewarn you that even early in the season, beautiful warm days can turn into clear, cold nights. So act like a cowboy and remember the longjohns if you'll be camping under canvas. We stayed here in 2006 and I swam at 8:00 p.m. when the entire lake was mine. Bliss. Be warned, though, that mosquitoes affect certain areas of the park, but that problem can be avoided by changing locations.

Bowron Lake

Location

Bowron Lake Provincial Park is famous for its wilderness canoe circuit, which covers over 116 kilometres around 11 different lakes, but there's also a vehicle-accessible campground anyone can use. The park is located 120 kilometres east of Quesnel and 30 kilometres beyond Wells, reached by taking a 27-kilometre dirt road found at the end of Highway 26. Two resorts and some stores on Bowron Lake offer a selection of services, including food and camping supplies, while a full range can be found in Wells.

Facilities

Twenty-five wooded secluded campsites suitable for vehicles and tents are located near the park entrance and start of the canoe circuit. Facilities are basic (picnic tables, fire pits, drinking water and pit toilets) and reservations are not accepted. There are 54 wilderness sites located elsewhere in the 149,207-hectare park for those undertaking the canoe circuit.

Recreational activities

Near the campground, which is on the eastern shore of Bowron Lake, there is a canoe-landing dock, and it is possible to swim, canoe and fish for Dolly Varden, rainbow trout and lake char. Boat and canoe rentals are available nearby, as is a public boat launch (though powerboats are only permitted on Bowron Lake). Wildlife includes moose, deer, caribou, black and grizzly bears, and coyotes. There are bald and golden eagles, ospreys and hawks, as well as a wealth of waterfowl and songbirds. The visitor centre has an informative video about the park that is well worth watching.

Additional information

To be able to fully appreciate the beauty of Bowron Lake Provincial Park, you should spend a week or more here. The park's reputation grows annually, both within North America and Europe; consequently, it is becoming increasingly difficult to get a canoe-circuit reservation and only a few first-come, first-served spots are offered each day. Advance planning is required if you want to canoe the circuit (in its entirety, or just the west side) and you should make a reservation by phoning 1-800-435-5622. This campground is a delightful place to stay in even if you're not a canoeing enthusiast, but for those who just want to visit the area, it may be easier to stay at Barkerville, which has two private campgrounds. Wells is a neat little community where canoe-rental companies also operate, delivering canoes and kayaks to Bowron Lake for those interested in paddling the circuit or just spending a day paddling and enjoying the beauty of the area.

BULL CANYON

Location

Bull Canyon Provincial Park has a particularly beautiful setting on the Fraser Plateau by the Chilcotin River. It is an excellent overnight stop for those travelling between Williams Lake and Bella Coola along Highway 20, as it has the only provincial campground between Williams Lake and Tweedsmuir Provincial Park. This pleasantly treed 123-hectare park is found 6 kilometres west of Alexis Creek. The nearest full range of services is at Williams Lake, 122 kilometres away, but gas and basic food items can be purchased at Alexis Creek.

Facilities

Bull Canyon was given provincial-park status in 1993 and has 20 basic campsites in an open camping area overlooking the azure blue Chilcotin River. Facilities are rudimentary (drinking water, fire pits, picnic tables, pit toilets). There is one wheelchair-accessible pit toilet but no sani-station, and water is obtained from a pump. The campground is really quiet with only the sound of the river lulling you to sleep, as the road isn't busy and is a little ways away from the campground.

Recreational activities

The fast-flowing Chilcotin River is suitable for fishing, canoeing and kayaking (as are the lakes in the area), but special fishing restrictions apply. Archaeological sites apparently exist in the park, but when we stayed here in 2006 we couldn't find them. Although insects often plague this area of the province, the pleasant breeze we had while camping here meant we didn't have any problems. There is good birdwatching and wildlife viewing, and a wonderful array of wildflowers can be found here at certain times of the year. This is a good picnic spot even if you don't want to camp. In the winter, this region experiences very cold temperatures, sometimes as low as -50°C.

Additional information

While staying at another provincial park, I met a retired gentleman from Germany who had been holidaying by RV in BC for the past 10 years, and claimed to have travelled on every road other than Highway 20. The year I talked with him, he was about to undertake that journey. One of the more pleasant aspects of staying in BC provincial parks is having the opportunity to meet people from all over the world, who often give advice on travelling in the province, including which campgrounds are their favourites.

CEDAR POINT

Location

This is one of BC's newest provincial parks and labelled Category C, which means it is jointly administered with a board from the local community of Likely. As it is co-operated, the facilities it offers and the general "feel" is different to other BC Provincial Parks. The 8-hectare park is located on Quesnel Lake, 6 kilometres from Likely, which is 120 kilometres on a paved road northeast of 150 Mile House. Services are found in Likely. The campground administrator's house is in the park.

Facilities

Camping exists for 40 parties, with sites varying in size. Besides the basics you'd expect (drinking water, picnic tables, fire pits, pit toilets), there is a sani-station but no showers. Surprisingly, firewood is provided free of charge, which means this is the only campground I know of to still offer this service!

Recreational activities

One of the major attractions here is Quesnel Lake, which is huge, and there is a boat launch in the park. Be prepared: because of the size, the lake can get quite windy. The campground provides access to short and multi-day canoe and kayaking trips. Whitewater kayaking on the adjacent Cariboo and Quesnel rivers is also an option. A good sandy beach and public dock provide excellent swimming opportunities, and fishing for rainbow trout, char and kokanee is good in the park. There is also a playground, a baseball diamond and grassy playing areas.

Additional information

I have not visited this campground, which is more than a little out of the way, but in researching it I found that the area was once a rendezvous point for trappers and fur traders, first included on Hudson's Bay Company maps in 1832. Gold was discovered in 1858 in Cedar Creek, which runs through the park, and there is a small outdoor mining museum with old mining machinery and mock mine shafts. If you are looking for an out-of-the-way location for a while, this could be just the spot.

DOWNING

Location

The scenery at this 100-hectare park is quite lovely. Mount Bowman, which can be seen to the north, is, at 2,243 metres, the highest mountain in the Marble Range. Downing Provincial Park almost completely encircles Kelly Lake and is located 18 kilometres southwest of Clinton off Highway 97 on a paved road. Services are available in the quaint town of Clinton and include restaurants, a post office, a grocery store, a pub, a bakery, gas station and an ice cream store.

Facilities

There are 18 campsites on an open grassy area next to the lake, with limited space for RVs. Facilities are restricted to the basics (drinking water, picnic tables, fire pits, pit toilets), and there's a 20-metre walk from the parking lot to the camping area. There is no sani-station and only limited wheelchair accessibility.

Recreational activities

Things to do here include fishing for rainbow trout, hiking, swimming and sunbathing on the small beach. There is a boat launch at Kelly Lake and canoeing and kayaking are possible. The nearby community of Clinton has a small museum and excellent ice cream shop and is a pleasant place to while away a few hours. The town also boasts the largest log building in BC, which is a combination hotel, pub and restaurant. It offers a really good breakfast and is a pleasant place to play pool in the evening should you decide to escape from your tent for a while.

Additional information

Located on Shuswap First Nation land, Downing Park was donated to the province by C.S. Downing in 1970, and his family still owns the adjoining property. BC Rail runs along one side of the lake, so you may be lulled to sleep by the sound of trains. If you don't have time to stay here, this site is an ideal spot to rest, picnic and bathe, and is particularly inviting to travellers who have taken the unpaved road between Pavilion, north of Lillooet, to Clinton. Drivers should be warned that the unpaved road between Downing Park and Pavilion is at times very steep and has hairpin bends that can be nerve-racking, but Pavilion has a beautiful little church well worth a photograph.

GREEN LAKE

Location

The Green Lake area was recognized as bountiful by Canada's indigenous population many years ago; today, campers of every age continue to appreciate its bounty. Green Lake Provincial Park is situated among groves of aspen and lodgepole pine, 15 kilometres northeast of 70 Mile House off a paved road and adjacent to the 14-kilometre lake from which it takes its name. Three campgrounds are available on both sides of the lake. Information about the exact location of the campgrounds is available at the road junction 10 kilometres east of 70 Mile House. Services are available at 70 Mile House, and a store and restaurant are located at Emerald Bay.

Facilities

Each of Green Lake's three campgrounds has something different to offer. The most popular, Arrowhead, is fairly open and relatively small, with just 16 spots, all situated on the beachfront. (Probably the best family swimming is to be found here.) The second camping area is Emerald Bay. Like Arrowhead, Emerald Bay is situated on North Green Lake Road, but it has 51 sites, several of them on the water's edge. Sunset View, on South Green Lake Road, has 54 sites and is usually the last campground to fill up. All campsites are relatively private and situated amongst aspen trees. There is a nearby sani-station (with adjacent flush toilets) and the pit toilets at Emerald Bay and Sunset View campgrounds are wheelchair-accessible. Reservations are accepted at the Sunset View and Emerald Bay campgrounds.

Recreational activities

Boredom should not be a problem here, as there are numerous activities to entertain every age group. The lake has moderately good fishing for rainbow trout and is restocked annually. There are two boat launches (one at Sunset View, the other at the Little Arrowhead picnic site) and waterskiing is allowed, but boats and skiers should keep well away from the swimming areas. There are children's playgrounds at both Emerald Bay and Sunset View, and hiking trails leading from the park. The shallow west area of the lake attracts numerous waterfowl and migratory birds and is a magnet for ornithologists. Horseshoe pits are located at each campground, but you have to bring your own horseshoes.

Additional information

Green Lake is 14 kilometres long and averages 1.5 kilometres in width. It has minimum outflow, which enables a high buildup of algae and other microorganisms. This, along with the composition of the water itself, gives the lake its greenish tinge. BC Parks suggests using the park in the spring, when large rainbow trout spawning in the creeks attract large numbers of bald eagles, and in the fall, when the aspens turn fantastic shades of red and orange, each occurrence being quite beautiful for those with an appreciative eye (and, hopefully, a camera at hand).

Horsefly Lake

Location

Horsefly Lake is a delightful 148-hectare provincial park set amongst an assortment of trees including western hemlock, redcedar, various types of spruce and subalpine fir. It is accessed by turning off Highway 97 at 150 Mile House and travelling 52 kilometres on paved road to Horsefly, then 13 kilometres along a good gravel road. Services at Horsefly include a café, grocery store and gas station.

Facilities

Horsefly Lake has 23 private vehicle-accessible sites in a coniferous forest, and seven walk-in tenting sites along the lakeshore. Up until recently, there were just the basic facilities (pit toilets, drinking water, picnic tables, fire pits) but coin-operated showers and laundry facilities were installed recently. One of the pit toilets is wheelchair-accessible.

Recreational activities

There is a short hike up to a lookout above the lake, and other park trails lead to Viewland Mountain and Eureka Park; details are available at the information board at the park entrance. Anglers visit the park to fish for rainbow trout in Horsefly Lake and in the smaller adjacent lakes. There's a boat launch so canoeing and boating are also possible, and the beach has a change room and roped-off area for swimmers. Just outside the community of Horsefly there are spawning channels for salmon, with a system of dikes for walking and viewing. The best viewing is in mid-September when the salmon are spawning, and there are often festivals that month to celebrate the return of the sockeye. There is also a horseshoe pit and basketball hoop in the day-use area.

Additional information

This area was once a centre for gold mining. The first gold in the Cariboo was discovered here in 1859, and even today some people arc drawn to the area in search of gold. Horsefly was originally called Harper's Camp after one of the early settlers, but was renamed by later pioneers when they discovered one of the area's drawbacks. Seriously, don't be put off by the name. Recent information supplied by the park's administration notes that there are few biting flies in the park, and when I visited in June 2002, there were none (there were also no other campers). The park covers a considerable area, most of which is semi-wilderness and inaccessible to the visitor. More recent visits have shown this provincial park and the area to be loved by fishers.

LAC LA HACHE

Location

Lac la Hache means "axe lake," and numerous stories have been advanced to explain how this name came to be. According to one, the name is based on the shape of the lake; another story holds that it gained its name when a trapper lost his axe through the frozen lake when trying to reach into the water. To local First Nations people, the lake is known as *Kumatakwa*, which means "chief" or "queen of the waters." Whichever name you prefer, this is a wonderful provincial park. It's situated 13 kilometres north of the community of Lac la Hache on Highway 97. Services can be found in Lac la Hache, and there is a small store opposite the campground, which has been open whenever I have visited or driven past.

Facilities

There are 83 campsites here and good facilities, including wheelchair-accessible flush toilets, tap water and a sani-station. All sites are large, relatively private and set in open Douglas fir and aspen woodlands. Some sites are close to the road, however, and it is possible there to hear the traffic from busy Highway 97. You can reserve campsites at this park, but when I visited in August 2007, spaces were readily available and park staff said reservations are not really necessary.

Recreational activities

Small trails lead around the park, which allow you to see and walk remnants of the historic Cariboo Wagon Road. There is an adventure playground and a self-guided interpretive trail. There is a boat launch, and the lake is popular for waterskiing, boating and fishing. Rainbow trout, kokanee and burbot can be caught here. There is a pebbly beach and excellent swimming to be had in fairly weed-free water. A change house and showers are located near the beach, which is on the other side of the highway from the campground but connected to it by a tunnel since 2004. Three kilometres north of the campground is the Cariboo Nature Park, which is an excellent location for birdwatching. Lac la Hache also claims to be BC's longest town. Unfortunately, with the exception of some small cafés and restaurants, I find there is little in the town to attract visitors.

Additional information

I am sentimentally attached to this park, as it was the first BC provincial park I ever stayed in. That time, and on the rare occasions I have had the opportunity to visit again, I have been impressed by the friendly and informative camp hosts. The lack of other provincial parks on Highway 97 coupled with this one's good family facilities make it a popular location. The small store is a magnet for children walking to and from the lake, and during the early evening pop and candy seem to be the store's most popular wares. Swimmer's itch can be a problem here in July and August, and the dreaded mosquito is often around in the evenings.

Ten Mile Lake

Location

Looking for somewhere to camp with children? Then look no further than Ten Mile Lake Provincial Park. Situated in an area of pine and aspen forest 11 kilometres north of Quesnel on Highway 97, the park's large campground is popular with both RVers and tenters, and it is particularly appealing for those with little ones to entertain. Services are available in Quesnel, and a small store in the park sells chips, pop, ice cream, bread, milk and other supplies.

Facilities

Ten Mile Lake has two campgrounds with a total of 144 campsites offering excellent facilities: Lakeside (62 spots) is near the lakeshore and Touring (82 slightly larger spots) is set among pine trees. Both campgrounds offer flush toilets and a pressurized water system, but Lakeside also has pay-to-use showers (coin-operated: $1.00 for four minutes) and wheelchair-accessible flush toilets. There are a number of pull-through sites and a sani-station near the park's entrance. Reservations are accepted

Recreational activities

As is common among the larger provincial parks, a variety of leisure pursuits for both old and young are available, but 260-hectare Ten Mile Lake is particularly attractive for those with children. There is a playground and horseshoe pits, and a gently sloping beach gives swimmers easy access to the lake. There is a boat launch, and fishers can cast their lines for rainbow trout. An extensive 10-kilometre network of trails leads explorers through mixed forest; the trail to a huge beaver dam and lodge is only half a kilometre long and well worth the effort. Mountain bikes can be ridden on a number of oher trails. Ducks Unlimited has placed nesting boxes in the area to encourage avian wildlife. When I visited the park, I discovered musical jam sessions taking place in the pavilion. Ten Mile Lake also has park hosts, who welcome campers, answer questions and give advice.

Additional information

At the start of the 1900s, Ten Mile Lake was a milepost for the Pacific Great Eastern Railway, evidence of which can still be seen in the day-use area. This campground is a delight, as there are numerous activities within the park itself, as well as in the immediate vicinity. The town of Quesnel, named after Jules Maurice Quesnelle, a member of Simon Fraser's exploration party, is only a short distance away. It is rich in pioneer gold-rush history and has a museum, historical markers and, for those less interested in the past, a couple of golf courses. When we stayed here in 2004, we met Gord, the wonderful park administrator, who told me that in the summertime, he works from 5:30 a.m. to 11:00 p.m. When we returned two years later, he was still there offering his brilliant service. Keep it up, Gord, campers like me really appreciate your efforts!

Ts'yl-os

Location

Do not expect to explore much of Ts'yl-os (pronounced "sigh-loss") when you visit, as this provincial park, approximately 200 kilometres from Williams Lake, is roughly the size of Prince Edward Island (233,240 hectares) and, for the most part, is a vast undeveloped wilderness. There are huge mountains, glaciers, clear blue lakes, waterfalls and meadows, many of which are inaccessible to the common camper. Ts'yl-os is accessed either from Highway 20 at Hanceville by driving 150 kilometres of rough gravel road, or from Tatla Lake via a 60-kilometre slightly better rough gravel road (which is the only option for those without a four-wheel-drive vehicle). Both routes take 4–6 hours from Williams Lake, and BC Parks actually recommends using four-wheel-drive vehicles in the park. Limited services are available at Tatla Lake.

Facilities

There are 16 campsites at the Nu Chugh Beniz site on the east side of Chilko (reached by driving in from Hanceville), and 8 "rustic" ones at the Gwa Da Ts'ih at the north end of the lake (reached by driving in from Tatla Lake). Campers staying at Nu Chugh Beniz have access to gas, propane, laundry and Internet access at the Nemiah Valley Tl'ebayi Community Centre while those staying at Gwa Da Ts'ih are close to commercial lodges, where they may find meals and basic supplies. BC Parks informed me that Gwa Da Ts'ih may be closed during the salmon season because of the threat of bears (mid-August to mid-September). Reservations aren't accepted, and despite its away-from-it-all location, the campgrounds do get full.

Recreational activities

The most popular recreational activity here is fishing. At 50 kilometres long, Chilko Lake is the largest natural high-elevation freshwater lake in North America and has lake and rainbow trout and Dolly Varden. Other activities include hiking and wildlife viewing. BC Parks does not recommend canoeing, as the lake is frequently prone to rough conditions. For those who really want to get a feel of the place, a five-day hiking trail leads through the Yohetta Valley, Spectrum Pass and Tchaikazan Valley. (To make arrangements to undertake this route, contact Ts'yl-os Park Lodge at 1-800-487-9567.) There are also horseback riding opportunities.

Additional information

The park takes its name from the mountain, Mount Tatlow, which stands over 3,000 metres high. Legend tells how a man, his wife and six children watch over the people of the Tsilhqot'in First Nation and intervene when necessary. A number of private lodges operate in the area for those who want to experience the park in relative luxury.

TWEEDSMUIR (SOUTH)

Location

It is not just people who are attracted to this area. In salmon-spawning season, grizzly bears can often be seen fishing in the numerous streams that flow through Tweedsmuir, so be careful. When we visited, there were numerous "Beware of Bears" signs and posters with instructions for safe camping. Tweedsmuir, one of the largest parks in the province at 506,000 hectares, is named after the 15th Governor General of Canada, John Buchan, Baron Tweedsmuir of Elsfield, who travelled in the area in 1937 and was impressed by its beauty. The park is divided into north and south regions, but only the south is accessible by road. The southern section is located on Highway 20, approximately 400 kilometres west of Williams Lake and 50 kilometres east of Bella Coola (which can be reached from Vancouver Island by taking the ferry from Port Hardy). Services are found in Bella Coola. There is also a small lodge in the park.

Facilities

There are two campgrounds accessible from Highway 20: Atnarko is 28 kilometres from the eastern entrance of the park and has 24 sites set amidst a grove of old-growth Douglas fir, while the Fisheries campground is located near to Stuie, 44 kilometres from the park's eastern entrance, and has 12 high-density open sites. Facilities at both sites are basic (picnic tables, fire pits, pit toilets, pump water). There is a sani-station near Atnarko.

Recreational activities

As one would expect in a provincial park of this size, there is a wealth of things to see and do. The park is home to a wide variety of wildlife, including deer, moose, caribou, black and grizzly bears, wolves and cougars. Rainbow trout, cutthroat trout and Dolly Varden are found in the park's many lakes and streams, while the Atnarko and Dean rivers are spawning grounds for trout and salmon. Water sports including swimming (although the water is very cold), canoeing and kayaking. The area is known as one of BC's most outstanding for alpine hiking, and numerous trails take backpacking enthusiasts into the spectacular mountain scenery. Rustic wilderness campsites exist along these trails. For the less energetic, a number of less arduous day hikes are also available. The park is also popular for horseback riding.

Additional information

With some superb scenery and varied terrain, the South Tweedsmuir area definitely is worthy of more than an overnight stop. The area is a real delight for those who enjoy backcountry exploration. Details of all the facilities and activities available can be obtained from the park's headquarters near the Atnarko River campground. Tweedsmuir's two vehicle-accessible campgrounds are very much adult-oriented but ideal if you're a serious outdoorsperson.

Naikoon Provincial Park on the Queen Charlotte Islands is a photographer's paradise.

Tyhee Lake's campsites are suitable for all sizes of RVs. (BC Parks photo)

NORTHERN BC

Famous for excellent fishing and big game, the Northern BC region stretches from the Canadian Rockies to the Pacific Ocean and incorporates mountain ranges, deep valleys, majestic fjords, glaciers, dense forests, lakes and rivers. In addition to its natural beauty, it is an area rich in First Nations history and culture. Although there are not a lot of large settlements, excellent wildlife viewing opportunities compensate for the lack of people, and travellers are usually blessed with an open road. Even at the peak of summer it is not unusual to drive for 30 minutes without seeing another vehicle. This region includes campgrounds accessible from the minor roads leading off the Trans-Canada/Yellowhead Highway (Highway 16) and from the highway itself west of McBride, all the way to and including the Queen Charlotte Islands. This region also encompasses Highway 37, a mix of gravel and paved road that goes from Kitimat to the road's junction with the Alaska Highway, and Highway 97 north of Prince George, which leads all the way to Dawson Creek and beyond, following the Alaska Highway up to the Yukon border. Finally, it includes Highway 29 from Fort St. John to Tumbler Ridge and Highway 2. So hop in your car or RV and go enjoy a region of BC that feels like it has been created with only you in mind.

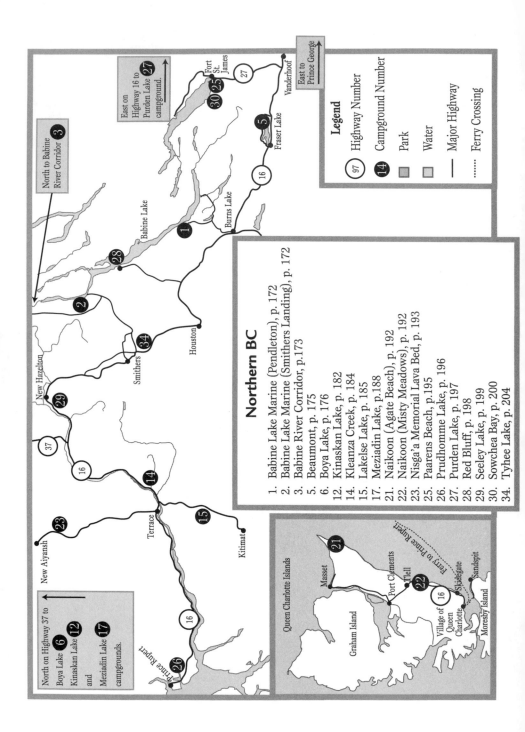

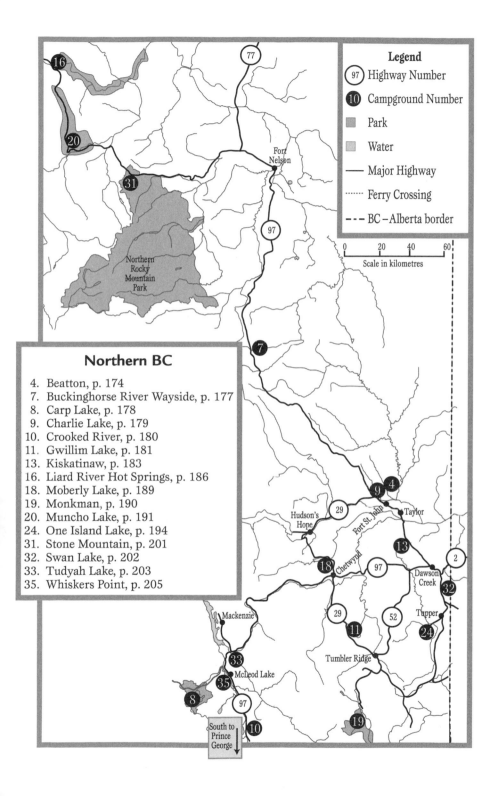

Legend

- (97) Highway Number
- (10) Campground Number
- ▪ Park
- ▪ Water
- —— Major Highway
- ······ Ferry Crossing
- —·—· BC–Alberta border

0   20   40   60
Scale in kilometres

Fort Nelson

Northern Rocky Mountain Park

Northern BC

Hudson's Hope

Fort St. John

Taylor

Chetwynd

Dawson Creek

Mackenzie

Tupper

Tumbler Ridge

Tudyah Lake

McLeod Lake

South to Prince George

BABINE LAKE MARINE

Location

Campers who choose to stay on the banks of the longest natural lake in BC have the choice of three campgrounds: two are in Babine Lake Marine Provincial Park, while the third is in Red Bluff Provincial Park (described separately). Babine Lake's two campgrounds are Pendleton Bay at the southern end of the lake and Smithers Landing to the north. To reach Pendleton Bay, turn off Highway 16 at Burns Lake and travel 35 kilometres north on a gravel road. To reach Smithers Landing, turn off Highway 16 at Smithers and travel 35 kilometres northeast on a gravel road. Services are available in Burns Lake and Smithers, and Tukii Lodge has a store near Smithers Landing.

Facilities

The two camping locations provide 28 sites: 20 at Pendleton Bay and 8 at Smithers Landing, some under the cover of trees and others at the edge of the beach. Facilities are rudimentary and consist of pit toilets, water access, picnic tables and fire pits.

Recreational activities

The BC Parks website says this park is "ideal for those wanting a slower pace," and the two campgrounds on Babine Lake are perfect for those who want to get away from it all and fish. If you prefer other recreational pursuits, you should stay somewhere else. Both campgrounds have boat launches, and Babine Lake provides angling opportunities for rainbow trout and char. Because of the park's somewhat remote location, Babine Lake campers have an opportunity to see a wide array of wildlife, including moose and bear. Swimming and sailing can also be enjoyed here. Numerous commercial resorts in the area offer fishing, canoeing, horseback riding and skiing excursions.

Additional information

The distance to these campgrounds and their limited facilities dissuade some people from coming to Babine Lake. But if you can undertake the drive, the scenery and tranquility are very rewarding. Bears frequent the area, so you must take all the necessary precautions for storing food. The community of Burns Lake, originally called Burnt Lake after a nearby fire, now serves as the major retail source of fishing equipment and supplies. The town of Smithers is larger and a little more geared toward tourists. It has a delightful main street to wander along that has restaurants, stores specializing in merchandise for enjoying the outdoors (including rainwear) and gift shops.

BABINE RIVER CORRIDOR

Location

This park must win an award for being one of the most remote provincial parks in the province with vehicle-accessible camping facilities; however, if your passion is fishing or wildlife, particularly bears, this is the place for you! The nearest town is Smithers, 130 kilometres away. Access the park from Smithers by taking Babine Lake Road east, then taking a gravel Nilkitkwa Forest Service Road for 58 kilometres.

Facilities

Four kilometres from the 14,523-hectare park's entrance is a small vehicle-accessible campground with 10 spots and basic facilties (picnic tables, fire pits, drinking water and pit toilets). Because of the prevalence of bears in the area, all food and garbage must be stored in a vehicle, dogs must be kept on a leash, and children should be with adults at all times. Wilderness camping is permitted, if you are brave enough.

Recreational activities

The primary pastime here is fishing. There is a boat launch in the park and BC Parks describes "world-class angling opportunities" for steelhead and sockeye salmon. Rafting and kayaking opportunities exist, and there are commercial operators offering guided trips in the park. Be warned: the river can be quite challenging. Hiking is also possible.

Additional information

While this provincial park has all the facilities required to be included in this guide, it is very remote and I have not camped here or even visited. However, in undertaking the research for this guide, it seems the area is spectacular for fishing. It is not only anglers who seek fish: numerous grizzly bears inhabit the area and are frequent visitors to the park; indeed, the park is closed for fishing for one hour after sunrise and one hour before sunset as BC Parks claims this "gives the bears some time to fish during daylight hours without the disturbance of humans." Anyone with a bear phobia may want to go elsewhere.

BEATTON

Location

For the angler, Beatton Provincial Park boasts the best fishing for walleye in British Columbia. For those who do not fish, Beatton is a lovely camping retreat that has been enjoyed by campers for decades. Established on September 14, 1934, this is one of BC's oldest provincial parks. Beatton is located 13 kilometres northwest of Fort St. John off Highway 97 on a paved road access. Limited services can be found along Highway 97, but a more comprehensive range is available at Fort St. John.

Facilities

Thirty-seven campsites are found here on the eastern side of Charlie Lake, set among poplar and spruce trees. Some spots are on the lakeside; all are large and very private. There is no sani-station and facilities are restricted to the basics (fire pits, drinking water, pit toilets and picnic tables). Some park facilities are wheelchair-accessible and reservations are accepted.

Recreational activities

Aspen-lined trails lead from the campground to a 300-metre beach on the banks of Charlie Lake, which is suitable for waterskiing, windsurfing and paddling. Although it is possible to swim, the high algae content of the lake at times may make it unappealing. A boat launch is available, and there is excellent fishing for northern pike and walleye. In addition to over 40 species of birds and waterfowl, moose, mule and white-tailed deer can be seen in the park. Hikers will enjoy the 12 kilometres of trails and mountain bikers have 12 kilometres of cross-country ski trails available to them in the summer. Beatton Provincial Park also has an adventure playground in the day-use area, a horseshoe pit and a baseball field.

Additional information

Nearby Charlie Lake Provincial Park has similar facilities, but I prefer Beatton. This 310-hectare park is not just popular in summer: during the colder months, visitors can go tobogganing, cross-country skiing, ice fishing for walleye and northern pike, and snowshoeing. Both moose and deer frequent the park during winter months. The park provides "warm-up huts" (which, for someone from the south of the province, conjure wonderful images).

BEAUMONT

Location

This 192-hectare provincial park is located on Fraser Lake, west of Vanderhoof, 134 kilometres from Prince George on Highway 16. Early people named the area "Natleh" and used trails in this area to trade with the people of neighbouring settlements. During the last century, fur traders used the same trails. The remains of Fort Fraser, which was established by Simon Fraser in 1806, are situated within the park. Food, gas and accommodation are available just a few kilometres away at Fort Fraser to the west of the park, or at Fraser Lake to the east.

Facilities

There are 49 large campsites at this location. Some are quite open and exposed and others are situated amongst trees. The park has a sani-station, flush toilets and facilities for those in wheelchairs (including accessible flush toilets). Reservations are accepted.

Recreational activities

A range of recreational activities is available, including swimming in a designated swimming area (a change house is located close to the beach), sunbathing, windsurfing, boating and fishing for kokanee, char, burbot, rainbow trout and sturgeon. There is a boat launch in the park, but boaters should be aware that strong winds can easily transform the generally calm waters of Fraser Lake and cause a serious hazard. In addition, there are hiking trails, a children's play area, a volleyball net and horseshoe pits. Information on the park's notice board informs campers that bears, wolves and moose inhabit the area.

Additional information

The campground is surrounded by the Hazelton, Skeena and Omineca mountains and is set amidst an abundance of willow, poplar, birch, spruce and aspen trees. The site was originally chosen by early pioneers for its commanding view and because of the breezes that kept mosquitoes at bay. When I visited in late August, there were no signs of the dreaded bug; other campers, however, may tell a different story. Beaumont is an ideal location to stop for a picnic or take a stroll. The play area and beach make it particularly attractive for parents who have young children to entertain, with sandy shores and clear waters adjacent to a grassy picnic area. This campground never feels busy or crowded—an ideal place for every age group.

Boya Lake

Location

A stunningly beautiful sight awaits the camper who heads for Boya Lake, described by BC Parks as a "must-see" location. The lake is remarkable for its clarity and aquamarine colour, the result of light being reflected from the lake bottom, which is composed of silt and shell fragments. In this regard Boya is quite unlike the lakes found in many other BC provincial parks, and it is a wonderful lake to photograph. Boya Lake Provincial Park is situated 150 kilometres north of Dease Lake and 34 kilometres from the Cassiar–Alaska Highway junction, which is where the nearest services are located. Two kilometres of gravel road (rudimentary when we visited in 2004) east of Highway 37 lead to the campground itself, which sits adjacent to Boya Lake and affords truly spectacular views of the Cassiar Mountains.

Facilities

Boya Lake has 44 spaces of a variety of shapes and sizes. Some are close to the lake, some are just for tents, and most are private and set amongst black and white spruce trees. There is no sani-station and only basic facilities (picnic tables, pit toilets, drinking water, fire pits).

Recreational activities

Because the lake is so clear, fishing here is not good for the serious angler, although my children had a ball catching small toe-biters. Fishing for grayling can be enjoyed a short distance away, in Dease River. A short 1.5-kilometre lakeside trail introduces the multitude of songbirds and waterfowl attracted to the area by its topography, vegetation and mild climate. Moose and beaver are found in the park, as are mountain goats and caribou. The lake is ideal for boating (as long as you observe the 10-horsepower-motor restriction) and swimming (although the water's somewhat cold), and photographers will enjoy the mix of spectacular scenery and plant life. In 2004, we found park administrators had built a small children's play area.

Additional information

The quietest campground on Highway 37, Boya Lake also seems to have been personally cared for. For example, a box where campers can deposit and select reading material is placed at the entrance. I love these personal touches; they make camping special. In 2004, the four-day weather forecast was posted on the campground notice board—again, a lovely touch. The main draw of this campground, though, is still the crystal-clear lake and stunning views. Boya is a gorgeous place to camp.

BUCKINGHORSE RIVER WAYSIDE

Location

Buckinghorse River Wayside Provincial Park's campground is oriented very much toward overnighters travelling the Alaska Highway. When I stayed, I recognized a number of vehicles that I had passed or that had passed me during the course of the day. The campground is located 200 kilometres northwest of Fort St. John at Mile 173 of the highway. A restaurant and gas station are conveniently situated near the campground.

Facilities

One of the better roadside campgrounds, Buckinghorse River Wayside has a different "feel" as the local community manages it cooperatively with BC Parks. There are 33 spots here, all with a view of the river. They are quite closely positioned with no interspersed vegetation and have little privacy; the better ones are toward the end of the campground. Because the campsite is set a short distance away from the highway, noise is not a problem. All the basic amenities are provided (fire pits, drinking water, pit toilets, picnic tables), and some park facilities are wheelchair-accessible.

Recreational activities

This campground is primarily for travellers en route to other destinations, so there are limited recreational activities. There is a boat launch and the river provides an opportunity to fish for Arctic grayling, and if you take a short walk downstream you can find areas in which to swim. As is the case in many provincial parks in the north, it is possible to spend hours stargazing. The sky seems bigger in this area of the world. Peaceful evenings with only the noise of flowing waters and a crackling fire provide the ideal setting for this astronomical pursuit.

Additional information

BC Parks warns that both black bears and grizzly bears inhabit the area, so caution must be exercised. During the winter months, moose graze here. For those who do not wish to cook their own breakfast or dinner, there is a restaurant conveniently located across the road from the campground. Although the camping spots are close to each other, when I stayed (early September), there were only 10 spots taken, so it did not feel crowded.

CARP LAKE

Location

Why not camp on top of the world? At an elevation of 841 metres, Carp Lake is a picturesque island-dotted lake covering over 38,000 hectares of the Nechako Plateau. Two hours' drive north of Prince George, the park is accessed by turning off Highway 97 at McLeod Lake and then travelling along a gravel road for 32 kilometres. This gravel road is single lane and not particularly good in places. There are a number of tight corners, and the route is not suitable for cars or trailers during the spring breakup period. Services can be found at Prince George and McLeod Lake.

Facilities

This provincial park has two campgrounds from which to choose. Carp Lake, the main one, is situated at Kettle Bay and has a sani-station and 90 large sites that can accommodate most recreational vehicles. At the east end of War Lake, there are 12 smaller sites, which are not suitable for larger vehicles. If you have a boat, wilderness camping is possible on three of the islands in Carp Lake. There is no wheelchair access and the facilities are the basic ones found in parks of this type (fire pits, drinking water, pit toilets, picnic tables).

Recreational activities

Visitors do not lack for something to do here. Two sandy beaches are located along the beach trail, a 20- and a 40-minute walk from the main campground respectively. Boat launches are available at both campgrounds, and powerboating and canoeing can be enjoyed on the lake. Fishing is good, as rainbow trout, burbot and northern squawfish are plentiful in the lake. There's also a short trail to McLeod River that leads anglers to an ideal fly-fishing spot. In addition, there are numerous trails for those who wish to hike or mountain bike. One of these trails follows a section of a route used long ago by the Carrier First Nation between Fort McLeod and Fort Stewart. Wildlife viewing is good, and moose are often seen at the lake, especially at dawn and dusk. The main campground has a playground and horseshoe pit.

Additional information

In his journal of 1806, Simon Fraser wrote of the Carrier people who visited the area to catch large quantities of fish similar to carp. The park is still a magnet for those who enjoy fishing. The summertime temperature at Carp Lake can be cool, averaging 12–18°C in July, and can drop considerably at night, so be sure to bring enough warm clothing.

Charlie Lake

Location
Naturalists love this area for the chance of seeing a wide variety of wildlife, including white-tailed and mule deer, black bears, beavers, moose and an array of waterfowl. It is easy to see why this provincial park situated on the southwestern shore of Charlie Lake in the broad valley of the Peace River is popular with both locals and visitors. It is conveniently located 11 kilometres north of Fort St. John on the Alaska Highway at its junction with Highway 29. All services can be found at Fort St. John, while more limited facilities are available closer to the campground on Highway 97.

Facilities
The 58-site campground is set amongst a heavily treed deciduous forest of aspen, birch, alder, lodgepole pine and spruce on the southwestern shore of the 13-kilometre Charlie Lake. A few sites are located close to the road, but most are not. The well-appointed sites are large and suitable for every type of recreational vehicle; some have grassy areas for tents. There is also a sani-station and a wheelchair-accessible pit toilet. Reservations are accepted.

Recreational activities
Fishing in summer and winter is popular here; northern pike and walleye inhabit the lake. BC Parks calls Charlie Lake the walleye "hot spot" of the province (what a claim to fame!). A 2-kilometre trail leads from the campground to the lakeside day-use area, where there is a boat launch. You can swim in the lake, although the high algae content of the water may put you off. The campground has a play area for children and a horseshoe pit. During the peak summer months, interpretive programs are offered. For those who choose activities away from the campground, an 18-hole golf course and country club can be found at Mile 54 of the Alaska Highway.

Additional information
Archaeological research in the area has revealed First Nations habitation dating back 10,000 years. If you succeed in obtaining a campsite away from the road, Charlie Lake is a delightful place to camp. A variety of berries grow in the vicinity, but remember that picking the vegetation in BC parks is prohibited.

CROOKED RIVER

Location

There are two kinds of campgrounds: those geared for overnight camping and those where you want to spend time relaxing and overdosing on BC's wonderful scenery. Crooked River falls into the second category. This delightful spot is found in the Fraser Basin amid a forest of lodgepole pine interspersed with alder, birch, aspen and spruce. Recently, the area has been ravaged by the mountain pine beetle, which can be easily evidenced by the numerous brown trees in the area of the park. Crooked River is situated 70 kilometres north of Prince George on Highway 97. The nearby community of Bear Lake provides accommodation, gas and food (try the Grizzly Inn for a good breakfast).

Facilities

There are 90 spots of various sizes here. A tarmac approach road gives way to a gravel road upon entering the camping area. As with all BC provincial-park campgrounds, a map at the entrance to the park illustrates where the largest sites are and where the pull-throughs are located. Some sites overlook the lake, and trees provide privacy and shade. There is a sani-station, as well as flush and pit toilets and showers. Some park facilities, including the washrooms, are wheelchair-accessible. During the peak summer months, campers register at a booth upon entering the park. Reservations are accepted.

Recreational activities

The park is on Bear Lake, which has two good sandy beaches ideal for children. It is possible to canoe and kayak, and boats can be rented in the park. With powerboats prohibited, paddlers are assured of a tranquil visit, as are windsurfers. Fishing is good and not just confined to Bear Lake: nearby Squaw and Hart lakes and Crooked River have rainbow and brook trout, Dolly Varden, Arctic grayling and whitefish. There are a number of trails that take about an hour to complete, as well as longer hikes. The trail around Squaw Lake is great for viewing wildlife and birds (amateur ornithologists may be rewarded by sightings of bald eagles and ospreys), while the Crooked River Trail follows the same route that early Canadian explorers, such as Simon Fraser and Alexander Mackenzie, took in the 19th century. Youngsters will enjoy the park's adventure playground, volleyball court and horseshoe pits.

Additional information

BC Parks literature states that Crooked River Provincial Park was originally established to protect the area's attractive lakes and surrounding landscape. I stayed at this location in June one year and got completely bitten from head to toe by mosquitoes, despite dressing in layers of clothing and standing over the fire pit. This experience tainted my opinion of the park, although I have not had the same problem on subsequent visits.

Gwillim Lake

Location

With its stunning location, 32,458-hectare Gwillim Lake Provincial Park is definitely a place to include on your camping itinerary. Set in the Rocky Mountain foothills, at an elevation of 765 metres, the park offers breathtaking mountain views and 25 kilometres of shoreline. It is found on Highway 29, a 40-minute drive from Chetwynd to the north and Tumbler Ridge to the south. Services are available in both these centres.

Facilities

Gwillim Lake's 49 campsites are located in an area lightly forested with pines; many have commanding views of the lake and the Rocky Mountains. There are also numerous walk-in camping spots. All the basic facilities found within BC parks are available (fire pits, drinking water, pit toilets, picnic tables), and some park facilities are wheelchair-accessible. No sani-station is provided.

Recreational activities

A perfectly wonderful time can be had here just reading, relaxing and enjoying the beauty of BC, but Gwillim Lake also has a designated swimming area and a boat launch. Arctic grayling, northern pike, Dolly Varden, burbot and mountain whitefish can all be caught, although anglers should be warned that the deep blue waters of the lake do not yield fantastic fish populations. The park has hiking trails, too, and the area is very good for observing wildlife, particularly deer and moose, which are most often spotted in the early morning. For children, there is an adventure playground in the middle of the campground.

Additional information

This park provides some panoramic views of the Rocky Mountains. Above the northwestern shore, an open meadow creates a viewpoint of the western part of the lake. The park is beautiful to visit in the fall when the colours are spectacular, but it really is a gem of a location any time of the year. The town of Chetwynd is basically a forestry community with a relatively small population (under 3,000), yet it boasts a museum, a railway museum and a trapper's cabin—all open to the public. The town also displays a number of interesting chainsaw sculptures by BC artists.

KINASKAN LAKE

Location

For those who have bounced along the gravel section of Highway 37, the remote lakeside campground at 1,800-hectare Kinaskan Lake Provincial Park is a gift from the gods. Set in the south Stikine Plateau and Iskut River Valley between the Skeena and Coast mountains, this park is found 100 kilometres south of Dease Lake, the "jade capital of the world," which offers amenities such as gas, propane, food, lodging and a huge SuperValu store that has everything the camper needs. More limited amenities are available at Iskut, approximately 40 minutes north of Kinaskan Lake.

Facilities

The campground is situated in a desirable location on the lake itself, and a large number of the 50 campsites are on the water's edge where the views are wonderful. The sites, which are quite large and surrounded by trees, afford more privacy than those of Kinaskan Lake's nearest competitor, Meziadin Lake, which is a three-hour drive away. There is no sani-station and only the basic facilities exist (picnic tables, pit toilets, drinking water, fire pits).

Recreational activities

Lake fishing for rainbow trout in Kinaskan and Natasdeleen lakes is reputed to be excellent. For boaters, there is a floating wharf and a boat launch, and swimming is possible, although the lake is prone to high winds and waves that can develop quite suddenly. This is the provincial park closest to Mount Edziza Park, established to conserve spectacular volcanic landscapes that include lava flows, cinder fields and basalt plateaus. The Mowdade Trail leads from Kinaskan Lake to the Coffee Crater area of this 230,000-hectare park.

Additional information

This area also offers beautiful scenery and is a welcome rest for those who have endured the gravel section of Highway 37. It was established in 1987, and its remote location makes it a magnet for fishermen, moose, black and grizzly bears, wolves, coyotes, minks, goats and Stone sheep. Staying here lets campers see the BC featured in the tourist literature. I have only stopped to picnic here, which is a great pity, because it is a stunning location (if a little cool). There is little for children to do here, so I don't think I will be experiencing this campground fully for quite a few years.

KISKATINAW

Location

Kiskatinaw Provincial Park is located on the old Alaska Highway. Nearby, aromatic cottonwood trees on the edge of the river exude a delicate perfume in the summer (a delight for most people except those with allergies). Primarily used as an overnight camping spot, this 54-hectare provincial park is located on the northern Great Plains, 28 kilometres north of Dawson Creek. A 5-kilometre paved access road leads to the campground. Services can be found at Dawson Creek to the south or Taylor to the north.

Facilities

Kiskatinaw offers 28 spots, secluded in groves of poplar and spruce. Camping facilities are basic and include pit toilets, drinking water, fire pits and picnic tables but no sani-station or wheelchair access. Sites are reserved by calling the campground operator at (250) 843-0074.

Recreational activities

There are limited swimming possibilities, but the water is warm so tubing and wading are popular, and the campground has swings, a sandbox and a horseshoe pit. An archaeological site is also located in the park. From the campground you can walk to the scenic deep-walled canyon of the Kiskatinaw River and view the historic curved wooden bridge that was developed for the original Alaska Highway in 1942. The bridge was built in just nine months by a Canadian construction company and was the first curved wooden bridge built in Canada. It is 190 feet long with a banked nine-degree curve to conform to the bend of the highway and is the only curved banked trestle bridge remaining in western Canada.

Additional information

The town of Dawson Creek was established in 1931 when the Northern Alberta Railway Line was extended, and it flourished in 1942 when American soldiers and engineers arrived to build the Alaska Highway. Dawson Creek is now home to the Mile Zero Post, a 3-metre-high marker that identifies the beginning of the Alaska Highway, and the Dawson Creek Station Museum gives information on the construction of this famous road. Many tourists visit Dawson Creek to have their photographs taken at Mile Zero before heading north to the Yukon and Alaska.

Kleanza Creek

Location
At the beginning of the 20th century, the area around Kleanza Creek was inhabited by gold seekers. Some years later, in 1934, a 180-gram gold nugget was taken from the creek, and there may still be some more gold left. This wonderful peaceful campground is situated on Highway 16,15 kilometres east of Terrace, where all amenities can be found.

Facilities
Tall fir trees provide shade and privacy to the 32 large campsites of Kleanza Creek Provincial Park. Many sites overlook the clear bubbling waters of the creek itself—a calming sound that will lull you to sleep. Facilities are basic (pit toilets, drinking water, picnic tables, fire pits); there is limited wheelchair access and no sani-station.

Recreational activities
There is a relaxing ambience here. Leisure pursuits include a 1-kilometre trail leading up to a viewpoint above the creek, and there is also a smaller trail running alongside the creek. If you look hard, the remains of the Cassiar Hydraulic Mining Company's operations can be seen above the canyon. Pink salmon are often observed in the creek during the fall, and there is limited fishing potential. Swimming is possible in cool pools. The campground has a basketball hoop, horseshoe pit and checkerboards. If it happens to be raining, visit Mount Layton Hot Springs or the Heritage Park Museum in Terrace.

Additional information
Kleanza means "gold" in the Gitxsan language. Maybe it is because I visited this park during good weather, but the campground lives in my memory as serene and quite beautiful. Even if you are not intending to stay the night, the park is great for a picnic stop and BC Parks has conveniently placed benches to face the tumbling creek. The only note of caution is that bears occasionally pass through the area. Otherwise, a highly recommended and exquisite place to camp.

LAKELSE LAKE

Location

For people craving hot springs and camping, this is the place to be. Lakelse Lake Provincial Park is just 3 kilometres from Mount Layton Hot Springs, and given the comprehensive range of facilities the 354-hectare park offers, it is a very attractive camping location for all ages. Set amidst majestic old-growth forest and located 20 kilometres south of Terrace on Highway 37, the park provides a beautiful haven for travellers. Services are available either in Terrace or in Kitimat, 40 kilometres to the south.

Facilities

Within a forest of cedar, hemlock and Sitka spruce, the Furlong Bay campground offers 156 large, well-organized and well-maintained campsites catering to every type of recreational vehicle. A full range of facilities is provided, including a sani-station, flush toilets and showers. As well, the toilets, shower buildings and the Furlong Beach day-use area are wheelchair-accessible. Reservations are accepted.

Recreational activities

The lake offers excellent canoeing, sailing and waterskiing, and there is a paved boat launch. There are wonderful golden sandy beaches, picnic shelters and a children's playground. A 45-minute educational trail that leads through the park allows closer exploration of the old-growth forest, and there are also interpretive programs offered in the summer. In the lake, and in the nearby Skeena and Kitimat rivers, anglers can catch steelhead, rainbow trout, Dolly Varden and all five species of Pacific salmon. In August, hundreds of sockeye salmon can be seen in Williams Creek at the end of the park. The adjacent Mount Layton Hot Springs Resort has waterslides and mineral pools, as well as a café and pub. The resort offers $1.00 off the admission price to those camping in the provincial park. A 30-minute drive away, Kitimat offers a variety of activities, including tours of a salmon hatchery.

Additional information

Lakelse really is a delight to visit for the wide array of activities it provides both within the confines of the park's boundaries and in the larger vicinity. It is easy to spend an entire day at the hot springs: children (and some adults) will be entertained for hours by the resort's waterslides and play areas, while the older generation will appreciate soaking in the therapeutic waters of the springs, which are open well into the evening. I spent a wonderful Wednesday evening in mid-September being one of just six people enjoying the hot springs. After our soak, we played darts and shuffleboard in the pub over food and drinks. Returning to the uncrowded campground at 10:00 p.m., I was met at the gate by a BC Parks representative ready to collect my camping fee and ensure that I was having a good time, making me feel rather like a teenager whose father had waited up for her to return home!

LIARD RIVER HOT SPRINGS

Location

For any BC parks enthusiast, Liard River Hot Springs must be one of the biggest jewels in the crown. It certainly ranks as one of the top provincial parks for me. The only disadvantage to this beautiful park is that it is the most northerly in BC and therefore not easily accessible for most people. However, those who do travel as far as Mile 496 (Kilometre 765) on the Alaska Highway will be rewarded amply for their efforts. Liard River Hot Springs is situated 20 kilometres north of Muncho Lake and is the second-largest hot springs in Canada (after Banff). A restaurant and small shop are located across the road from the park itself, while more comprehensive services can be found at Muncho Lake.

Facilities

At Liard River Hot Springs there are 53 large, well-appointed and totally private campsites set amongst trees and suitable for every type of recreational vehicle. The park is wheelchair-accessible, but facilities are restricted to the basic ones (fire pits, drinking water, pit toilets, picnic tables) and there is no sani-station. There are also no showers . . . but here they aren't needed! Reservations are accepted.

Recreational activities

The park's biggest attraction is, of course, the hot springs, which have been beautifully maintained in their natural setting. A boardwalk takes campers from the campground to the two bathing pools, one an 8- and the other a

12-minute walk from the campground. Both have change rooms. At the larger Alpha pool, bathers can choose which area of the water to sit in and which temperature to endure (from an almost unbearable 52°C, where the waters emerge, to a far more comfortable heat). The smaller Beta circular pool is at a constant temperature (approximately 42°C). It is possible to swim here. In addition to these two mineral pools, a variety of fauna and flora unique to the region can be seen. More than 100 bird species visit the park. Moose and black bear also live here, and BC Parks literature states that over 28 species of mammals and 250 species of boreal forest plants are found here. A hanging garden displays this vegetation at certain times of the year, which is loved by photographers. For children, there is a play area, a horseshoe pit and interpretive programs in the summer.

Additional information

Travellers have enjoyed the hot springs here for centuries: many hundreds of years ago, the Kaska people bathed here, and in 1835 the waters were charted by Robert Campbell, a Hudson's Bay Company factor. In 1942, the American army stationed in the area to build the Alaska Highway constructed the first boardwalk to the pools. I have extremely affectionate memories of the one time I was lucky enough to stay here. We went to the hot pools at 7:00 a.m., before most people were up. A thunderstorm was passing, and we sat in the hot waters watching the lightning as the cold rain fell into the warm pools. After this therapeutic experience, we took our clean glowing bodies for breakfast in the funky little restaurant across the road from the campground—a perfect start to the day. Liard River Hot Springs is well worth a visit, and unlike many of the commercially developed hot springs in the south of the province, it remains in a totally natural environment. This is one of my favourite provincial parks; however, in 1997, two people were killed here in a bear attack and the park received some negative publicity. Such incidents are rare but remind us of the potential hazards in camping outdoors. The Beta Pool hot springs is now closed each year from approximately August 1 to May 1, in part because of bear activity. Liard River's hotsprings are ranked among the top five in North America, but if you don't camp here, you'll have to pay the day-use fee to access them (in 2008, the fee was $5 for adults, $3 for children or $10 for families).

Meziadin Lake

Location

Ever seen a live bear trap? When I visited Meziadin Lake, a trap was being kept at the park, although the BC Parks attendant informed me that it had not been used for a while. Meziadin Lake Provincial Park is in the Nass Basin and rewards the visitor with excellent views of the Coast Mountains. As you travel north from Highway 16, this is the first of three provincial park campgrounds on Highway 37. It is just south of Meziadin Junction, the turnoff for Stewart, which has a shop, café, gas station and tourist information. The park also has a small convenience store, but the widest range of services are found in Stewart, 50 kilometres to the west.

Facilities

This 335-hectare park has 66 open gravel campsites, which offer little privacy although a few are situated on the lakeshore and views of the lake are breathtaking. There is no sani-station, and because of the prevalence of bears in the area, garbage has to be stored in a concrete structure on the site and all items used for cooking, eating and drinking must be kept in a vehicle day and night. The pit toilets are wheelchair-accessible, and the park offered wireless Internet access in 2008. There is also a "travel trailer" that sleeps up to six people available (in 2008, the rate was $75.00/night), which can be booked by contacting the park facility operator at 1-866-500-7302.

Recreational activities

Recreational pursuits offered by the lake include swimming, boating and fishing for rainbow trout and Dolly Varden. There is a boat launch, a small dock and the nearby Meziadin River has a salmon-counting fence. The road to Stewart provides a breathtaking view of more than 20 glaciers, including Bear Glacier, which comes right down to the road. Stewart and Hyder are early gold- and silver-mining communities located 65 kilometres from the campground, and Stewart has a number of pleasant cafés and restaurants.

Additional information

This campground seems to be the busiest on Highway 37 and is a popular place for those interested in fishing. Bears are particularly active during the salmon-spawning season, so visiting Hyder at this time of year provides the best chance of seeing both black and grizzly bears. We spent an unforgettable three hours in Hyder watching grizzly bears fish salmon out of the stream, rip them apart and devour them. It is an image I will never forget. When we got back to our tent at 8:00 p.m., it was dark and raining heavily. A couple in a neighbouring RV took pity on us and invited us in for the remains of their chicken stew and alcohol. We retired to our tent two very happy campers. We stayed again in August 2004, swam in the lake with a beaver, had brilliant weather and saw grizzly and black bears. A truly wonderful location.

Moberly Lake

Location

This campground is well maintained and a real delight to stay in, but at certain times of the year watch out for black bears, which feed on the abundant berries growing in the area. Positioned in the valley of the Moberly River on the south shore of the lake, between the foothills of the Rocky Mountains and the northern Great Plains, Moberly Lake Provincial Park is reached by turning off Highway 29, 24 kilometres northeast of Chetwynd, and taking a good gravel road 3 kilometres. All services are available at Chetwynd, 25 kilometres away, and more limited ones are at the Moberly Lake townsite, 11 kilometres from the campground.

Facilities

One hundred and nine large private camping spots set in a forest of mature white spruce and aspen make this a desirable destination. Streams flow through the campground and a few sites overlook the lake. Grassy sites are available, and there is ample space for the longest RV. There is a sani-station, some facilities are wheelchair-accessible, and reservations are accepted.

Recreational activities

A number of activities can be undertaken both within the 104-hectare park and in the surrounding area. The park has a boat launch, and it is possible to fish for Dolly Varden, whitefish and char. A developed beach and changing facilities make swimming a delight. There are also a number of walks and trails, and a children's play area has been built near the lake. A wealth of bird life can be observed in the area, including bald eagles, American kestrels, belted kingfishers and common loons. Close to the park, the W.A.C. Bennett Dam, one of the largest earth-filled dams in the world, houses a visitor centre with interpretive programs and a restaurant, and the nearby Peace Canyon Dam is also well worth a visit. There are also opportunities to go golfing in the area.

Additional information

Moberly Lake was named after Henry Moberly, a trader and trapper working for the Hudson's Bay Company, who settled on the shores of the lake in the mid-1800s. It has special significance to the Dunne-za First Nation, who knew it as "the lake that you could depend on" because it was a consistent food source. They also believed it had a hole in its bottom (or, no bottom at all) and that a mythical creature lived in the lake—so be careful when you go swimming . . .

MONKMAN

Location

Monkman Provincial Park is a wonderland of waterfalls and scenic lakes surrounded by the Hart Range of the central Rocky Mountains. The park was established in 1981; 22,000 hectares were added in 1999 to take in the Upper Fontiniko Creek Valley and Limestone Lakes area, which contains an area of old-growth spruce and unique geological forms. Accessing this massive park requires travelling 60 kilometres south from Tumbler Ridge on a gravel road, a trip that may deter some visitors. Services are located at Tumbler Ridge.

Facilities

Twenty camping spots are found here, a number of them less than 50 metres from the Murray River. All accommodate every type of recreational vehicle, and some have specific areas for tents. Backcountry campsites are also available. At the time of writing, the campground was user-maintained, meaning that there is no staff or services. As a result no fees are charged, although campers will still find fire pits, firewood, picnic tables, hand-pumped drinking water and pit toilets.

Recreational activities

Among the biggest attractions here are the hiking trails. A short trail leads to the spectacular 60-metre-high Kinuseo Falls, where a viewing platform ensures excellent photography opportunities. A 7-kilometre (one-way) trail leads to the Murray River, where a suspension bridge can be crossed, taking hikers along the Mount Head Trail into the park's backcountry. The latter route follows the original one of the Monkman Pass Highway (see below). Powerboats can be launched on the Pine and Murray rivers, and the Murray River can be canoed below the falls. Fishing in the lakes and rivers yields trout, char, grayling and whitefish. The campground also has a playground and horseshoe pit, and the area is very rich in wildlife, including grizzly and black bears, mountain goats, moose and caribou.

Additional information

In 1922, Alex Monkman, a fur trader, farmer and visionary, dreamed of creating a route to link the farms of the Peace River to Hansard, northeast of Prince George. In 1936, he formed the Monkman Pass Highway Association, and a year later work started. Unfortunately, the project was plagued by a lack of funds, and all work ceased in 1939 with the outbreak of the Second World War. Today, the Monkman Lake Trail follows much of the original highway, while the pass bears the name of the pioneer whose dream was never realized.

Muncho Lake

Location
Muncho Lake is an area of parkland covering over 85,000 hectares in the Terminal and Muskwa ranges of the Rocky Mountains, an area noted not only for its wildlife but also for its classic Rocky Mountain features, such as folded and vaulted rock and alluvial fans. Like many provincial parks along the route, it owes its existence to the Alaska Highway and is situated at Mile 422 (Kilometre 681) of the Alaska Highway, 250 kilometres west of Fort Nelson. A gas station, restaurants and small shops are located, quite unusually, in the park itself. When travelling to or from Muncho Lake, stop near Mile 474 (Kilometre 650) of the Alaska Highway and look for Stone sheep licking the mineral rocks. The best time for viewing is at dawn or dusk in the late spring and early fall.

Facilities
Thirty campsites are positioned in two campgrounds on the shores of Muncho Lake. The more northerly campground, MacDonald, has 15 spots that are quite close to the road and provide little privacy. Strawberry Flats (my preference) is the more southerly location, with 15 spots that are more private, some on the waterfront. There is no sani-station, and facilities are basic in both campgrounds (fire pits, drinking water, pit toilets, picnic tables).

Recreational activities
Muncho Lake, 12 kilometres long and over 2 kilometres wide in places, is typical Canadian Rocky Mountain scenery and offers endless photo opportunities. The 90-kilometre drive through the park on the Alaska Highway is often described as the most scenic stretch of that route. While staying here, campers can follow hiking trails, go boating (there is a boat launch at MacDonald campground) and fish for trout, Arctic grayling, Dolly Varden and whitefish. The lake tends to be cold in the summer, so it is not a popular swimming location. The park is also noted for its wildlife, including black bears, Stone sheep, mountain goats, caribou, deer and wolves.

Additional information
Muncho Lake takes its name from the Kaskan language: *muncho* means "big lake." The lake's jade-green colour comes from the copper oxides leached in from the surrounding bedrock, coupled with the refraction of sunlight on sediments brought into the lake by glacial meltwater. The scenery here is spectacular, but the weather can be quite cool and windy.

NAIKOON

Location
Naikoon Provincial Park is a photographer's paradise: the atmospheric conditions and the variety of plants and wildlife yield fantastic photography opportunities. The only provincial park with camping facilities on the Queen Charlotte Islands (now called Haida Gwaii), Naikoon is found on Graham Island, the most northerly of the Charlottes, which is served by scheduled ferries from Prince Rupert. The park has two campgrounds: Misty Meadows is located near Tlell, 42 kilometres north of Skidegate on Highway 16, while Agate Beach is 26 kilometres northeast of Masset on a secondary road. Services are available in Port Clements, Tlell, Masset and Village of Queen Charlotte (formerly called Queen Charlotte City).

Facilities
The 43 sites at Agate Beach are close to the ocean and somewhat exposed; in contrast, the 30 vehicle and 30 tent sites at Misty Meadows are situated under pine trees. Misty Meadows is my preference, as it is less exposed. When I was here, each campsite had a hanging basket full of flowers at its entrance—a wonderful touch. Neither site has a sani-station or flush toilets. There is limited wheelchair access at Agate Beach. Wilderness camping is also permitted throughout the park, and three wilderness shelters are located along East Beach near the mouths of the Cape Ball and Oeanda rivers and at Fife Point.

Recreational activities
Numerous recreational activities can be enjoyed in this 69,166-hectare park, and visitors frequently spend a week or more here. The visitor centre is located on Highway 16, 2 kilometres south of Tlell, and is open from June 15 to September 15. Hiking trail details are posted on the information board at the entrance to each campground, and the park has 100 kilometres of beach to explore. It is possible to dig for clams and to swim, and coho salmon and steelhead can be caught in the Tlell River. Opportunities to see wildlife abound: the Tow Hill Ecological Reserve and Rose Spit Ecological Reserve have been established in the park to protect the flora and fauna. It is illegal to camp, fish, hunt or use motorized vehicles in these ecological reserves.

Additional information
The Queen Charlottes, renowned for overcast skies and frequent fogs, are often referred to as "the misty islands." Campers should come well prepared for cold damp conditions, even if you're planning to visit in July and stay in a vehicle. If you wear the correct gear, you can enjoy walking along deserted windswept beaches, and there are excellent opportunities to see an assortment of sea mammals and birds—the Charlottes boast the second-highest eagle population in the world. Naikoon means "long nose" and is derived from the Haida name *Naikun*.

Nisga'a Memorial Lava Bed

Location

North of Terrace, you can camp adjacent to Canada's most recent volcanic eruption, which experts believe took place in the mid-1700s. The Nisga'a Memorial Lava Bed is the first provincial park to be managed jointly by a First Nation and BC Parks. Also known as *Anhluut'ukwsim Laxmihl Angwinga'asanskwhl Nisga'a*, this 17,683-hectare park is reached by turning off Highway 16 at Terrace, travelling 55 kilometres north and then driving another 55 kilometres on a gravel road. There is a visitor centre and information kiosk at the entrance to the park. Full services can be found at Terrace; grocery stores, restaurants and gas stations are in the four local Nisga'a villages. Watch for logging trucks, especially if you're driving the road on a weekday.

Facilities

This campground was established beside Vetter Creek in 2000, and has 16 vehicle/tent spaces. Facilities include flush and pit toilets, and picnic tables. One campsite and one pit toilet are wheelchair-accessible.

Recreational activities

This park is the first in the province to combine an interpretation of natural features and First Nations culture. The Nisga'a Tribal Council has established a visitor centre (open from mid-June to Labour Day) to illustrate its traditional culture, display aspects of the Nisga'a lifestyle and arrange tours of the volcano (3-kilometre-long guided walks are offered daily in the summer). In addition to touring spectacular lava beds, there are other hiking options, and Lava Lake offers opportunities for swimming, boating and fishing for salmon and trout. The lake has one gravel boat launch and there's another one at Nass River.

Additional information

It is believed the Tseax Cone erupted in 1775, destroying two Nisga'a villages and killing as many as 2,000 people. The lava flow rerouted the Nass River and dammed other waterways. Visitors now see a sparsely vegetated lava plain that stretches over 10 kilometres. Be forewarned: walking on the lava beds, although fascinating, is hard on the feet, so be sure you have appropriate footwear. This is another fascinating and unique area of BC to visit.

ONE ISLAND LAKE

Location

I still have not had the opportunity to visit this park (indeed it is one of only a handful I haven't visited), but all of the people I have spoken to who know the area stress the cleanliness of the lake's water. I recently learned it is now a Category C park, jointly maintained by BC Parks and the local community, so while it is called a provincial park, the services it provides may not be the same as at other provincial parks. Somewhat off the beaten track, One Island Lake does not have the advantage of being a conveniently situated roadside campground for one night's stop, but it will guarantee a quiet night's rest. The 59-hectare park is situated 60 kilometres southeast of Dawson Creek in the foothills of the Rockies. Turn off Highway 2 at Tupper, where services are available, and take an unpaved road 33 kilometres to the campground.

Facilities

There are 36 campsites available on the east side of the lake, some backing onto the lake. Services are limited to the basics (drinking water, fire pits, picnic tables, pit toilets).

Recreational activities

This park is popular with residents of Dawson Creek in summer and winter. It is possible to swim, fish, waterski, windsurf and go boating here. There is a boat launch, and, since the lake is stocked annually, fishing for rainbow and brook trout is reputed to be excellent (with catches reaching over two kilograms in size). A fish-cleaning stand is provided near the boat launch, and there's an annual Father's Day fishing derby. There are no developed hiking trails, but there is a small playground, should you have small children or the urge to stop fishing and play yourself.

Additional information

One Island Lake Provincial Park is representative of the Kiskatinaw Plateau ecosystem, and moose, white-tailed and mule deer, and beaver are found here. The lake's original name was "HOP Lake," after the first letters of the last names of the three men who helped build the first access road: Len Hodsgon, Bill Oakford and Art Pearson. It was renamed "One Island Lake" by government surveyors, after the small island in one corner of the lake. The first settlers of Tupper were Sudetens (Czechoslovakians from the Czech/Poland border) who escaped Hitler by settling here in the 1930s. For those who do not like travelling on gravel roads, Swan Lake is a nearby alternative campground.

Paarens Beach

Location

Watch the sun go down and the stars come out from this lovely campground on the warm southern shores of Stuart Lake, one of the largest lakes in the province, amidst the Nechako Plateau Hills. It's a little less than two hours from Prince George on Highway 27. Approximately 15 minutes away by car is the historic town of Fort St. James, which has all services.

Facilities

The campground contains 36 sites; six are close to the water's edge. With a few exceptions, the sites are large, private and partly wooded. Only the basic amenities are provided (pit toilets, drinking water, picnic tables, fire pits). Reservations are accepted.

Recreational activities

This provincial park boasts a large sandy beach, and BC Parks has made it ideal for families by providing a change house, a picnic shelter, multiple picnic tables, horseshoe pits, a play area for children and a large grassy area perfect for ball games. Stuart Lake is also an ideal location for sailing and windsurfing, but users must be cautious because sudden strong winds can easily develop on this large lake. Campers can also fish for rainbow trout and lake char, and there is a concrete boat launch at the south end of the park. Nearby, the reconstructed Hudson's Bay Company trading post at Fort St. James provides an account of pioneer life and is well worth a visit. Guides dressed in period costume give accounts and anecdotes of the lives of the early settlers. For the more energetic, the Mount Pope trail just north of the community takes hikers on a two- to four-hour hike (one way) up to the top of the mountain, which offers spectacular views of Stuart Lake below.

Additional information

Swimmer's itch can sometimes be a problem in Stuart Lake at certain times of year. Stuart Lake is one of the largest in the province and is part of the Stuart–Takla chain of lakes, along with Trembleur Lake and Takla Lake (almost 90 kilometres long). With so much water, this area is a fishing nirvana. Paarens Beach is very close to Sowchea Bay, where there are comparable facilities, and it is easy to travel between the two to determine which provincial park provides the best camping location for your needs.

PRUDHOMME LAKE

Location

Twenty kilometres east of Prince Rupert there is a small coniferous-forested lakeside campground at Prudhomme Lake. Access from Highway 16 is immediate, and all amenities are available in Prince Rupert, 16 kilometres to the west. By staying here, campers can enjoy the best of two provincial parks: Diane Lake Provincial Park is a stone's throw away, accessed by a 2.5-kilometre gravel road off Highway 16.

Facilities

Prudhomme Lake offers 24 spacious campsites on the water, though large RVs may have difficulty accessing some of these spots. There is no sani-station and only basic facilities (picnic tables, pit toilets, pump water, fire pits). One campsite and pit toilet are wheelchair-accessible. Noise from passing traffic is easily audible, although the road is not that busy, especially at night.

Recreational activities

Although the activities at Prudhomme Lake are limited to fishing for steelhead, rainbow trout and Dolly Varden, Diane Lake has a day-use area that's good for swimming, canoeing and sunbathing. From Diane Lake Park it is possible to take a trail that meanders through the coastal rainforest to Diane Creek Falls, or to fish in the creeks that run through the park. A short drive away, Prince Rupert offers many leisure activities, including the Museum of Northern BC, a railway museum, a self-guided walking tour and an 18-hole golf course. In the nearby community of Port Edward, you can visit one of the BC coast's oldest fishing canneries. Open daily from May to September (and Sundays year-round), this site is well worth a visit as it represents a unique piece of BC history (for more information visit www.cannery.ca).

Additional information

In August and September, it is possible to see salmon spawning in Diane Creek, and black-tailed deer also inhabit this area. From Prince Rupert, air charters to the Khutzeymateen, 45 kilometres north of the city, can be arranged. This area of 445 square kilometres is home to the largest known grizzly bear population on the BC coast and one of the largest in the world. I see Prudhomme Lake primarily as a convenient overnight camping location for visiting Prince Rupert, or if you need a place to spend the night prior to catching a ferry.

PURDEN LAKE

Location

Exceptional photography opportunities can be had at Purden Lake, especially in the early morning as the mist slowly clears over the calm waters of the lake. Situated in the foothills of the Rockies, less than an hour's drive from Prince George on a paved road 2 kilometres off the Yellowhead Highway, this popular campground is regularly used by both Prince George residents and visitors. Services such as gas, propane and restaurants are conveniently located less than 5 kilometres from the campground, although its proximity to Prince George means campers are within an hour's drive of every amenity.

Facilities

This 2,581-hectare park has 78 campsites set amongst trees. All sites are relatively private, and some sites are set aside specifically for tents. There are flush toilets and a sani-station but no showers. Some park facilities are wheelchair-accessible.

Recreational activities

Park amenities include an adventure playground and a horseshoe pit. There's also a sandy beach with a designated swimming area and changing rooms in the day-use area. Lakeside walking trails offer beautiful views of the surrounding area and make it possible to investigate a variety of plant life. There is a concrete boat launch, and waterskiing is permitted on the lake. Anglers can fish for rainbow trout and burbot. The city of Prince George, 64 kilometres away, provides a wealth of things to see and do, including the Fraser–Fort George Regional Museum and the University of Northern British Columbia, which affords spectacular views of the surrounding landscape.

Additional information

Thanks to the park's beautiful setting amidst undulating forested mountains, and its easy access to Prince George, Purden Lake is one of the region's most popular parks. Consequently, it is regularly full on weekends, and reservations are not taken. The lakeshore is very picturesque and its beauty quite haunting.

RED BLUFF

Location

Like Babine Lake Provincial Park, Red Bluff is situated on Babine Lake, the longest natural freshwater lake in British Columbia. So-called because of the dramatic reddish cliffs under which it nestles, the park is a few kilometres south of the village of Granisle, a 45-minute drive from Highway 16 on a paved road reached by turning off at Topley. The 148-hectare park is jointly managed by the local community and BC Parks, which means services may vary from those at other provincial parks.

Facilities

The campground has 27 large sites set in woodland; a few overlook the lake, while others are more open and closer to the day-use area. There is also an overflow camping area. Facilities are limited to the basic ones generally found in BC parks (picnic tables, fire pits, drinking water, pit toilets) so there is no sani-station, flush toilets or wheelchair access. However, campsite reservations may be possible if you call the Village of Granisle at (250) 697-2248.

Recreational activities

Visitors can engage in numerous pursuits involving the lake, such as fishing (BC Parks boasts that cutthroat trout weighing up to one kilogram, rainbow trout of up to six kilograms and char up to 13 kilograms can be caught here), boating (there is a somewhat rudimentary boat launch) and swimming. Hiking is possible, and a number of small trails provide the opportunity to see wildlife—black bears and moose being particularly abundant—and one trail overlooks a marsh area, where your patience may be rewarded by a sighting of elusive birds and waterfowl. However, at certain times of the year, when the water level is high, this trail can be flooded. The Fulton River Salmon Hatchery just south of the park also deserves a visit if you want to view salmon leaping up a series of channels and learn about salmon spawning.

Additional information

Granisle was a copper-mining town until the mine closed in 1992, and the surrounding area is known for its wildlife. Wild animals are regularly sighted along the quiet drive from Highway 16 to the park, and we saw black bears when we drove here. The lake can become extremely rough, as high winds are easily whipped up in the area. I spent a somewhat uneasy night at this campground listening to the winds high in the trees and wondering which tree was going to crash down on top of me. My fears were totally unfounded.

Seeley Lake

Location

Seeley Lake is nestled amongst the Hazelton Mountains and located on Highway 16, 10 kilometres west of New Hazelton, where services are located. It's a quaint picturesque 24-hectare park with fantastic views. Bring your binoculars to this park, as you will be rewarded with sightings of bald eagles, ospreys, kingfishers and a variety of waterfowl.

Facilities

The campground is relatively small, containing only 20 sites. All of them are large, private and wooded, and about half of the sites overlook the lake. There is no sani-station and only the basic amenities (pit toilets, drinking water, fire pits, picnic tables). The only downside to the location is that the campsites are quite near the road.

Recreational activities

The fish that can be caught here include cutthroat and rainbow trout. Swimming is also possible as there is a small sandy beach. In May, ice can still be found on the lake, so be prepared for a cold dip if you're camping early in the season. A short trail starting at the day-use area leads to a wildlife-viewing platform. Seeley Lake is only a short drive from 'Ksan, a recreated village illustrating characteristics typical of a historic Gitksan community. There are six longhouses with painted fronts and totem poles, a gift shop and a carving school. In the summer, 'Ksan dancers perform in the early evenings. (For more information, visit www.ksan.org.) For those interested in exploring First Nations culture further, Seeley Lake makes an ideal base from which to travel to see the totem poles of Kispiox, Kitwanga and Kitwancool.

Additional information

I stopped here early one morning as the mist was rising over the lake and the surrounding snow-topped mountains were just coming into view; the moment was magical. Seeley Lake also makes a lovely picnic spot for those who choose not to camp.

SOWCHEA BAY

Location

This region is full of historical accounts of early European settlers and is an educational and relaxing recreational destination. Sowchea Bay is 70 kilometres from the Yellowhead Highway and just a five-minute drive from Paarens Beach Provincial Park. The park's location and the recreational facilities it provides are similar to those of its neighbour; campers can easily travel between the two provincial parks to decide which campground to choose. The nearest community to both is Fort St. James, 20 kilometres away.

Facilities

This is a particularly attractive campground with 30 sites. The advantage Sowchea Bay has over Paarens Beach is that all sites here are located on the water's edge. They are also quite large, relatively private and set amongst trees. There is no sani-station. Unlike Paarens Beach, Sowchea Bay campground does not accept reservations.

Recreational activities

Aside from the lack of day-use picnic facilities, Sowchea Bay's recreational opportunities are similar to those available at Paarens Beach. They include fishing for rainbow trout, lake char, burbot and kokanee in Stuart Lake, as well as swimming, sunbathing, sailing and boating (there is a boat launch at the site). In addition, the nearby community of Fort St. James provides historical interest, as well as a nine-hole golf course with views of Stuart Lake.

Additional information

Although Paarens Beach seems to be the more popular site—perhaps because it has a day-use area and accepts reservations—I prefer Sowchea Bay. With all sites on the beach, it is an ideal place to watch the sun set while taking a stroll along the shoreline. The views are quite spectacular, and on a clear night the stargazing from this vantage point is awe-inspiring. Caution must be exercised by those who plan to windsurf or sail on Stuart Lake, as it is prone to high winds and waves. Swimmer's itch can also be a problem here.

STONE MOUNTAIN

Location

High amongst the breathtaking Rocky Mountain scenery at Mile 373 of the Alaska Highway is 25,690-hectare Stone Mountain Provincial Park. Camping here can either be bleak or beautiful, depending on the weather and your personal camping preferences. Full services are available at Fort Nelson, 140 kilometres east of the park, while gas and food can be obtained a few kilometres from the park.

Facilities

The Stone Mountain campground is situated at the end of Summit Lake. The 28 campsites here are very exposed and close to the road. All overlook the lake to varying degrees but have little privacy, as there are no trees or vegetation. Facilities here are basic (fire pits, picnic tables, pit toilets, drinking water).

Recreational activities

The area is known for five hiking and backcountry exploration trails, accessed from the campground. These trails take up to a week to complete and let you appreciate the full beauty of this area of the Rocky Mountains. Summit Lake has a boat launch, and fishing for trout and whitefish in the lake, and Arctic grayling and Dolly Varden in MacDonald Creek, can be attempted. The fishing is not fantastic because the waters are too cold to yield high fish populations. Mountaineering, horseback riding, photography and wildlife observation are other popular activities possible in the park.

Additional information

This campground, located on the highest part of the Alaska Highway (elevation: 1,267 metres), is exposed to very cold winds. The scenery, char-

acterized by steep bare mountain slopes, is quite beautiful, and the location provides easy access into the backcountry. The park features erosion pillars and hoodoos, plus subalpine lakes and waterfalls. One of the primary attractions of the area is the abundant wildlife, but visitors have to be patient in order to see any of the hundreds of mountain caribou, Stone sheep, moose, mule deers, black and grizzly bears, lynx, wolverines, beavers and elk that live in the region.

Swan Lake

Location
Swan Lake is probably the BC provincial park closest to the Alberta border, and it has a colourful history spanning 50 years. The park is found 35 kilometres southeast of Dawson Creek on Highway 2, just north of Tupper, which has basic services. A 2-kilometre gravel road leads from the highway to the campground. A comprehensive range of services is available at Dawson Creek.

Facilities
Situated on the lakeside are 42 campsites catering to every type of recreational vehicle. There is no sani-station and only limited access for those in wheelchairs. Facilities are limited to the basic ones found in BC parks (fire pits, picnic tables, pit toilets, drinking water).

Recreational activities
Five-kilometre-long Swan Lake has an average depth of 2 metres and is only 3 metres at its deepest point. The lake favours water-oriented activities, including boating, swimming from an excellent beach and fishing for northern pike, walleye and perch. The park has a boat launch, and waterskiing and powerboats are permitted. Hikes around the lake can be taken from the campground. A large grassy area attracts daytrippers and picnic parties, and there is an adventure playground for children, as well as horseshoe pits and a baseball diamond. The vast number of waterfowl and migratory birds in the area makes this location attractive to the birding community.

Additional information
This 65-hectare park was established on June 19, 1918, making it BC's third-oldest provincial park. It's popular with residents of Dawson Creek and has a long history of hosting local social events. For those who are visiting the area for the first time, the town of Dawson Creek at Mile Zero of the Alaska Highway has an interesting pioneer village open during the summer months that's worth a visit.

TUDYAH LAKE

Location

Close to the junction of Highway 97 and Highway 39, between the Hart Range and the Nechako Plateau of the Rocky Mountains, this 56-hectare lakeside provincial park is perfect for the weary traveller. Tudyah Lake is 9 kilometres north of McLeod Lake on Highway 97 and 157 kilometres from Prince George. The nearest services are found at McLeod Lake.

Facilities

Primarily used for overnight stays, this campground has a somewhat unusual feel to it because the 36 spaced-out sites are set in an open grassy meadow with a creek running through it, creating a pleasant pastoral atmosphere with good privacy. There is no sani-station or wheelchair access, but the park includes all the basic amenities (fire pits, drinking water, pit toilets, picnic tables).

Recreational activities

It is possible to swim (be aware of the sharp drop-off), kayak and canoe in Tudyah Lake. Anglers will enjoy fishing for rainbow trout, Dolly Varden and whitefish in the lake and at the nearby Parsnip River. Tudyah Lake has a boat launch, and ice fishing is popular in the winter. There is a large group-camping facility and day-use area with horseshoe pits. The town of Mackenzie, 30 minutes away, has a nine-hole golf course and a recreation centre, and is situated on the banks of Williston Lake, a prime fishing spot.

Additional information

The community of Mackenzie is at the south end of Williston Lake, a huge artificial reservoir that supplies water to the hydroelectric plant at Hudson's Hope. The town is named after Alexander Mackenzie, the first white person to reach Canada's Pacific coast by land. Mackenzie was built in 1965 in an area of wilderness as a centre for pulp, paper and lumber manufacturing. It has a museum and is home to the world's largest tree crusher, seen on Mackenzie Boulevard, but it has little to recommend it architecturally. In 2008, the town's mill closed and with the loss of Mackenzie's main employer, the town's future is uncertain.

TYHEE LAKE

Location

Children adore Tyhee Lake for the beach, anglers love it for the fish, and birdwatchers are attracted to the abundant bird life. But for me, Tyhee Lake's biggest attraction is its friendly atmosphere. While it is the convention in BC parks to say hello and pass the time of day with other campers, when I stayed at Tyhee everyone I met was happy and communicative. Consequently, Tyhee Lake lives in my memory as being the "very friendly provincial park." This provincial park's family-oriented campground is a 15-minute drive east of Smithers on Highway 16 near the quaint settlement of Telkwa in the Buckley River Valley. All amenities are therefore available within a few kilometres of the park itself.

Facilities

This large and well-maintained campground is set amidst an aspen forest on the side of Tyhee (Maclure) Lake. There are 59 campsites, a few with views over the lake, accommodating every kind of recreational vehicle, as well as tents. In addition to all the usual facilities found in provincial parks, Tyhee Lake has a sani-station, flush toilets and showers. Reservations are accepted.

Recreational activities

A beautiful 200-metre beach provides access for swimming. Waterskiing is permitted on the lake, and there is also a boat launch. Fish found in the lake include cutthroat and stocked rainbow trout, while smaller anglers can go for minnows and sticklebacks. Horseshoes and volleyball are also available, as is a play area for children. An interpretive trail has been developed around the campground, and there is a marsh-viewing platform where you may see loons, red-necked grebes, ruffed grouse and beavers. In addition, the communities of Smithers and Telkwa are pleasant places to visit. Smithers houses a wildlife museum that displays a variety of big game animals, and Telkwa dates back to the 1860s. Both are lovely places to wander around in, and they have good restaurants if you're getting bored of camping fodder.

Additional information

The large well-kept day-use area and the park's proximity to the Yellowhead Highway also make it an ideal picnic spot if you do not have time to spend the night. But with the many activities available here, Tyhee Lake is a perfect place for family camping, and visitors usually spend more than one night. For me, the only downsides of Tyhee were the jet skiers who dominated the lake in the early evening hours when I last stayed and the Canada goose droppings littering the grass.

WHISKERS POINT

Location

Rich in First Nations and pioneer history and situated on a sandspit jutting out into McLeod Lake, Whiskers Point is an extremely agreeable location. The campground is 130 kilometres north of Prince George on Highway 97 and about 10 kilometres south of McLeod Lake, where gas, food and lodging are available.

Facilities

Sixty-nine large secluded sites set in a mature forest of spruce and pine are available. A number of them overlook the lake or are near Whiskers Creek, which runs through the campground. There is a sani-station, flush and pit toilets, and some facilities are wheelchair-accessible. Reservations are not accepted.

Recreational activities

McLeod Lake provides a wealth of opportunity for the water enthusiast. There is a good beach and excellent swimming, a concrete boat launch has been built, and windsurfing, canoeing, kayaking and fishing for Dolly Varden and rainbow trout are all possible. (A note of caution: the lake is subject to suddenly changing conditions, and strong winds can easily transform the calm water.) For younger campers, there's a children's play area, horseshoe pits and a volleyball net. The area is rich in bird and animal life, and there's also a 20-minute-long nature trail.

Additional information

I have visited Whiskers Point but have not stayed in the campground. All the literature on this area stresses the beauty of the sunsets visible from the park, which have been described as "spectacular," "magnificent" and "breathtaking." The community of McLeod Lake, 10 kilometres north of the campground, was first established in 1805 by Simon Fraser. Known first as Trout Lake Fort and later as Fort McLeod, it was the first trading post and first European settlement west of the Rocky Mountains at the time. Although the Hart Highway (Highway 97) was developed in the 20th century, the local Sekani people had a system of trails developed in this region long before the Europeans came. You will not be disappointed in your decision to stay here.

MULTI-DAY
CAMPING TOURS

Designed for individuals travelling in a vehicle, this chapter provides suggestions for one-, two- and three-week camping excursions starting in the Lower Mainland. However, these itineraries can easily be amended to accommodate personal preferences or alternative starting points.

While I offer brief synopses of the roads to take for each of the recommended tours, a good map is required for anyone planning to camp and travel in BC. One excellent resource is the *British Columbia Recreational Atlas*, which provides comprehensive coverage of the province's major and minor highways, as well as data on places, area boundaries, trails, elevations, lakes and parks. The fact that it is an 8-by-11-inch bound mapbook and not a four-by-four-foot paper map makes it easy to consult in the car (and helps keep it in one piece). Alternately, Tourism British Columbia sells a *Road Map and Parks Guide*, which lists all provincial parks. Both publications are readily available at tourist information offices, and the *British Columbia Recreational Atlas* is carried by most bookstores in BC (and from greatbooks@heritagehouse.ca). Travellers should also check road conditions and potential closures by calling the Drive BC automated phone service at 1-800-550-4997, or by consulting the equivalent website: www.drivebc.ca.

For those campers uncomfortable travelling without a reservation, each of the one-, two- and three-week tours has a "fully reserved" option, where it is possible to book all camping spots in advance. Anyone planning to vacation in the popular peak months of July and August without reserving ahead should be prepared to encounter some full campgrounds and plan alternative options on the fly.

7-Day Tours

Trip 1: A Little Taste of the Province

Although this route may appear to involve a lot of driving, for those who like this pastime it provides a good introduction to the province, a taste of some of the best scenery and an introduction to lovely provincial parks. It is a circular tour: you start by travelling north to Highway 97, east on the Yellowhead Highway, south on Highway 93 then west on Highway 3.

Day 1	Lac la Hache	Day 5	Moyie Lake
Day 2	Mount Robson	Day 6	Kettle River Recreation Area
Day 3	Mount Robson	Day 7	Manning
Day 4	Kootenay (National)		

Trip 2: Popular Provincial Parks (Fully Reserved)

This itinerary gives campers the security of knowing they have accommodation in some of the most popular campgrounds in the province. It includes campgrounds on BC's mainland, Vancouver Island and the Gulf Islands, making for wonderful ferry trips and minimal driving. After staying at Alice Lake, travel south on the Sea to Sky Highway to Horseshoe Bay and take the ferry to Vancouver Island. From there, it is just a short drive north on Highway 19 to Rathtrevor. After Rathtrevor, head south on Highway 19 to Goldstream. To reach Montague Harbour, take a ferry from Swartz Bay to Galiano Island.

Day 1	Alice Lake	Day 5	Goldstream
Day 2	Alice Lake	Day 6	Montague Harbour Marine
Day 3	Rathtrevor Beach	Day 7	Montague Harbour Marine
Day 4	Rathtrevor Beach		

Swim in weed-free water at Lac la Hache Provincial Park.

Trip 3: Vancouver Island and Gulf Island Hopping

Like Trip 2, this route has some fantastic ferry rides through breathtaking scenery. Montague Harbour on Galiano Island is reached by ferry from Tsawwassen. Ruckle Provincial Park is on Salt Spring Island, and ferries regularly leave from Galiano for Salt Spring. From Salt Spring, take a ferry to Swartz Bay; from here, the Island Highway leads to Goldstream and Bamberton. French Beach is located south of Victoria on Highway 14.

Day 1	Montague Harbour Marine	Day 5	Goldstream
Day 2	Montague Harbour Marine	Day 6	Bamberton
Day 3	Ruckle	Day 7	French Beach
Day 4	Ruckle		

Trip 4: Circle Tour

This easy-to-complete circular excursion takes campers to some of the less popular camping spots that are still easily accessible from Vancouver. It involves driving north on the lovely Sea to Sky Highway turning briefly off Highway 99 to access Birkenhead, and continuing along this scenic road until it joins Highway 97 just north of Cache Creek. At Cache Creek, you take Highway 97C south to Kentucky–Alleyne. From this campground, travel south on Highway 5A to Highway 3, which leads through Manning Park and back to Vancouver.

Day 1	Nairn Falls	Day 5	Manning
Day 2	Birkenhead Lake	Day 6	Manning
Day 3	Birkenhead Lake	Day 7	Emory Creek
Day 4	Kentucky–Alleyne		

Kentucky–Alleyne Provincial Park is within easy reach of Vancouver.

Trip 5: The Hiker's Dream

This trip is designed for driving one day and hiking the next. To reach Wells Gray, take the Coquihalla (Highway 5) to Kamloops and then head north on Highway 5. After Wells Gray, continue north on Highway 5 until it joins the Yellowhead Highway (Highway 16). After Mount Robson, take the fantastic Glacier Highway (Highway 93) south until it meets Highway 1. (Pray for good weather, as the views along this road are some of the best in the province.) Travelling west on Highway 1 leads to Yoho. From Yoho it is possible to drive back to Vancouver in a day. For those who want a less hurried route, take Highway 1 as far as Kamloops, then Highway 97 until it reaches Highway 99, which you can follow to Vancouver.

Day 1	Wells Gray	Day 5	Yoho (National)
Day 2	Wells Gray	Day 6	Yoho (National)
Day 3	Mount Robson	Day 7	Marble Canyon
Day 4	Mount Robson		

The spectacular beauty of Mount Robson Provincial Park draws outdoor enthusiasts from all over the world.

210

14-Day Tours

Trip 1: A Bigger Taste of the Province

Two weeks is a good length of time for touring the province. On the first day of this itinerary, there is little driving involved, as campers head out of Vancouver on Highway 7 to nearby Golden Ears. After camping here, continue on Highway 7 to the junction with Highway 3 and then take Highway 3 through Manning. After Manning, travel north to Kamloops. A number of routes are available, but my advice to those who have time is to take 5A. From Kamloops, take Highway 5 north until it joins the Yellowhead Highway. Travel east on the Yellowhead until you get to Highway 93, which can be taken all the way south to Kootenay National Park and beyond, where it meets Highway 95. From Jimsmith Lake, follow Highway 3, then 3A to Crawford Bay and the longest free ferry ride in the world over Kootenay Lake, where Highway 31 leads to Kootenay Lake Provincial Park. Travel south from Kootenay Lake on Highway 3A and take a slow drive along Highway 3 back to Vancouver, with a stop at Haynes Point in Osoyoos.

Day 1	Golden Ears		Day 8	Mount Robson
Day 2	Manning		Day 9	Kootenay (National)
Day 3	Manning		Day 10	Kootenay (National)
Day 4	Paul Lake		Day 11	Jimsmith Lake
Day 5	Wells Gray		Day 12	Kootenay Lake
Day 6	Wells Gray		Day 13	Kootenay Lake
Day 7	Mount Robson		Day 14	Haynes Point

Wells Gray is one of the best provincial parks in BC.

Trip 2: Stress-free BC (Fully Reserved)

This itinerary only includes campgrounds that accept reservations. Travel along Highway 7 to Highway 3 and continue east on this road until it meets Highway 97. At this juncture, you will adopt a northward direction as the road leads toward Highway 1, dividing into highways 97, 97A and 97B. All these roads lead in the direction of Shuswap Lake. After staying at Shuswap Lake, drive west on Highway 1 to Kamloops, then take Highway 5 north to the Yellowhead Highway and the stunningly beautiful Mount Robson Park. Retrace your steps to Kamloops and follow Highway 5A south to Princeton and the nearby Otter Lake Provincial Park. The return journey to Vancouver leads you back on Highway 3.

Day 1	Golden Ears	Day 8	Shuswap Lake
Day 2	Golden Ears	Day 9	Shuswap Lake
Day 3	Manning	Day 10	Shuswap Lake
Day 4	Manning	Day 11	Mount Robson
Day 5	Okanagan Lake	Day 12	Mount Robson
Day 6	Okanagan Lake	Day 13	Mount Robson
Day 7	Okanagan Lake	Day 14	Otter Lake

Trip 3: Vancouver Island and Gulf Island Hopping

On this lovely relaxed excursion you will be able to explore the camping highlights of Vancouver Island and the Gulf Islands. Montague Harbour on Galiano Island is reached by ferry from Tsawwassen. Ruckle Provincial Park is on Salt Spring Island, and ferries regularly leave from Galiano for Salt Spring. From Salt Spring, a ferry is needed to reach South Pender Island, the last Gulf Island on the tour. Travel from South Pender Island to Vancouver Island's Swartz Bay by ferry. At Swartz Bay the Island Highway (Highway 1) leads south to Victoria. Take Highway 14 from Victoria to French Beach. From here the return journey north starts, taking the Island Highway as far as Parksville. At Parksville head west on Highway 4, which meanders across Vancouver Island to Pacific Rim National Park (the road from Port Alberni to the coast is particularly lovely). Return along this road to the Island Highway and continue north until reaching Campbell River. Highway 28 just north of this town leads into Strathcona Park. Return to the Lower Mainland by ferry from Nanaimo.

Day 1	Montague Harbour Marine	Day 8	Bamberton
Day 2	Montague Harbour Marine	Day 9	Pacific Rim (National)
Day 3	Ruckle	Day 10	Pacific Rim (National)
Day 4	Ruckle	Day 11	Miracle Beach
Day 5	Prior Centennial (National)	Day 12	Strathcona
Day 6	French Beach	Day 13	Strathcona
Day 7	Goldstream	Day 14	Strathcona

Trip 4: Fruit and Freedom—The Okanagan and the Kootenays

This tour offers the best of both worlds, as the somewhat more populated Okanagan is visited in conjunction with the calm quiet Kootenays. The quickest way to reach Bear Creek, the first provincial park campground on the itinerary, is to take Highway 1 out of Vancouver then the Coquihalla Highway to Merritt. Turn east on Highway 97C toward Kelowna. Alternatively, instead of the Coquihalla, take Highway 3 through Manning Park to Princeton then Highway 5A north to Highway 97. From Bear Creek, drive north to Vernon, and then take Highway 6 east to reach Mabel Lake. After staying here, continue on Highway 6 until the turnoff for Highway 31A; this leads to Highway 31 and, by travelling north, to Kootenay Lake Provincial Park. From Kootenay Lake, travel south on Highway 31 and take Highway 3A to find Kokanee Creek. A short drive south on this road leads to Champion Lakes. Continue the journey back to Vancouver on Highway 3, stopping at Otter Lake and Manning or any other campgrounds that look appealing.

Day 1	Bear Creek	Day 8	Kootenay Lake
Day 2	Bear Creek	Day 9	Kokanee Creek
Day 3	Mabel Lake	Day 10	Champion Lakes
Day 4	Mabel Lake	Day 11	Otter Lake
Day 5	Rosebery	Day 12	Otter Lake
Day 6	Kootenay Lake	Day 13	Manning
Day 7	Kootenay Lake	Day 14	Manning

The small town of Coalmont, near Otter Lake Provincial Park, sprang to life during the gold rush.

Trip 5: Rocky Mountains and the National Parks

It is easily possible to visit all the "big" parks in a two-week period, but a few long days in the car are required. This tour has been designed to compensate for these long travelling times with two- or three-night stays in some of the largest and most spectacular parks in the province. To take this excursion, leave Vancouver on Highway 1, and then take the Coquihalla north to Kamloops. Just north of Kamloops is Paul Lake Provincial Park. The following day, take Highway 1 east to Glacier, and a few days later proceed the few kilometres to Yoho. From Yoho, Highway 1 east leads to Lake Louise. From here, head south on Highway 93 to Kootenay National Park. Continue on Highway 93, which eventually becomes Highway 95 and joins Highway 3. Highway 3 travels across the bottom of the province and leads back to Vancouver.

Day 1	Paul Lake	Day 8	Kootenay (National)
Day 2	Glacier (National)	Day 9	Kootenay (National)
Day 3	Glacier (National)	Day 10	Kootenay (National)
Day 4	Glacier (National)	Day 11	Moyie Lake
Day 5	Yoho (National)	Day 12	Kettle River Recreational Area
Day 6	Yoho (National)	Day 13	Manning
Day 7	Yoho (National)	Day 14	Manning

Beautiful Manning Provincial Park is a hiker's paradise.

21-Day Tours

Trip 1: A Huge Taste of the Province

If travelling hundreds of kilometres a day across remote regions of the province is a pleasurable notion for you, then this trip will be a dream. I undertook it in 19 days, which required a lot of driving—over 6,500 kilometres. It is not an itinerary for those who suffer from motion sickness. Leave Vancouver on the Sea to Sky Highway and travel north on what I believe to be one of the best roads in the world. When the road joins Highway 97, head north. This is the Gold Rush Trail. After stopping at Lac la Hache and turning east just north of Quesnel on Highway 26 to visit Barkerville, return to Highway 97 and proceed north to Prince George. From here, turn west on the Yellowhead Highway (Highway 16). At Terrace, take Highway 97 south to Lakelse, after which you should be prepared to travel north on this highway as far as the Alaska Highway. (Be warned that sections of Highway 37 between Dease Lake and Meziadin Junction are unpaved.) Upon reaching the Alaska Highway, head south as far as Dawson Creek, then drive Highway 97 south to Prince George. At Prince George, travel east on the Yellowhead Highway to Mount Robson, and then head south on Highway 5 to Kamloops. At Kamloops you can choose between returning to Vancouver via the fast Coquihalla or on Highway 1 through the Fraser Canyon.

Day 1 Lac la Hache
Day 2 Ten Mile Lake
Day 3 Ten Mile Lake
Day 4 Sowchea Bay
Day 5 Sowchea Bay
Day 6 Tyhee Lake
Day 7 Lakelse Lake
Day 8 Lakelse Lake
Day 9 Meziadin Lake
Day 10 Boya Lake
Day 11 Liard River Hot Springs
Day 12 Liard River Hot Springs
Day 13 Buckinghorse River Wayside
Day 14 Gwillim Lake
Day 15 Bear Lake
Day 16 Bear Lake
Day 17 Mount Robson
Day 18 Mount Robson
Day 19 Wells Gray
Day 20 Wells Gray
Day 21 Emory Creek

Magnificent falls in Wells Gray
Provincial Park.

Trip 2: Best of the Mainland (Fully Reserved)

Many of the campgrounds that are part of this itinerary are ideal for families and those who require more comfort when camping, such as flush toilets, showers and nearby stores. To reach the first campground, leave Vancouver on Highway 1, then take Highway 3, which meanders through Manning Park. Continue east along this road until you reach Osoyoos, and then head north on Highway 97. After staying at Ellison, continue the journey north on Highway 97 until you reach the junction with Highway 1. At this stage, head west as far as Kamloops, then north on Highway 5 to the Yellowhead Highway and Mount Robson. After Mount Robson take the Yellowhead Highway west to Prince George, then travel north on Highway 97 as far as Crooked River. On the next stage of the journey, take Highway 97 south as far as the turn for Highway 99, just north of Cache Creek. You will spend the final days of your camping tour driving the wonderful Highway 99 back to Vancouver.

Day 1	Manning	Day 12	Crooked River
Day 2	Manning	Day 13	Crooked River
Day 3	Manning	Day 14	Ten Mile Lake
Day 4	Okanagan Lake	Day 15	Ten Mile Lake
Day 5	Okanagan Lake	Day 16	Green Lake
Day 6	Okanagan Lake	Day 17	Green Lake
Day 7	Ellison	Day 18	Green Lake
Day 8	Ellison	Day 19	Alice Lake
Day 9	Mount Robson	Day 20	Alice Lake
Day 10	Mount Robson	Day 21	Porteau Cove
Day 11	Mount Robson		

Trip 3: Vancouver Island, the Gulf Islands and the Sunshine Coast

An easy-to-complete excursion featuring beautiful drives and numerous ferry rides, this route follows the same one detailed in the 14-night Vancouver Island and Gulf Island Hopping itinerary. However, upon leaving Strathcona Provincial Park, travellers extend their tour by taking the ferry from Courtenay to Powell River on the Sunshine Coast. Next, drive south on Highway 101. To end the journey, take the ferry back to Horseshoe Bay.

Day 1	Montague Harbour Marine	Day 12	Pacific Rim (National)
Day 2	Montague Harbour Marine	Day 13	Pacific Rim (National)
Day 3	Ruckle	Day 14	Miracle Beach
Day 4	Ruckle	Day 15	Strathcona
Day 5	Prior Centennial (National)	Day 16	Strathcona
Day 6	Goldstream	Day 17	Strathcona
Day 7	Goldstream	Day 18	Saltery Bay
Day 8	Bamberton	Day 19	Saltery Bay
Day 9	Rathtrevor Beach	Day 20	Porpoise Bay
Day 10	Rathtrevor Beach	Day 21	Porpoise Bay
Day 11	Pacific Rim (National)		

Trip 4: Gold Rush Trail and the Queen Charlotte Islands
The drawback of this trip is that the same roads have to be travelled on the outbound and the return journeys. However, the scenery en route to the Queen Charlotte Islands more than compensates. From Vancouver, go north via highways 99 and 97 as far as Prince George, and then follow the Yellowhead Highway west to Prince Rupert, where a six-hour ferry ride connects you to the Queen Charlottes. Retrace the same route back until just north of Cache Creek, where you can continue on the Gold Rush Trail south (Highway 1) down the Fraser Canyon all the way to Hope.

Day	1	Lac la Hache	Day 12	Naikoon
Day	2	Sowchea Bay	Day 13	Naikoon
Day	3	Sowchea Bay	Day 14	Kleanza Creek
Day	4	Tyhee Lake	Day 15	Beaumont
Day	5	Lakelse Lake	Day 16	Beaumont
Day	6	Lakelse Lake	Day 17	Ten Mile Lake
Day	7	Lakelse Lake	Day 18	Ten Mile Lake
Day	8	Prudhomme Lake	Day 19	Green Lake
Day	9	Naikoon	Day 20	Green Lake
Day	10	Naikoon	Day 21	Emory Creek
Day	11	Naikoon		

Dress warmly when strolling Naikoon's windswept beaches.

Illecillewaet is just one of three campgrounds in Glacier National Park. (Parks Canada/Rick Reynolds photo)

Trip 5: The Rockies and the Larger Provincial and National Parks

Designed with the hiker in mind, this itinerary features some of the best parks in the province. On leaving Vancouver, take either Highway 1 or the quieter Highway 7 to the junction with Highway 3. Travel east on Highway 3 to Castlegar, then take Highway 3A to Kokanee Creek. Continue along Highway 3A until it rejoins Highway 3, which turns into Highway 95 and leads north into Kootenay National Park. Next, travel north to meet Highway 1, and then drive west through Yoho and Glacier national parks as far as Kamloops, where Highway 5 leads north to the Yellowhead Highway and Mount Robson. From Mount Robson head west on Highway 16 (the Yellowhead Highway) as far as Prince George and then south on Highway 97, back through the Fraser Canyon to Vancouver.

Day 1	Manning	
Day 2	Manning	
Day 3	Kokanee Creek	
Day 4	Kokanee Creek	
Day 5	Moyie Lake	
Day 6	Kootenay (National)	
Day 7	Kootenay (National)	
Day 8	Kootenay (National)	
Day 9	Yoho (National)	
Day 10	Yoho (National)	
Day 11	Yoho (National)	

Day 12	Glacier (National)	
Day 13	Glacier (National)	
Day 14	Wells Gray	
Day 15	Wells Gray	
Day 16	Wells Gray	
Day 17	Mount Robson	
Day 18	Mount Robson	
Day 19	Mount Robson	
Day 20	Ten Mile Lake	
Day 21	Downing	

SPECIAL-INTEREST CAMPING RECOMMENDATIONS

Although many campers are content to explore any and every provincial park they find, a number of people have special needs or interests and seek camping facilities that will accommodate them. Here are some suggestions for those folks.

Hiking

Numerous provincial and national parks offer superb hiking. Most offer easier walking, but among the best known for varied hikes are the larger provincial parks such as Wells Gray, Manning, Mount Robson, Strathcona and Tweedsmuir (South), as well as Yoho, Glacier, Kootenay and Pacific Rim national parks. It is easy to spend a week or more at any of these locations and only begin to touch the beauty they offer.

Diving

A number of campgrounds in BC offer diving potential, but the most notable ones in the province are Saltery Bay on the Sunshine Coast (home to Canada's first underwater statue), Ellison in the Okanagan (the country's only freshwater dive park) and Porteau Cove (less than one hour's drive from Vancouver).

Hot Springs

What better way to relax than in warm mineral pools? Kootenay (National), Whiteswan Lake, Lakelse Lake and Liard River Hot Springs parks all offer this idyllic environment within their boundaries. If you don't mind a short drive, Dry Gulch is close to Radium Hot Springs (in Kootenay National Park); Martha Creek is close to Canyon Hot Springs; Kootenay Lake and Kokanee Creek are close to Ainsworth Hot Springs; Arrow Lakes, McDonald Creek and Summit Lake are all close to Nakusp Hot Springs; and McDonald Creek also has Halcyon Hot Springs nearby.

Canoeing and Kayaking

With an abundance of lakes, the possibilities for canoeing and kayaking are almost limitless. Those who seek serious paddling excursions should consider Champion Lakes, Wells Gray, Bowron Lake, Okeover Arm (with access to Desolation Sound) and Sasquatch. BC Parks offers canoes for rent at a number of provincial parks, including Manning and Golden Ears, and you can rent canoes at Yoho National Park's Emerald Lake.

Gold Panning

Although the potential to pan for gold exists in many provincial parks, Emory Creek, Kettle River, Stemwinder and the aptly named Goldpan are good places to try.

Horseback Riding

Relive that pioneer spirit by exploring BC parks on horseback. Horses can be rented from businesses adjacent to Babine Lake, Tweedsmuir (South), Golden Ears and Manning provincial parks and Yoho National Park for riding on specifically designated trails in these parks. Other parks also allow horseback riding, including Big Bar Lake, Tunkwa, Tsy'los and Glacier National Park.

Birdwatching

You can spot wonderful birdlife almost everywhere in BC, but the parks that are particularly notable include Vaseux Lake, Manning, Kootenay (National), Big Bar Lake, Green Lake, Inkaneep, Kilby, Rolley Lake, Paul Lake and Naikoon. All are excellent destinations for amateur ornithologists.

If you don't own a canoe or kayak, some parks have rentals available.

To catch your dinner, all you need is a fishing rod and some luck.

Fishing

All anglers have their own tips for the best fishing location, and BC parks provide thousands of spots to choose from. Of particular note are Elk Falls, Stamp River, Wells Gray, Charlie Lake, Babine River Corridor, Kokanee Creek, Whiteswan Lake, Tunkwa, Jewel Lake, Summit Lake, Vaseux Lake, Beatton, Premier Lake, Cowichan River, Skagit Rive, Bridge Lake and Goldpan.

Islands

Island campgrounds are magical, since the neighbouring communities (if any) on these quiet oases are quite distinct from those of the Mainland. Smelt Bay, Montague Harbour Marine, Newcastle Island, Fillongley, Ruckle and Sidney Spit Marine (National) all provide fantastic camping retreats.

Beaches

Tidal beaches are attractive to every age group, but especially to children. The following recommended sites are all on Vancouver Island: French Beach, Pacific Rim (National), Rathtrevor Beach, Miracle Beach and Sidney Spit Marine. There are also spectacular lakeside beaches to be enjoyed at Gordon Bay, Haynes Point, Okanagan Lake and Birkenhead Lake on the Mainland.

Family

BC Parks has a number of family-oriented campgrounds that have activities for children, playgrounds and numerous safe environments to explore. Alice Lake, Kokanee Creek, Rathtrevor Beach, Shuswap Lake, Tyhee Lake, Porpoise Bay, Cultus Lake, Golden Ears, Wasa, Miracle Beach, Manning, Sasquatch, Champion Lakes, Bear Creek, Paul Lake, Kikomun Creek, Monck and Ten Mile Lake are but a few fantastic locations.

USEFUL INFORMATION

Maps

Tourism British Columbia produces a map of the province that details all of the provincial parks and summarizes their facilities. *British Columbia Road Map and Parks Guide* is available from most tourist offices and bookstores for $3.95. The *British Columbia Road and Recreational Atlas*, is an excellent guide of the province, featuring up-to-date colour maps (1:600,000 scale).

Websites

Several informative websites give details about camping in BC. For the majority of the parks listed in this book, the BC Parks website has the most up-to-date information on all of the provincial park campgrounds and can be accessed at www.bcparks.ca. For current details about the national parks included in this book, visit www.pc.gc.ca.

Make provincial park reservations through www.discovercamping.ca. For national parks, the equivalent is www.pccamping.ca.

The following websites are also useful:

www.travel.bc.ca
www.canadianrockies.com
www.bcadventure.com
www.gocampingbc.com
www.bc-camping.com

www.camping.bc.ca
www.britishcolumbia.com
www.spacesfornature.org
www.hellobc.com

GROUP CAMPING

I celebrated my 40th birthday in 2001 in a number of different ways, one of which was renting the group campsite at Alice Lake Provincial Park for a weekend party with my friends and their families. Twenty adults and 16 children between the ages of eight months and nine years spent two days—one wonderful and one wet—at this location. We hiked, swam, made trips to Tim Hortons, fished, babysat each other's children, played games, sang, cooked and, of course, drank and told tales into the wee hours. A fantastic, economical time was had by all. This has become a regular event. Each August, between 10 and 20 adults and 20 children descend on Alice Lake—it's our own private camp.

Following is a list of campgrounds that offer group-camping facilities, which are generally located a short distance away from the main campground (ideal if you have noisy kids) and usually have their own toilets, water source and cooking pits. Some parks situate their group-camping section in a large open area, while others provide a more private location.

Requirements for reserving these spots vary depending on the park and some have minimum/maximum group sizes. The BC government contracts out the day-to-day operation and administration of BC Parks to private park administrators, who are responsible for booking groups at these facilities. To reserve a group site, consult the following website for reservation details and contact information: www.env.gov.bc.ca/bcparks/reserve/group.html.

Provincial parks included in this book that offer group-camping facilities

Alice Lake
Conkle Lake
Cowichan River
Cultus Lake
Fintry
French Beach
Golden Ears
Goldstream
Gordon Bay
Green Lake
Kentucky–Alleyne
Kettle River Recreation Area
Kikomun Creek
Lakelse Lake
Loveland Bay
Mabel Lake
Manning

Miracle Beach
Montague Harbour Marine
Mount Assiniboine
Mount Robson
Nairn Falls
Newcastle Island Marine
Paul Lake
Porpoise Bay
Rathtrevor Beach
Ruckle
Sasquatch
Shuswap Lake
Skagit Valley
Strathcona
Syringa
Tudyah Lake
Tyhee Lake

In addition, reservable group-camping facilities are available at the following national parks:

Kootenay, Crook's Meadow: call (403) 522-1203
Pacific Rim, Green Point (Long Beach): fax request to (250) 726-4270
Sidney Spit: call 1-877-559-2115

CAMPGROUND
COOKING

Appetites increase when you're outdoors, especially after an enjoyable day of hiking or swimming, and the fun continues if you let everyone help out with the cooking. The secret of campground food is simplicity. If you want to savour the best veal in cream and mushroom sauce, save this desire until you return home; do not attempt it while camping, for disappointment will ensue.

Although there are a couple of camp cooking books to guide the enthusiast, I find them far too complicated to be practical, with recommendations that included anchovy-and-tomato-stuffed eggplant and peaches in spiced brandy sauce! These recipes I have difficulty with at home, let alone in an open-air kitchen. I believe experimentation is the order of the day when cooking outdoors yet the best results are achieved when you keep it simple.

Along those lines, I have a few suggestions on preparations that can be done before leaving home and advice on a few basic necessities you'll want to have on hand. Following this advice will help to ensure that your meal preparation will be relatively problem free, whether you're cooking over an open fire, using a hibachi or relying on a camp stove.

1. Purchase a large roll of heavy-duty aluminum foil. This will be used frequently and is invaluable.

2. Before leaving home, pack salt, pepper, olive oil and any herbs and spices you think you will need (plastic film containers make excellent herb jars). Also take a couple of tins of tuna or cooked meat, rice, noodles and pasta as standbys.

3. Buy bottles of ready-made salad dressing, barbecue sauce and any other sauces you deem appropriate (e.g. Thai peanut sauce, mustard, mayonnaise, HP sauce, lemon juice) to keep in your camping food box. A few years ago we found Dragon sauce. It went on everything we grilled over the fire—I have no idea who made it, what was in it or whether it was

A campground cooking spot at Mount Robson Provincial Park looks cozy.

Cooking outdoors is easier than it may seem.

good for us, and I doubt we would have used it at home, but outdoors it tasted great and only cost a dollar.

4. Sachets of salt, pepper, tomato sauce, relish, vinegar, milk, etc., are also useful. The camper with initiative will easily be able to access these items.

5. Purchase ready-made salads in sealed plastic bags, available from large supermarkets. If kept cool, these provide good supplies of fresh vegetables that do not require washing.

6. Metal grills with wooden handles (from old hibachis) are useful for cooking food on the fire pit and ensure that sausages are less likely to fall into the fire. In addition, long toasting forks are mandatory instruments for turning food.

7. Take a pan with a lid for boiling water. Alternatively, a couple of flasks can be easily replenished with coffee or boiling water at gas stations or cafés when travelling, to be consumed later in the day.

8. Plastic food containers are useful not only for keeping food but also as bowls for marinade or dips. Bring an assortment.

9. Remember to pack newspaper, matches, dish detergent, tea towels, plastic plates, cups, bowls, cutlery, a sharp knife, wet wipes, a can opener, bottle opener and plastic bags (for collecting the garbage that has to be disposed of after every meal—do not leave it until the next morning, as this attracts animals).

10. Remember that vegetables last, meats rot and seafood should be eaten fresh.

11. Pita bread, flour tortillas and enchiladas keep very well, and even when a bit stale, they come to life once heated over an open fire.

12. Fruit such as bananas (delicious when baked whole on the fire), apples, pears, peaches and grapes are ideal desserts. In the Okanagan, it is difficult to resist the numerous fruit stands.

13. Buy boxed wine, as this is easier to transport and unbreakable (it also has the advantage of not disclosing how much has been drunk).

14. To round off the evening, don't forget the marshmallows. However, for a really good night's sleep, oblivious to the unfamiliar sounds of the forest, a tot of good malt whisky just before bedtime is an excellent sleeping potion.

Cooking Over an Open Fire

Whether the results are stupendous or disastrous, cooking over an open fire is tremendous fun. Using this method requires a bit of trial and error, which is the enjoyable part. Campers soon learn from mistakes and develop their own unique recipes. Following are seven easy and appetizing evening meal suggestions designed primarily for the novice camper and which require only an open fire and one pan. A fire can take awhile to get started, especially if the wood is damp, so be sure you have a few appetizers designed to reduce, not enhance, the appetite.

Tortilla Wraps

Flour tortillas	Can of tuna
Cheese	Bacon
Tomatoes	Salad
Condiments	

Flour tortillas keep well and offer easy meal options. Heat them until soft on the grill (2 minutes), then fill with salad, tuna, cheese, bacon and tomatoes, and whatever condiments you have available. While these wraps are better warm, if it's raining too hard to start a fire, they are good cold and also offer sustenance for hiking.

Happy Hamburgers

Hamburgers	Bacon
Mushrooms	Buns
Salad	Tomatoes
Cheese	Condiments

Grill hamburger patties along with bacon and mushrooms (cooked whole), then place in a bun (or pita bread) with salad, tomatoes, cheese and condiments, and serve with chips. What could be easier?

Steak and Potatoes with Vegetable Surprise

Steak	Potatoes
Zucchini	Onions
Red and green peppers	Tomatoes
Mushrooms	Bacon

A meal guaranteed not to taste the same twice. Make a concoction of sauces for the steak marinade, including any or all of the following: red wine, olive oil, mustard, salt, pepper, garlic, mixed herbs, tomato purée/sauce. Soak the steak for as long as possible then place directly on the grill and baste as required. Wrap the potatoes in foil and place in the fire. Use a fork to test for when they are done (30 to 60 minutes). Layer a large piece of foil with sliced zucchini, sliced onions, cut peppers, mushrooms, sliced tomatoes and bacon. Season with garlic, herbs and sauces. Fold the foil to create a tight parcel and place on the grill. Turn upside down once. Cook for about 15 minutes.

Bacon cooks well over an open fire, as do sausages.

Cooking outdoors and sharing meals is one of the joys of camping, and it need not be stressful. (BC Parks photo)

Saucy Sausages in Pita Bread

Sausages   Red peppers
Tomatoes   Pita bread
Salad

Place the sausages and sliced red pepper on the grill and start to cook. Put the tomatoes on the grill or on a piece of foil placed on top of the grill. When everything is cooked, warm the pita bread on the grill. Fill the warm pitas with the sausages, tomatoes and red peppers. Serve with salad.

Campground Chicken with Zucchini and Yams

Chicken pieces   Yams
Zucchini

Marinate the chicken pieces to taste (see steak recipe) and place on the grill. Wrap the yams in foil and place in the fire until soft (20 to 60 minutes). Place the zucchini on the grill and cook until just beginning to turn brown (10 to 15 minutes).

Spare Ribs with Sweet Corn and Noodles

Marinated spare ribs   Sweet corn
Noodles

Place marinated spare ribs directly on the grill until cooked. Remove the green leaves from the sweet corn and place on the grill. Cook until tender (15 minutes), turning regularly. Cook the noodles in the pan as directed.

Salmon Steaks with Spicy Vegetables and Rice

Salmon steaks   Broccoli
Cauliflower   Mushrooms
Peppers   Tomatoes
Rice

Place the salmon steaks on a large piece of foil and season with salt, pepper, lemon juice and mustard. Place on the grill and turn the fish until cooked. Wash and marinate vegetables (see recipe for steak marinade and amend as desired) and cook on the grill. Cook the rice in the pan as directed.

Bon appétit!

Facts and Figures on BC Parks

- Nearly 14 percent of BC's land base (more than 13.09 million hectares) is dedicated park or protected area.

- BC has the second-largest parks system in Canada, after Canada's national parks.

- As of June 2007, there were 893 provincial parks, recreational areas and ecological reserves in BC.

- In 1960, approximately 3 million visits were made to provincial parks. By 2006, this figure had increased over seven times to 23.5 million.

- Approximately 6 out of every 10 BC residents use a provincial park at least once a year.

- There are 11,125 vehicle-accessible campsites located in BC provincial parks.

- In 2001, 2,639,293 camping parties visited BC provincial parks.

- Over 234 provincial parks have facilities for people with disabilities.

- More than 7,000 kilometres of hiking trails are available in BC provincial parks.

- The highest concentration of grizzly bears is found in Khutzeymateen Provincial Park (no camping facilities), which is Canada's only grizzly bear sanctuary.

- Tweedsmuir Provincial Park is BC's largest provincial park, covering 974,046 hectares.

- Canada's second-highest waterfall, Della Falls, is found in Strathcona Provincial Park, which was BC's first provincial park, created in 1911.

- Roderick Haig-Brown Provincial Park has the world's most productive sockeye salmon run.

- Golden Ears is the most popular provincial park with camping facilities in BC, followed by Manning, Rathtrevor Beach and Cultus Lake.

- Rathtrevor Beach is the most popular provincial park with camping facilities on Vancouver Island.

- Okanagan Lake is the most popular provincial park campground in the Okanagan.

CAMPER NOTES

CAMPER NOTES

CAMPER NOTES

CAMPER NOTES

ALSO AVAILABLE FROM HERITAGE HOUSE

Country Roads of British Columbia
Exploring the Interior

Author Liz Bryan explores and celebrates the amazing landscapes and traces the early history of Canada's westernmost province, taking readers on 18 picturesque country journeys, mostly between the Rockies and the Coast Mountains. Through her text and full-colour photographs, Bryan showcases some of the most diverse and beautiful scenery in the country. With 100 colour photos and 18 maps, the book is a wonderful way to get familiar with BC.

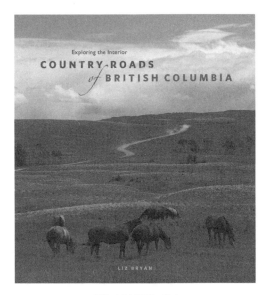

978-1-894974-43-1
$24.95 (softcover)

Great Seashore Books

Available from Heritage House

Charlie White's
103 Fishing Secrets
978-1895811-61-2
$14.95

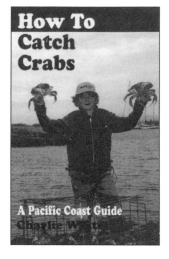

How to Catch Crabs
A Pacific Coast Guide
978-1-895811-51-3
$8.95

How to Catch Shellfish
Along the Pacific Coast
978-1-895811-49-0
$9.95

How to Catch
Bottomfish
978-1-894384-60-5
$15.95

Road and Recreational Atlases

Indispensable for travellers exploring the province, these information-packed atlases feature the most up-to-date BC road maps, including serviced logging and back roads. Each book has a comprehensive names index for cities, towns, creeks, rivers, lakes, bays and islands, plus the locations of all eco reserves, hot springs, wildlife viewing areas, major ski areas, BC Forest Service campgrounds and provincial and national parks.

The *Southwestern British Columbia Road & Recreational Atlas* covers all of Vancouver Island and the Lower Mainland north to Lillooet and east to Manning Park with 1:200,000 scale (1 cm = 2 km) shaded relief maps and a 4,000 + names index. Includes all of the features listed above plus core city maps for Vancouver, Victoria, Whistler, Campbell River, Powell River, Courtenay, Comox and Nanaimo.

The *British Columbia Road & Recreation Atlas* covers all of British Columbia plus parts of the Yukon (Whitehorse), Alaska (Ketchikan to Juneau) and Alberta (Banff National Park to Calgary) with 1:600,000 scale (1 cm = 6 km) shaded relief maps and a 10,000 + names index. Includes all of the features listed above plus provincial circle-tour routes and a 24-page spread highlighting national parks and historic sites.

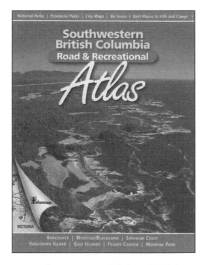 

Southwestern British Columbia
Road & Recreational Atlas
978-0-9680772-5-2
$22.95 (softcover)

British Columbia
Road & Recreation Atlas
978-0-9680772-6-9
$24.95 (softcover)

Jayne Seagrave moved to Canada from England 20 years ago. She lives in Vancouver with her husband, Andrew, and their sons, Jack and Sam. She has a Ph.D. in criminology and divides her time between working as the marketing manager for the Vancouver Tool Corporation (www.vancouvertool.com), the business she owns with her husband, speaking on innovation and the home-improvement industry (www.jayneseagrave.com) and enjoying her family and the province of British Columbia.

She is also the author of *Camping with Kids: The Best Family Campgrounds in British Columbia and Alberta* and *From the Mind to the Marketplace: The Story of an Inventor, the Home Improvement Industry, His Wife and Her Lovers.*

"If it's a park campground, chances are Jayne Seagrave has pitched her tent there. *Camping British Columbia* is a classic for families eager to explore this remarkable province. Jayne's eagle eye for detail guides us to the best camp-sites, including some great suggestions for activities and attractions. Let's go!"
—MARK FORSYTHE, *BC ALMANAC*, CBC RADIO ONE

Your guide to 150+ provincial and national park campgrounds

Fully revised and updated, this sixth edition of *Camping British Columbia* describes the location, amenities and recreational activities of every BC provincial and national park that offers vehicle-accessible camping.

- **Camping with kids?** Learn which campgrounds have interpretive programs, playgrounds and safe swimming beaches.

- **Don't want to rough it too much?** Pick out the provincial and national parks with flush toilets, hot showers and restaurants nearby.

- **Exploring the province in an RV?** Find out which campgrounds have sani-stations, hookups and pull-through sites.

Presented alphabetically region by region, with maps and easy-to-follow driving directions, these campground listings provide all the information anyone could want and make it easy to compare parks.

ISBN 978-1-894974-60-8

9781894974608

$19.95

www.heritagehouse.ca